CONTEMPORARY'S

Top 50 Writing Skills

for GED SUCCESS

 Wright Group

TIM COLLINS

Editor: Martha Flynn Trydahl
Executive Editor: Linda Kwil
Interior Design: Linda Chandler
Cover Design: Tracey Harris-Sainz

ISBN: 0-07-704478-9
ISBN: 0-07-704479-7 (with CD)

Send all inquiries to:
McGraw-Hill/Contemporary
One Prudential Plaza
130 E. Randolph St., Suite 400
Chicago, IL 60601

4 5 6 7 8 9 0 POH/POH 09 08 07

The **McGraw·Hill** Companies

Table of Contents

Top 50 Skills
Part 1: Editing

Sentence Structure

Usage

Mechanics

Organization

Part 2: The Essay

About the GED Writing Test

Test Overview

The GED Language Arts, Writing Test is divided into two parts:

Part I: 75 minutes; 50 multiple-choice questions

Part II: 45 minutes; 1 essay

In Part I, test-takers find and correct errors in reading passages of 200 to 300 words in a multiple-choice format. In Part II, test-takers write an essay in response to an essay topic.

Test Content

Reading passages in Part I include workplace, how-to, and informational documents. Multiple-choice questions on the GED Language Arts, Writing Test are taken from four major content areas:

- **Mechanics** (25%): correcting errors such as incorrect punctuation, capitalization, and spelling of homonyms and contractions
- **Usage** (30%): correcting errors such as incorrect subject-verb agreement, pronoun use, and verb tenses
- **Sentence Structure** (30%): correcting errors such as run-on sentences, comma splices, improper parallel structure, and sentence fragments
- **Organization** (15%): correcting errors such as lack of unity and coherence, and improper topic sentences

In Part II, test-takers plan, write, and revise an essay on a topic of general interest. The essay topic is designed so test-takers can answer using their own knowledge, experience, opinions, and ideas. No specialized knowledge is needed. Essays are evaluated using the GED Essay Scoring Guide. For more information on the GED Essay Scoring Guide, see pages ix–xi.

Multiple-Choice Question Types

There are three types of multiple-choice questions on the GED Language Arts, Writing Test:

- **Correction** (45%): presents a sentence with several possible changes, which may include making specific corrections to the sentence, moving it to another location in the passage, or removing the sentence entirely.
- **Revision** (35%): consists of one or more sentences with a section underlined. Answer options present alternative ways of revising the underlined section, which may or may not contain an error.
- **Construction Shift** (20%): presents one or more sentences that should be rewritten, combined, moved, or inserted into a paragraph. Options may also ask for paragraphs to be divided, joined, or moved.

Here are examples of each kind of item:

Correction

❶ Sentence 1: **Members of the West Suburban Parent-Teacher Organization will have their fall meeting at Burbleson Middle School on Saturday, october 10 at 9:30 A.M.**

Which correction should be made to sentence 1?

① replace <u>Organization</u> with <u>organization</u>
② replace <u>their</u> with <u>they're</u>
③ change <u>their</u> to <u>its</u>
④ replace <u>fall</u> with <u>Fall</u>
⑤ replace <u>october</u> with <u>October</u>

The answer is Option ⑤. Because October is a month, it is a proper noun and should be capitalized.

Revision

❷ Sentence 2: **At the meeting, the group's president will report on progress the group <u>is making</u> last year getting new books and supplies for teachers.**

Which is the best way to write the underlined portion of this sentence? If the original is the best way, choose option (1).

① is making
② has made
③ made
④ will make
⑤ will have made

The answer is Option ③. This part of the sentence is about what happened last year, so the simple past tense is required.

Construction Shift

❸ Sentences 3 and 4: **The meeting will address ways to improve test scores in area schools. We will also address ways for sending more needy students to college.**

The most effective combination of sentences 3 and 4 would include which group of words?

① schools because sending
② schools and to send
③ schools and more needy students
④ schools, and will focus to send
⑤ schools, and improving sending

The answer is Option ②. This option uses parallel structure correctly. Two infinitive phrases *(to improve* and *to send)* are joined correctly with *and.*

How to Use This Book

Top 50 Writing Skills for GED Success is a short, test-directed course in GED writing preparation. The 50 skills chosen are those most representative of the type and difficulty level of skills tested on the GED Language Arts, Writing Test. Each of the 30 multiple-choice questions on Part I of the GED Language Arts, Writing Test addresses a particular editing skill. On Part II of the test, the essay addresses the assessment criteria identified in the GED Essay Scoring Guide (page x).

Top 50 Writing Skills for GED Success is divided into four main sections:

- **Pretest:** The Pretest and Pretest Evaluation Charts help instructors and learners identify the exact skills learners need to work on.
- **Top 50 Skills:** This section includes instruction on the top 50 skills needed for success on the GED Language Arts, Writing Test. Learners can complete only those skills identified in the Pretest or work through all of the skills in order. GED Readiness exercises for each skill provide immediate practice and reinforcement. The complete answers and explanations in the Answer Key provide immediate feedback and clarification of all correct and incorrect answer options.
- **GED Posttest:** A short, two-part Posttest shows readiness to take the GED. Use the Posttest for practice under test-like conditions. Learners and instructors can use the GED Posttest Evaluation Charts to determine which skills need additional review and reinforcement prior to taking the GED test.
- **Supporting Material:** Also included are an annotated Glossary of important writing terms and an extensive Answer Key with complete explanations of all correct and incorrect answers for all items in the Pretest, GED Readiness exercises, and GED Posttest.

To the Instructor

Top 50 Writing Skills for GED Success is instructor-friendly, organizing for you in 50 lessons a core of writing skills identified by the GED Testing Service. Each lesson addresses a single skill and provides follow-up practice. One or more lessons can be completed in a single study period.

To the Learner

Follow these steps to use *Top 50 Writing Skills for GED Success* to maximum advantage:

- Take the Pretest to determine your strengths and weaknesses. Then use the Pretest Evaluation Charts to determine the skills you need to review.
- Review the lesson for each skill identified on the Pretest Evaluation Charts, or go through all of the skills in order. Use the Answer Key to review your answers to each question in the GED Readiness exercises in each lesson.
- Take the GED Posttest. For best results, take the test under timed, test-like conditions. The Answer Key allows you to check your answers, and the GED Posttest Evaluation Charts tell you which skills you need to review again.

Using the Writing Process

When you write your GED essay, you will have only 45 minutes. This is not enough time to write a first and final draft of your essay, so you should use your time effectively to write your essay in a single draft. The writing process: a series of steps to plan, write, and revise an essay, can help you structure your work so you can write a high-scoring essay in 45 minutes.

The writing process has four steps:

- Gathering ideas
- Organizing your ideas
- Writing your essay
- Revising your essay

Gathering Ideas

This is probably the most important step in writing a good essay. In order to write an essay that is long enough to address the essay question, you need plenty of good ideas. Brainstorming is one way to gather ideas. When you brainstorm, you gather as many ideas as you possibly can in a short period of time. You simply jot the ideas down. At this point, you should focus on getting ideas down on paper. Don't be concerned about sentence structure, spelling, or other details. You can take care of that later in the process. Here is a list of ideas about someone's favorite food:

Favorite food: pizza

Nice to eat on a Sunday night
Many great toppings: sausage, pepperoni, mushrooms, green pepper, olives, broccoli
Good for you: has bread, vegetables, cheese, and meat
Tastes delicious
Many different kinds: thin crust, thick crust

Other ways to gather ideas include:

- Asking *wh*-questions (*who, what, where, when, why,* and *how*)
- Using the five senses (What does it sound like, smell like, taste like, look like, and feel like?)

Organizing Ideas

After you have a list of ideas, your next step is to organize them in a logical order. There are many ways to organize ideas. You can organize ideas according to

- Time (the way things happened)
- Process (steps in how to do something)
- Order of importance

You can organize your ideas by numbering or drawing lines on your idea list.

Favorite food: pizza

5. Nice to eat on a Sunday night
3. Many great toppings: sausage, pepperoni, mushrooms, green pepper, olives, broccoli
2. Good for you: has bread, vegetables, cheese, and meat
1. Tastes delicious
4. Many different kinds: thin crust, thick crust

Writing Your Essay

Once your ideas are organized, you are ready to begin writing. You should write your ideas following your organizational plan. Your essay should have an introductory paragraph, one or more body paragraphs, and a concluding paragraph (For more information, see Skills 44 to 48).

It seems like everyone likes to eat, and I am no different. Like most people, I like many kinds of foods. However, my very favorite food is pizza.

Why do I like pizza so much? One reason is taste. There is nothing like biting into a fresh, hot slice of pizza. The flavors of all the ingredients blend together into a delicious taste.

I also like pizza because it's very nourishing. Pizza has bread in the crust and can have many vegetables, such as onion and green pepper. Some pizzas even have eggplant or broccoli. Pizzas also have meat and cheese.

toppings

Another reason I like pizza is because of the many different kinds of crusts and ~~topings~~ you can get. My family likes to order a vegetarian pizza from a restaurant near our home. That pizza has eight kinds of vegetables. I also like to order a mushroom and sausage pizza from a carry-out place near my job.

Finally, pizza is nice to eat at certain times. I like to order a pizza for my family on Sunday nights. Then I settle back, watch a few good TV shows, and help my kids with their homework. It's a relaxing way to start a family evening at home.

Pizza is my favorite food because it's delicious, nourishing, and fun to eat. In fact, I think I will have some pizza after I finish this essay.

There are many different kinds of crust, such as thin, thick, deep-dish, and whole wheat.

Revising Your Essay

After you write your essay, you can then focus on details such as sentence structure and spelling. You should go back and revise your work to make sure it's organized, stays on topic, includes all of your ideas, has good word choice, and uses correct spelling. For example, in this essay, the writer has gone back to add information about kinds of pizza crust, which was in the idea list but not in the essay. The writer also corrected the spelling of *toppings*.

Using the GED Essay Scoring Guide

The GED Testing Service will use the GED Essay Scoring Guide (see pages x–xi) to evaluate your essay. The scores on each part of the Scoring Guide will identify the essay writing skills you need to focus on in the instruction section of the book.

If possible, have your instructor evaluate your essay. If that is not possible, ask another learner to evaluate your writing or evaluate it yourself. If you are evaluating your own essay, let it sit for a few days before you assess it. That will allow you to experience your essay in much the same way an official reader would.

Use the Scoring Guide to score from 1 to 4 on each of the criteria:

- Response to the Prompt
- Organization
- Development and Details
- Conventions of Edited American English
- Word Choice

You can then average those scores (by adding them and dividing the total by 5) to find your estimated overall score. The lowest passing score on Part II of the GED Language Arts, Writing Test is 2. However, whether you pass the entire GED Language Arts, Writing Test depends on your score on both parts.

Use this information in the Scoring Guide to help you evaluate accurately:

Response to the Prompt

This focuses on your ability to stick to the GED essay topic. For example, if the topic asks you to discuss why you have or don't have a pet, your essay should focus on the topic of pets, not on your children.

Organization

This focuses on the organization of your essay. Your essay should have a definite beginning, middle, and end. This means that an essay has an introductory paragraph that introduces the topic and states the main idea, several body paragraphs that give details to back up the main idea of the essay, and a concluding paragraph that sums up the body paragraphs and reminds readers of the main idea.

Development and Details

This refers to the details and examples that back up, or support, your essay. Good writers always back up their ideas with plenty of specific examples. In addition, all of the details should be relevant, or related to, the main idea of each paragraph.

Conventions of Edited American English

Edited American English refers to what is also called "Standard English." Edited American English includes correct sentence structure, verb agreement, correct spelling, and so on.

Word Choice

When you write, you should vary your word choice to provide variety for the reader. In addition, you should use specific, detailed, and colorful words to make your writing come alive to readers.

Language Arts, Writing, Part II
Essay Scoring Guide

	1 Inadequate	2 Marginal	3 Adequate	4 Effective
	Reader has difficulty identifying or following the writer's ideas.	**Reader occasionally has difficulty understanding or following the writer's ideas.**	**Reader understands the writer's ideas.**	**Reader understands and easily follows the writer's expression of ideas.**
Response to the Prompt	Attempts to address the prompt but with little or no success in establishing a focus.	Addresses the prompt, though the focus may shift.	Uses the prompt to establish a main idea.	Presents a clearly focused main idea that addresses the prompt.
Organization	Fails to organize ideas.	Shows some evidence of an organizational plan.	Uses an identifiable organizational plan.	Establishes a clear and logical organization.
Development and Details	Demonstrates little or no development; usually lacks details or examples or presents irrelevant information.	Has some development but lacks specific details; may be limited to a listing, repetitions, or generalizations.	Has focused but occasionally uneven development; incorporates some specific detail.	Achieves coherent development with specific and relevant details and examples.
Conventions of EAE	Exhibits minimal or no control of sentence structure and the conventions of Edited American English (EAE).	Demonstrates inconsistent control of sentence structure and the conventions of EAE.	Generally controls sentence structure and the conventions of EAE.	Consistently controls sentence structure and the conventions of EAE.
Word Choice	Exhibits weak and/or inappropriate words.	Exhibits a narrow range of word choice, often including inappropriate selections.	Exhibits appropriate word choice.	Exhibits varied and precise word choice.

Language Arts, Writing, Part II
Essay Scoring Guide

Level 4 writing is effective because the writer presents a clearly focused main idea that addresses the prompt while controlling both the language and sentence structure. The response establishes a clear and logical organization and achieves coherent development with specific and relevant details and examples. Word choice is varied and precise, and there is consistent control of Edited American English (EAE), although a few minor errors may be present. As a result of these combined characteristics, the reader understands and easily follows the expression of ideas in the response.

Level 3 writing is adequate because the writer uses the prompt to establish a main idea and generally controls both the language and sentence structure. There is an identifiable organizational plan. The writer incorporates specific, focused detail, but the development may be uneven. Word choice is appropriate, and the conventions of EAE are generally correct, the errors that are present do not interfere with comprehension. The reader of the 3 response understands the writer's ideas.

Level 2 writing is marginal because the writer addresses the prompt but may lose focus or provide few specific details. The response shows some evidence of an organizational plan and has some development, but it may be limited to a listing, repetition, or generalizations. There is a narrow range of word choice, sometimes including inappropriate selections, and control of sentence structure or the conventions of EAE may be inconsistent. As a result of these combined characteristics, the reader occasionally has difficulty understanding or following the expression of ideas.

Level 1 writing is inadequate because the writer has little or no success in establishing and developing a focus, though there may be an attempt to address the prompt. The writer fails to organize ideas or provides little development; the response usually lacks details or examples and presents irrelevant information. There may be minimal, if any, control of sentence structure and the conventions of EAE, or word choice may be ineffective and often inappropriate. The reader of the 1 response has difficulty identifying or following the writer's ideas.

Reprinted with permission of the GED Testing Service.

GED Essay Examples

Here are some examples of essays and their scores:

Essay 1

Everyone has goals in life. Many of our goals are related to work, education, or family. Right now, my goal is to get my GED so that I can move ahead in my life.

After I left high school, I found out that I couldn't get a good job. I had several jobs in fast food restaurants. But the work was hard, and the pay was terrible. My sister, who has a GED, says that I can get a job at her company if I get my GED, too. Her company has lots of good jobs that require a GED. I am hoping to get a job as a file clerk or telephone sales representative. I will make more money with one of these jobs.

After I get my GED, I also hope to continue my education at City Community College. I like computers, so I want to take some computer classes. Then I will be able to get a job related to computers.

In order to achieve my goal I study every night. I have a preparation book that I work on after work. In addition, on Tuesdays, I have a GED math class at Community Adult School. In addition, I try to read the newspaper or a book every day in order to improve my reading skills.

If I am lucky, I will pass the GED test later this month. I have already passed 3 of the tests. I just have to pass math and reading, and I will be finished. I can't wait.

This essay scored a 4 on each of the criteria in the GED Essay Scoring Guide:

Response to the Prompt—This essay scored a 4 because it stuck to the topic of the writer's goal and how he or she will achieve it.

Organization—This essay scored a 4 because it had an introductory paragraph, three body paragraphs that give details about the main idea of the essay, and a concluding paragraph that sums up the essay. The organization was clear and easy to follow.

Development and Details—This essay scored a 4 because there were plenty of examples and details that back up the essay: the jobs he or she wants to get in the future, his or her plans for more education, and his or her plans for passing the GED Tests.

Conventions of Edited American English—This essay scored a 4 because of the correct and varied sentence structure, verb agreement, spelling, and so on.

Word Choice—This essay scored a 4 because it had varied word choice and used specific nouns and verbs, and colorful adjectives.

Essay 2

I have several goals that I want to achieve. Right now, my main goal is passing my GED

I want to pass my GED because I always felt bad that I didn't finish high school. Now my children are entering middle school. I want to set a good example for them. So I want to go back and get my GED so that they feel encouraged to stay in school.

I plan to get my GED by taking a class at the adult school in my neighborhood. The school opened last month, which is why I got the idea to go back for my GED now. The school is very nice, because it's new. The teachers are friendly. I think I will have to study for a long time. I am worried about the math test because math is hard for me.

But I know I can do it. After I get my GED, I will be very happy.

This essay scored 3 on each of the criteria in the GED Essay Scoring Guide:

Response to the Prompt—This essay scored a 3 because it stuck to the topic of the writer's goal and how he or she will achieve it.

Organization—This essay scored a 3 because it had an identifiable organization plan. It includes an introductory paragraph of two sentences, two body paragraphs, and a final concluding sentence. Though the organization could be better, the essay is clear and easy to follow.

Development and Details—This essay scored a 3 because there were some examples and details that back up the essay, but also an irrelevant sentence.

Conventions of Edited American English—This essay scored a 3 because it has correct and varied sentence structure, verb agreement, and spelling.

Word Choice—This essay scored a 3 because it has appropriate vocabulary.

Essay 3

Lately, my Goal has been to get my GED. I hated High School. so I didn't finish, and now I want to get my GED so I can achieve my Goals.

After I get my GED, I will look for a job with the City. In our town, you have to have a high school or a GED in order to get a job with the city. I want to become a truck driver or road worker. Those jobs pay good and the city gives good benefits. I really need insurance. City jobs are good because you don't have to work very hard

I am taking a GED class right now. It's not hard. I want to finish the class and take the test. After I pass, I will celebrate.

This essay scored 2 on each of the criteria in the GED Essay Scoring Guide:

Response to the Prompt—This essay scored a 2 because although it was about the essay topic, it had unrelated ideas in several places.

Organization—This essay scored a 2 because it showed some evidence of an organization plan. The essay has an introductory paragraph, but not a conclusion. Each of the paragraphs is about a different main idea, but each paragraph goes off topic. The essay is hard to follow.

Development and Details—This essay scored a 2 because there were few examples and details to support the main idea, and several ideas are irrelevant.

Conventions of Edited American English—This essay scored a 2 because the sentence structure is inconsistent. The essay contains many short, choppy sentences and some sentences exhibit errors of sentence structure. Some capitalization errors, misspelled words, and other errors interfere with understanding.

Word Choice—This essay scored a 2 because the vocabulary was narrow, and some words are repeated, inappropriate, or incorrect.

About the Pretest

This Pretest is an overview of the 50 skills you are most likely to see addressed on the GED Language Arts, Writing Test. The first 30 multiple-choice items address the four areas tested by the GED Testing Service:

- Mechanics
- Usage
- Sentence Structure
- Organization

The essay assesses the five areas identified on the GED Testing Service's Essay Scoring Guide:

- Response to the Prompt
- Organization
- Development and Details
- Conventions of Edited (Standard) American English
- Word Choice

This Pretest will help you identify specific skills in which you need more practice. The Pretest, unlike the actual GED Test, is not a timed test. In fact, you should take as much time as you need to answer each question and to write your essay.

Answer every question on this Pretest. If you are not sure of an answer, put a question mark by the item number to note that you are guessing. Then make your best guess. (On the actual GED, an unanswered question is counted as incorrect. So, making a good guess is an important skill to develop. For more hints on effective test-taking, see page 122.)

When you are finished, turn to the Answer Key (pages 146–174) and the GED Essay Scoring Guide (pages ix–xi) to check your answers. Then use the Pretest Evaluation Charts (pages 18–19) to figure out which skills to focus on in the instruction section of this book (pages 20–121).

After working through the instruction section, take the GED Posttest (GED practice test) on pages 124–139. Your success on the GED Posttest will indicate your readiness to take the actual GED Language Arts, Writing Test.

Pretest

Part I

Directions: Choose the <u>one best answer</u> to each question.
<u>Questions 1 through 8</u> refer to the following letter.

Manager
Value Inn Hotel
122 Massachusetts Avenue
Washington, DC 20027

Dear Manager,

(1) I am writing about a number of problems I had when I stayed at your hotel in May of this year. (2) The problems began at the front desk, where I had to wait in line for 10 minutes. (3) When I finally reached the desk, the employee was unable to find my reservation. (4) I spelled my name several times and gave her my reservation number. (5) She then said there were no more non-smoking rooms even though I had reserved one weeks ago. (6) My reservation was also for a room on a lower floor but she told me that only rooms on the twenty-second floor were available.

(7) Then I had trouble with my room key and had to return to the desk where more customers were in line. (8) The clerk who checked me in wasn't their, and another clerk was on duty. (9) Angrily he told me to wait in line with the others, so I had to wait 15 more minutes to get a key to my room. (10) When I finally entered my room, it was a terrible mess. (11) So, I returned to the front desk for a third time. (12) Imagine my surprise when the clerk offered me a non-smoking room on a lower floor!

(13) Your website said that Internet access was free, but I had to pay $9.95 in order to access the Internet. (14) When I made my reservation, I was told that the pool was working. (15) However, employees told me that the pool was not scheduled to open until the following weekend, which was memorial day. (16) That night, the air conditioner broke in my room. (17) I called the front desk, but the engineer was not able to repair it. (18) Since there were no other rooms available, I had to sleep in a warm, airless room that was uncomfortable.

Ⓓ

(19) I complained to a desk clerk about all of these problems, but she said that there was nothing she can do to solve them. (20) Because of the problems I experienced, I would like the cost of my stay refunded to me.

Sincerely,

Charles Walters, Jr.

Charles Walters, Jr.

1 Sentences 3 and 4: **When I finally reached the desk, the employee was unable to find my reservation. I spelled my name several times and gave her my reservation number.**

The most effective combination of sentences 3 and 4 would include which group of words?

① reservation if
② reservation until
③ reservation however,
④ reservation, but
⑤ reservation, since

2 Sentence 6: **My reservation was also for a room on a lower floor but she told me that only rooms on the twenty-second floor were available.**

Which correction should be made to sentence 6?

① insert a comma after lower floor
② insert a comma after but
③ replace she with he
④ change were to was
⑤ no correction is necessary

3 Sentence 8: **The clerk who checked me in wasn't their, and another clerk was on duty.**

Which correction should be made to sentence 8?

① change in to inn
② change wasn't to was'nt
③ change their to there
④ remove the comma after their
⑤ no correction is necessary

4 Sentence 9: **Angrily he told me to wait in line with the others, so I had to wait 15 more minutes to get a key to my room.**

Which correction should be made to sentence 9?

① insert a comma after Angrily
② insert a comma after line
③ remove the comma after others
④ insert a comma after minutes
⑤ no correction is necessary

The letter is repeated for your use in answering the remaining questions.

Manager
Value Inn Hotel
122 Massachusetts Avenue
Washington, DC 20027

Dear Manager,

A

(1) I am writing about a number of problems I had when I stayed at your hotel in May of this year. (2) The problems began at the front desk, where I had to wait in line for 10 minutes. (3) When I finally reached the desk, the employee was unable to find my reservation. (4) I spelled my name several times and gave her my reservation number. (5) She then said there were no more non-smoking rooms even though I had reserved one weeks ago. (6) My reservation was also for a room on a lower floor but she told me that only rooms on the twenty-second floor were available.

B

(7) Then I had trouble with my room key and had to return to the desk where more customers were in line. (8) The clerk who checked me in wasn't their, and another clerk was on duty. (9) Angrily he told me to wait in line with the others, so I had to wait 15 more minutes to get a key to my room. (10) When I finally entered my room, it was a terrible mess. (11) So, I returned to the front desk for a third time. (12) Imagine my surprise when the clerk offered me a non-smoking room on a lower floor!

C

(13) Your website said that Internet access was free, but I had to pay $9.95 in order to access the Internet. (14) When I made my reservation, I was told that the pool was working. (15) However, employees told me that the pool was not scheduled to open until the following weekend, which was memorial day. (16) That night, the air conditioner broke in my room. (17) I called the front desk, but the engineer was not able to repair it. (18) Since there were no other rooms available, I had to sleep in a warm, airless room that was uncomfortable.

D

(19) I complained to a desk clerk about all of these problems, but she said that there was nothing she can do to solve them. (20) Because of the problems I experienced, I would like the cost of my stay refunded to me.

Sincerely,

Charles Walters, Jr.

Charles Walters, Jr.

5 Which sentence would be most effective if inserted at the beginning of paragraph C?

(1) Internet access was my biggest problem.
(2) I didn't like my room, either.
(3) The pool and the Internet also were problems.
(4) Unfortunately, my problems did not end there.
(5) I will never stay at this hotel again.

6 Sentence 15: **However, employees told me that the pool was not scheduled to open until the following weekend, which was memorial day.**

Which correction should be made to sentence 15?

(1) remove the comma after <u>However</u>
(2) change <u>pool was</u> to <u>pool is</u>
(3) replace <u>weekend</u> with <u>Weekend</u>
(4) change <u>which was</u> to <u>which is</u>
(5) replace <u>memorial day</u> with <u>Memorial Day</u>

7 Sentence 18: **Since there were no other rooms available, I had to sleep in <u>a warm, airless room that was uncomfortable</u>.**

Which is the best way to write the underlined portion of this sentence? If the original is the best way, choose option (1).

(1) a warm, airless room that was uncomfortable
(2) a warm, airless, and uncomfortable room
(3) a warm and airless and uncomfortable room
(4) a warm airless uncomfortable room
(5) a warm room that was uncomfortable and airless

8 Sentence 19: **I complained to a desk clerk about all of these problems, but she said that there was nothing she can do to solve them.**

Which correction should be made to sentence 19?

(1) change <u>said</u> to <u>says</u>
(2) change <u>was</u> to <u>were</u>
(3) change <u>was</u> to <u>is</u>
(4) remove <u>can</u>
(5) change <u>can</u> to <u>could</u>

Questions 9 through 17 refer to the following information.

CHOOSING THE BEST TELEVISION SERVICE

A

(1) Consumers face a variety of bewildering options when choosing television services. (2) Each service has advantages and disadvantages, so it's important to choose wisely so that you and your family can see the programs they like.

B

(3) The most basic option is regular broadcast TV. (4) The biggest advantage of broadcast TV is that it's free. (5) You only need a television set with an antenna. (6) You can get all of the major TV networks, as well as a few local stations. (7) The disadvantage is the limited choices. (8) You cannot access any of the hundreds of stations available on cable or satellite networks. (9) In some locations your choices may be limited to four or five channels. (10) In addition, some of the major networks are now broadcasting in high-definition, so if you have a high-definition television set, you can watch those programs with better picture and sound.

C

(11) Cable television offers even more choices—up to 100 channels or more in some areas. (12) As technology improve, cable companies plan to increase the number of channels even more. (13) In many cities, you can now choose between two or more cable companies, each with slightly different programming options. (14) Therefore, if you want to watch a particular channel, you may have to choose the cable company that offers that channel. (15) This often happens with the more specialized channels.

D

(16) To help you find the programs you want, cable companies offer a variety of packages at various costs. (17) Basic cable has only a few programs, but it is very inexpensive. (18) Standard packages have more offerings other packages can include many more channels, including premium channels. (19) If you're not careful, the services you order can add up quickly. (20) Finally, cable companies allow parents to control the channels their children have access to. (21) Parents can simply not order an objectionable channel, or they can use blocking technology to prevent their children from watching them.

E

(22) The third alternative is a satellite network. (23) Using a satellite network, a special satellite dish is installed outside your home. (24) Satellite networks, offering the largest selection of programming, often costs more than cable. (25) In addition, you must be able to install the satellite dish. (26) Apartment dwellers, for example, may not be able to install a satellite dish where they live.

F

(27) What's the best deal for you? (28) It depends on how much you can afford to spend and the kinds of programming you want to see. (29) But choose wisely so that you get only the services you actually use at a price you can afford to pay.

9 Sentence 2: **Each service has advantages and disadvantages, so it's important to choose wisely so that you and your family can see the programs they like.**

Which correction should be made to sentence 2?

① change has to have
② replace it's with its
③ replace your with you're
④ replace they with you
⑤ no correction is necessary

10 Sentence 9: **In some locations your choices may be limited to four or five channels.**

Which correction should be made to sentence 9?

① insert a comma after some
② insert a comma after locations
③ replace your with you're
④ replace your with yours
⑤ no correction is necessary

11 Sentence 10: **In addition, some of the major networks are now broadcasting in high-definition, so if you have a high-definition television set, you can watch those programs with better picture and sound.**

Which revision should be made to sentence 10?

① move sentence 10 to the beginning of paragraph A
② move sentence 10 to follow sentence 5
③ move sentence 10 to follow sentence 6
④ move sentence 10 to follow sentence 8
⑤ remove sentence 10

12 Sentence 12: **As technology improve, cable companies plan to increase the number of channels even more.**

Which is the best way to write the underlined portion of this sentence? If the original is the best way, choose option (1).

① improve
② improves
③ improved
④ have improved
⑤ improving

13 Sentence 18: **Standard packages have more offerings other packages can include many more channels, including premium channels.**

Which revision should be made to sentence 18?

① change have to has
② insert a comma and and after offerings
③ change can include to could have included
④ remove the comma after more channels
⑤ no correction is necessary

The information is repeated for your use in answering the remaining questions.

CHOOSING THE BEST TELEVISION SERVICE

A

(1) Consumers face a variety of bewildering options when choosing television services. (2) Each service has advantages and disadvantages, so it's important to choose wisely so that you and your family can see the programs they like.

B

(3) The most basic option is regular broadcast TV. (4) The biggest advantage of broadcast TV is that it's free. (5) You only need a television set with an antenna. (6) You can get all of the major TV networks, as well as a few local stations. (7) The disadvantage is the limited choices. (8) You cannot access any of the hundreds of stations available on cable or satellite networks. (9) In some locations your choices may be limited to four or five channels. (10) In addition, some of the major networks are now broadcasting in high-definition, so if you have a high-definition television set, you can watch those programs with better picture and sound.

C

(11) Cable television offers even more choices—up to 100 channels or more in some areas. (12) As technology improve, cable companies plan to increase the number of channels even more. (13) In many cities, you can now choose between two or more cable companies, each with slightly different programming options. (14) Therefore, if you want to watch a particular channel, you may have to choose the cable company that offers that channel. (15) This often happens with the more specialized channels.

D

(16) To help you find the programs you want, cable companies offer a variety of packages at various costs. (17) Basic cable has only a few programs, but it is very inexpensive. (18) Standard packages have more offerings other packages can include many more channels, including premium channels. (19) If you're not careful, the services you order can add up quickly. (20) Finally, cable companies allow parents to control the channels their children have access to. (21) Parents can simply not order an objectionable channel, or they can use blocking technology to prevent their children from watching them.

E

(22) The third alternative is a satellite network. (23) Using a satellite network, a special satellite dish is installed outside your home. (24) Satellite networks, offering the largest selection of programming, often costs more than cable. (25) In addition, you must be able to install the satellite dish. (26) Apartment dwellers, for example, may not be able to install a satellite dish where they live.

F

(27) What's the best deal for you? (28) It depends on how much you can afford to spend and the kinds of programming you want to see. (29) But choose wisely so that you get only the services you actually use at a price you can afford to pay.

14 Sentence 21: **Parents can simply not order an objectionable channel, or they can use blocking technology to prevent their children from watching them.**

Which revision should be made to sentence 21?

(1) replace <u>objectionable channel</u> with <u>Objectionable Channel</u>
(2) remove the comma after <u>channel</u>
(3) insert a comma after <u>technology</u>
(4) change <u>their</u> to <u>there</u>
(5) replace <u>them</u> with <u>it</u>

15 Sentence 23: **Using a satellite network, a special satellite dish is installed outside your home.**

The most effective revision of sentence 23 would begin with which group of words?

(1) When you use a satellite network,
(2) When using a satellite network,
(3) When the satellite signal comes to your home,
(4) Using a signal, a satellite dish
(5) When the satellite dish uses a signal,

16 Sentence 24: **Satellite networks, offering the largest selection of programming, often <u>costs</u> more than cable.**

Which is the best way to write the underlined portion of this sentence? If the original is the best way, choose option (1).

(1) costs
(2) cost
(3) costing
(4) are costing
(5) will have cost

17 Which revision would improve the effectiveness of the information?

(1) join paragraphs A and B
(2) join paragraphs B and C
(3) join paragraphs C and D
(4) remove paragraph D
(5) move sentence 16 to the end of paragraph C

Questions 18 through 24 refer to the following information.

HOW TO CHOOSE THE RIGHT DOG FOR YOU

A

(1) Raising a puppy can be a great experience. (2) But choosing a puppy is a big decision. (3) You want to get the kind of dog that's right for you and your family. (4) In addition, you want to pick a healthy puppy. (5) That will grow up to be a loyal pet for many years. (6) How do you find the right puppy? (7) Experts agree that there is several steps you should follow to ensure you choose the right pet.

B

(8) First, before buying a dog, make sure you are getting the right kind of pet for your family. (9) Think carefully about the breeds you are interested in, and decide which one will be best for your home. (10) For example, if you have young children who like to romp and play, you will probably want to get a breed that is large enough play with your children. (11) A Chihuahua, for example, would not be a good choice, because it could be easily hurt while playing. (12) On the other hand, the dog you choose should not be a large or aggressive breed if your children are very small. (13) The dog could hurt your children. (14) You might get advice from a dog breeder, or veterinarian before making a choice.

C

(15) After choosing the kind of dog you want, begin looking around. (16) In general, large stores that sell puppies may not be the best place to find a puppy. (17) A dog from one of those stores might have health problems. (18) Instead, consider a private breeder. (19) Make sure that you are dealing with a reputable breeder. (20) Don't be afraid to ask for references. (21) If a private breeder is too expensive, you also might consider getting a dog from your city's animal shelter. (22) When you get a dog from the animal shelter you often only have to pay for the dog's license and required shots.

D

(23) When you pick out a puppy from a litter, observe the puppies carefully from a distance. (24) How do the puppies relate? (25) Choose a puppy whose character you like.

E

(26) Once you have narrowed your choice to one puppy, examine it carefully. (27) Does the puppy let you handle him or her? (28) Look over the dog to make sure their skin and fur look healthy. (29) Make sure the puppy doesn't have ticks or fleas. (30) Check the puppy's gums. (31) Pink gums indicate good health. (32) White gums could indicate anemia caused by heartworm.

F

(33) After you get your puppy home, continue to observe it to make sure it is the dog for you. (34) If you need further advice, check with the breeder or your vet. (35) With any luck, you will have a fine pet who will give you and your family years of loyalty and companionship.

18 Sentences 4 and 5: **In addition, you want to pick a healthy <u>puppy. That</u> will grow up to be a loyal pet for many years.**

Which is the best way to write the underlined portion of these sentences? If the original is the best way, choose option (1).

① puppy. That
② puppy that
③ puppy and
④ puppy. And that
⑤ puppy, and that

19 Sentence 7: **Experts agree that there is several steps you should follow to ensure you choose the right pet.**

Which revision should be made to sentence 7?

① change <u>agree</u> to <u>agrees</u>
② replace <u>there</u> with <u>their</u>
③ change <u>is</u> to <u>are</u>
④ change <u>choose</u> to <u>choosing</u>
⑤ replace <u>right</u> with <u>write</u>

20 Sentence 12: **<u>On the other hand,</u> the dog you choose should not be a large or aggressive breed if your children are very small.**

Which is the best way to write the underlined portion of this sentence? If the original is the best way, choose option (1).

① On the other hand,
② In addition,
③ As a result,
④ Therefore,
⑤ For that reason,

21 Sentence 14: **You might get advice from a dog breeder, or veterinarian before making a choice.**

Which revision should be made to sentence 14?

① replace <u>might</u> with <u>mite</u>
② remove the comma after <u>breeder</u>
③ insert a comma after <u>veterinarian</u>
④ replace <u>before</u> with <u>and</u>
⑤ no revision is necessary

The information is repeated for your use in answering the remaining questions.

HOW TO CHOOSE THE RIGHT DOG FOR YOU

(A)

(1) Raising a puppy can be a great experience. (2) But choosing a puppy is a big decision. (3) You want to get the kind of dog that's right for you and your family. (4) In addition, you want to pick a healthy puppy. (5) That will grow up to be a loyal pet for many years. (6) How do you find the right puppy? (7) Experts agree that there is several steps you should follow to ensure you choose the right pet.

(B)

(8) First, before buying a dog, make sure you are getting the right kind of pet for your family. (9) Think carefully about the breeds you are interested in, and decide which one will be best for your home. (10) For example, if you have young children who like to romp and play, you will probably want to get a breed that is large enough play with your children. (11) A Chihuahua, for example, would not be a good choice, because it could be easily hurt while playing. (12) On the other hand, the dog you choose should not be a large or aggressive breed if your children are very small. (13) The dog could hurt your children. (14) You might get advice from a dog breeder, or veterinarian before making a choice.

(C)

(15) After choosing the kind of dog you want, begin looking around. (16) In general, large stores that sell puppies may not be the best place to find a puppy. (17) A dog from one of those stores might have health problems. (18) Instead, consider a private breeder. (19) Make sure that you are dealing with a reputable breeder. (20) Don't be afraid to ask for references. (21) If a private breeder is too expensive, you also might consider getting a dog from your city's animal shelter. (22) When you get a dog from the animal shelter you often only have to pay for the dog's license and required shots.

(D)

(23) When you pick out a puppy from a litter, observe the puppies carefully from a distance. (24) How do the puppies relate? (25) Choose a puppy whose character you like.

(E)

(26) Once you have narrowed your choice to one puppy, examine it carefully. (27) Does the puppy let you handle him or her? (28) Look over the dog to make sure their skin and fur look healthy. (29) Make sure the puppy doesn't have ticks or fleas. (30) Check the puppy's gums. (31) Pink gums indicate good health. (32) White gums could indicate anemia caused by heartworm.

(F)

(33) After you get your puppy home, continue to observe it to make sure it is the dog for you. (34) If you need further advice, check with the breeder or your vet. (35) With any luck, you will have a fine pet who will give you and your family years of loyalty and companionship.

22 Sentence 22: **When you get a dog from the animal shelter you often only have to pay for the dog's license and required shots.**

Which correction should be made to sentence 22?

① insert a comma after <u>dog</u>
② insert a comma after <u>shelter</u>
③ replace <u>you often</u> with <u>one often</u>
④ replace <u>dog's</u> with <u>dogs'</u>
⑤ insert a comma after <u>license</u>

23 Sentence 28: **Look over the dog to make sure <u>their</u> skin and fur look healthy.**

Which is the best way to write the underlined portion of this sentence? If the original is the best way, choose option (1).

① their
② it's
③ its
④ there
⑤ hers

24 Sentence 30: **Check the <u>puppy's</u> gums.**

Which is the best way to write the underlined portion of this sentence? If the original is the best way, choose option (1).

① puppy's
② puppies'
③ puppies
④ puppies's
⑤ puppys

WHAT ARE COMETS?

(1) Comets are one of the most interesting bodies orbiting the sun. (2) A comet is a frozen chunk of rock, dust gases, and water that orbits around the sun. (3) Comets have an elliptical (oval-shaped) orbit, which takes them far from the sun. (4) Some comets' orbits are very large. (5) Those comets travel millions of miles beyond Pluto, the planet farthest from the sun. (6) When a comet gets near the sun, energy from the sun causes some of the ice and frozen gases to evaporate and form a long tail.

(7) People have known about comets for thousands of years. (8) For example, the Chinese have records of comets from as early as 240 B.C. (9) However, people didn't understand comets at first. (10) In fact, for many years people thought that the appearance of a comet in the sky meant that something terrible is going to happen.

(11) Among the most famous comets is Halley's Comet, which to this day becomes visible from Earth every 76 years. (12) In fact, Halley was the first person to figure out that comets had regular, elliptical orbits. (13) He predicted that the comet would reappear in about 1758, one year later the comet became visible in March, 1759. (14) Another famous comet was Comet Hale-Bopp, which was one of the brightest comets ever observed.

(15) Astronomers believe that there are millions of comets in orbit around the sun. (16) However, until now, they have catalog only about 1,000 of them. (17) They believe that most comets are far from the sun on long, slow orbits and will take many years to come close enough to become visible. (18) Each year, about 10 new comets are discovered, usually by amateur astronomers. (19) One famous comet, Hyakutake, was discovered by a Japanese man, Yuji Hyakutake, on January 30, 1996. (20) He was using only binoculars. (21) When someone finds a new comet, he or she can choose the name. (22) Many of the discoverers, such as Hyakutake, choose to name their comets after them. (23) Who will find the next comet? (24) It could be you.

25 Sentence 2: **A comet is a frozen chunk of rock, dust gases, and water that orbits around the sun.**

Which is the best way to write the underlined portion of this sentence? If the original is the best way, choose option (1).

① rock, dust gases, and water
② rock dust gases and water
③ rock, dust, gases, and, water
④ rock dust gases, and water
⑤ rock, dust, gases, and water

26 Sentences 4 and 5: **Some comets' orbits are very large. Those comets travel millions of miles beyond Pluto, the planet farthest from the sun.**

The most effective combination of sentences 4 and 5 would include which group of words?

① are so large that them
② are so large that they
③ are so large that it
④ are so large that them comets
⑤ are so large that their comets

27 Sentence 10: **In fact, for many years people thought that the appearance of a comet in the sky meant that something terrible is going to happen.**

Which is the best way to write the underlined portion of this sentence? If the original is the best way, choose option (1).

① is
② was
③ had been
④ would have been
⑤ were

28 Sentence 13: **He predicted that the comet would reappear in about 1758, one year later the comet reappeared in March, 1759.**

Which correction should be made to sentence 13?

① change reappear to reappeared
② remove the comma after 1758
③ insert and before one
④ insert since before one
⑤ remove the comma after March

29 Sentence 16: **However, until now, they have catalog only about 1,000 of them.**

Which is the best way to write the underlined portion of this sentence? If the original is the best way, choose option (1).

① have catalog
② having cataloged
③ have cataloged
④ had cataloged
⑤ have cataloging

30 Sentence 22: **Many of the discoverers, such as Hyakutake, choose to name their comets after them.**

Which is the best way to write the underlined portion of this sentence? If the original is the best way, choose option (1).

① them
② herself
③ himself
④ themselves
⑤ itself

Part II

Essay Directions and Topic

Look at the box on page 17. In the box is the assigned topic.
You must write on the assigned topic **ONLY**.

On the GED test, you will have 45 minutes to write on your assigned essay topic. However, on this Pretest, you may take as much time as you wish.

After you write your essay, you or your instructor will score your essay according to its overall effectiveness. Follow the evaluation instructions on pages ix–xi. The evaluation will be based upon the following criteria:

- Well-focused main points
- Clear organization
- Specific development of your ideas
- Control of sentence structure, punctuation, grammar, word choice, and spelling

Be sure to do the following:

- Write legibly in ink so that readers will be able to read your writing.
- Write on the assigned topic.
- Write your essay on ordinary lined paper or the Essay Answer Sheet (page 143).

IMPORTANT:

On the GED test, you may return to the multiple-choice section after you complete your essay if you have time remaining in the test period. However, on this Pretest, you may take as much time as you wish on both parts of the test.

Essay Topic

We all have different reasons for choosing our friends.

In your essay, identify three reasons you have for choosing your friends. Explain the importance of each reason. Use your personal observations, experience, and knowledge to support your essay.

Part II is a test to determine how well you can use written language to explain your ideas.

In preparing your essay, you should take the following steps:

- Read the **DIRECTIONS** and the **TOPIC** carefully.
- Plan your essay before you write. Use scratch paper to make any notes.
- Before you turn in your essay, reread what you have written and make any changes that will improve your essay.

Your essay should be long enough to develop the topic adequately.

Pretest Evaluation Charts

After you complete the Pretest, use these charts to figure out which skills you need to focus on in the instruction section of this book.

To complete the charts, use results from the Answer Key, pages 146–149 and the GED Essay Scoring Guide and Instructions, pages ix–xi.

Part I

In column 1, circle the numbers of the questions you missed. The second and third columns tell you the name of the skill and its number in the instruction section of this book. Focus your preparation on those skills. The fourth column tells you the page numbers to study. After you study the pages, put a check in the last column.

Question Number	Skill Name	Skill	Pages	Completed ✔
1	Subordination	4	26–27	
2	Commas Joining Independent Clauses	20	58–59	
3	Homonyms	26	70–71	
4	Comma Details	23	64–65	
5	Topic Sentences and Paragraphs	27	72–73	
6	Capitalization	18	54–55	
7	Parallel Structure	6	30–31	
8	Sequence of Verb Tense	12	42–43	
9	Avoiding Pronoun Shift	17	52–53	
10	Commas after Introductory Prepositional Phrases	22	62–63	
11	Unity and Coherence	28	74–75	
12	Subject-Verb Agreement	7	32–33	
13	Run-On Sentences	2	22–23	
14	Pronoun Agreement	15	48–49	
15	Misplaced and Dangling Modifiers	5	28–29	
16	Agreement with Interrupting Structures	8	34–35	
17	Joining and Dividing Paragraphs	29	76–77	
18	Sentence Fragments	1	20–21	
19	Agreement with Inverted Structures	9	36–37	
20	Transitions Within Paragraphs	30	78–79	
21	Avoiding Excess Commas	24	66–67	
22	Commas Joining Subordinate Clauses	21	60–61	
23	Possessive Pronouns	14	46–47	
24	Using Apostrophes	25	68–69	
25	Commas in a Series	19	56–57	
26	Subject and Object Pronouns	13	44–45	
27	Using Word Clues to Figure Out Tense	11	40–41	
28	Comma Splice	3	24–25	
29	Correct Verb Forms	10	38–39	
30	Reflexive and Indefinite Pronouns	16	50–51	

Part II

After you evaluate your essay by following the instructions on page ix, circle your score for each part of the Essay Scoring Guide in this chart. Then focus your preparation on the skills with a score of 2 or lower. The remaining columns tell you each skill's name, number, and page numbers to study. After you study the pages, put a check in the last column.

Criteria	My Score	Skill Name	Skill Number	Pages	Completed ✔
Response to the Prompt	1 2 3 4	What Is an Essay?	31	80–81	
		Understanding the Topic	32	82–83	
Organization	1 2 3 4	Parts of the Paragraph	35	88–91	
		Description	36	92–93	
		Narration	39	98–99	
		How-To	40	100–101	
		Giving Reasons	41	102–103	
		Checking the Organization	42	104–105	
		The Three-Paragraph Essay	44	108–109	
		The Introductory Paragraph and Thesis Statement	45	110–111	
		Writing Body Paragraphs	46	112–113	
		Writing Concluding Paragraphs	47	114–115	
		Writing Longer Essays	48	116–117	
Development and Details	1 2 3 4	Brainstorming	33	84–85	
		Support and Relevance	38	96–97	
		Raising Your Score: Content and Organization	49	118–119	
Conventions of Edited American English	1 2 3 4	Complete Sentences	34	86–87	
		Revising Mechanics	43	106–107	
		Raising Your Score: Sentence Structure	50	120–121	
Word Choice	1 2 3 4	Word Choice	37	94–95	

Sentence Fragments

A complete sentence

- has a complete subject and a complete verb
- expresses a complete thought
- can stand alone

Example:
Martha baked a delicious apple pie.

Martha is the subject; *baked* is the verb. The sentence expresses a complete thought and can stand alone.

A **sentence fragment** is an incomplete sentence. A sentence fragment

- lacks a complete subject or complete verb
- does not express a complete thought
- cannot stand alone

Examples:
- Nancy been my boss for the last three years.
  (lacks a complete verb, does not express a complete thought, and cannot stand alone)

- Although he likes candy a lot.
  (dependent clause: does not express a complete thought and cannot stand alone)

- That he bought at a discount store.
  (relative clause: does not express a complete thought and cannot stand alone)

Correcting a Sentence Fragment

There are three ways to correct a sentence fragment:

- Add a subject and/or a complete verb.
  Nancy **has** been my boss for the last three years.
  (added a complete verb)

- Add an independent clause.
  Although he likes candy a lot, **he never eats <u>it</u>**.

- Add a clause that completes the thought.
  He's wearing a brand-new sweater that he bought at a discount store.

A **sentence fragment** is an incomplete sentence.	

A **dependent clause** is introduced by a word such as *after, although, because, before, if, since, unless, until, when,* or *where.*	

A **relative clause** is introduced by a relative pronoun such as *who, whom, which, that, whoever,* or *whatever.*	

GED Readiness

Questions 1 through 5 refer to the following e-mail. Circle the number of the <u>one best answer</u> to each item.

To: Mark Bell (mbell@world.com)
From: Lee Phillip (lphillip@world.com)

(1) I am writing to invite you to a meeting tomorrow afternoon. (2) We discussing a number of important issues about the upcoming fall sales campaign. (3) Beginning next month, the campaign will run for six weeks. (4) The campaign is an important time for the company to get new customers. (5) Which we need to increase our income. (6) The meeting is in Conference Room A from 2:00 to 4:00. (7) Although we might have to move to the Executive Conference Room because of another meeting scheduled for Conference Room A. (8) I will send you another e-mail if the room changes. (9) Hoped you have a lot of good ideas to share.

Correction

1 Sentence 2: **We discussing a number of important issues about the upcoming fall sales campaign.**

Which correction should be made to sentence 2?

① change <u>discussing</u> to <u>discussed</u>
② change <u>discussing</u> to <u>is discussing</u>
③ change <u>discussing</u> to <u>will be discussing</u>
④ change <u>discussing</u> to <u>be discussing</u>
⑤ no correction is necessary

Correction

2 Sentence 3: **Beginning next month, the campaign will run for six weeks.**

Which correction should be made to sentence 3?

① change <u>Beginning</u> to <u>Will be beginning</u>
② insert <u>The campaign</u> before <u>Beginning</u>
③ change <u>Beginning</u> to <u>Begun</u>
④ remove <u>Beginning next month,</u>
⑤ no correction is necessary

Revision

3 Sentences 4 and 5: **The campaign is an important time for the company to get new <u>customers. Which we</u> need to increase our income.**

Which is the best way to write the underlined portion of these sentences? If the original is the best way, choose option (1).

① customers. Which we
② customers, so we
③ customers where we
④ customers, which we
⑤ customers

Revision

4 Sentences 6 and 7: **The meeting is in Conference Room A <u>from 2:00 to 4:00. Although we</u> might have to move to the Executive Conference Room because of another meeting scheduled for Conference Room A.**

Which is the best way to write the underlined portion of these sentences? If the original is the best way, choose option (1).

① from 2:00 to 4:00. Although we
② from 2:00 to 4:00 we
③ from 2:00 to 4:00, we
④ from 2:00 to 4:00 however we
⑤ from 2:00 to 4:00 although we

Correction

5 Sentence 9: **Hoped you have a lot of good ideas to share.**

Which correction should be made to sentence 9?

① replace <u>Hoped</u> with <u>Hopes</u>
② insert <u>I</u> before <u>Hoped</u>
③ replace <u>Hoped</u> with <u>I hope</u>
④ change <u>Hoped</u> to <u>Be hoping</u>
⑤ no correction is necessary

Run-On Sentences

A **run-on sentence** is two or more independent clauses joined together without connecting words or punctuation. (A **clause** is a group of words with a complete subject and complete verb. An **independent clause** can stand alone as a sentence.)

Example:

Going to a car race is a lot of fun it's exciting to see which driver will win.

The two independent clauses are: *Going to a car race is a lot of fun* and *it's exciting to see which driver will win.* Both of these clauses have complete subjects and complete verbs and can stand alone.

Correcting a Run-On Sentence

There are several ways to correct a run-on sentence:

- Divide the run-on sentence into two separate sentences.
  Going to a car race is a lot of fun. It's exciting to see which car will win.

- Join the two clauses with a semicolon.
  Going to a car race is a lot of fun; it's exciting to see which car will win.

- Join the clauses with a comma and a coordinating conjunction *(and, but, or, nor, for, yet,* and *so).*
  Going to a car race is a lot of fun, **and** it's exciting to see which car will win.

- Join the two clauses with a subordinating conjunction and a comma (if necessary). Common subordinating conjunctions include *although, because, before, even though, if, though, unless, when,* and *while.*
  Going to a car race is a lot of fun **because** it's exciting to see which car will win.

- When you join an independent clause and a dependent clause into a single sentence, use a comma only when the dependent clause comes first.
  Because it's exciting to see which car will win, going to a car race is a lot of fun.

A **run-on sentence** is two or more independent clauses joined together without connecting words or punctuation.

A **clause** is a group of words with a complete subject and complete verb.

An **independent clause** can stand alone as a sentence.

A **dependent clause** cannot stand alone as a sentence. It must be joined to an independent clause.

GED Readiness

Questions 1 through 5 refer to the following information. Circle the number of the one best answer to each item.

> ### KEEPING YOUR CAR IN GOOD REPAIR
>
> (1) Nothing is more frustrating than having your car break down it can ruin your entire day. (2) Several steps your car in good operating condition and will help you avoid trouble on the road. (3) First, you should have your oil changed and your fluid levels, air filter, and battery checked every three months or 3,000 miles. (4) Second, check your tire pressure regularly you should put air in your tires whenever the pressure looks low. (5) You check your tires make sure you check the air pressure in your spare tire, too. (6) Finally, make sure you take your car in for tune-ups and other scheduled maintenance.

Correction

1 Sentence 1: **Nothing is more frustrating than having your car break down it can ruin your entire day.**

Which correction should be made to sentence 1?

1. replace <u>down it</u> with <u>down. It</u>
2. replace <u>break</u> with <u>brake</u>
3. change <u>break</u> to <u>broke</u>
4. insert a comma after <u>down</u>
5. no correction is necessary

Correction

2 Sentence 2: **Several steps your car in good operating condition and will help you avoid trouble on the road.**

Which correction should be made to sentence 2?

1. insert <u>will keep</u> after <u>steps</u>
2. insert a comma after <u>condition</u>
3. remove <u>and</u>
4. replace <u>condition and will help you</u> with <u>condition. Help you</u>
5. change <u>will help</u> to <u>helps</u>

Revision

3 Sentence 3: **First, you should have your <u>oil changed and your fluid levels, air filter, and battery checked</u> every three months or 3,000 miles.**

Which is the best way to write the underlined portion of this sentence? If the original is the best way, choose option (1).

1. oil changed and your fluid levels, air filter, and battery checked
2. oil changed, your fluid levels, air filter, and battery checked
3. oil changed, and your fluid levels air filter and battery checked
4. oil changed and your fluid levels air filter, and battery checked
5. oil changed, and your fluid levels air filter, and battery checked

Correction

4 Sentence 4: **Second, check your tire pressure regularly you should put air in your tires whenever the pressure looks low.**

Which correction should be made to sentence 4?

1. insert a comma after <u>regularly</u>
2. insert a semicolon after <u>regularly</u>
3. change <u>regularly</u> to <u>regular</u>
4. remove <u>you should</u>
5. no correction is necessary

Construction Shift

5 Sentence 5: **You check your tires make sure you check the air pressure in your spare tire, too.**

If you rewrote sentence 5 beginning with
<u>When you check</u>
the next words should be

1. make sure you check
2. the air pressure in your spare tire
3. your tires, the air pressure
4. your tires, make sure
5. your spare tire

3

Comma Splice

A **comma splice** and a run-on sentence are very similar. They both involve two clauses that are improperly joined. A comma splice occurs when two independent clauses are joined together with a comma.

Example:

A tornado is a dangerous storm, a hailstorm can be dangerous, too.

The two independent clauses are: *A tornado is a dangerous storm* and *a hailstorm can be dangerous, too.* Both of these clauses have a complete subject and a complete verb and can stand alone.

Correcting a Comma Splice

There are several ways to correct a comma splice:

- Divide the comma splice into two separate sentences.
  A tornado is a dangerous storm. A hailstorm can be dangerous, too.

- Join the two clauses into a single sentence with a semicolon.
  A tornado is a dangerous storm; a hailstorm can be dangerous, too.

- If the two clauses are connected with a transitional word, such as *however, therefore,* or *for example,* use a semicolon and a comma.
  A tornado is a dangerous storm; **however,** a hailstorm can be dangerous, too.

- Add a comma and a coordinating conjunction *(and, but, or, nor, for, yet,* and *so).*
  A tornado is a dangerous storm, **but** a hailstorm can be dangerous, too.

- Add a subordinating conjunction and use a comma if necessary. Common subordinating conjunctions include *although, because, before, even though, if, though, unless, when, whether,* and *while.*

  If the subordinating conjunction is the first word in the sentence, a comma is needed.
  Although a tornado is a dangerous storm, a hailstorm can be dangerous, too.

  If the subordinating conjunction is in the middle of the sentence, no comma is needed.
  A tornado is a dangerous storm **although** a hailstorm can be dangerous, too.

> A **comma splice** occurs when you join two independent clauses with a comma.

GED Readiness

Questions 1 through 4 refer to the following information. Circle the number of the <u>one best answer</u> to each item.

BOYD MANUFACTURING COMPANY
Providing Good Customer Service

(1) Good customer service is part of our job, whether we work directly with customers or not. (2) Our company exists because of our customers, we must provide excellent customer service to keep their business. (3) Here are some ideas that will help you provide the outstanding service that our customers deserve:

- (4) First, smile when you are on the phone with a customer. (5) Smiling gives your voice a pleasant tone.
- (6) Second, prepare all customer orders carefully. (7) Make sure that orders are accurate and complete.
- (8) Third, listen carefully a customer has a complaint. (9) Try to resolve the complaint in a way that's fair for the customer and the company.

(10) Following these steps will help us become the best company in our growing industry. (11) Remember, it's easy to lose a customer, it's much harder to get a new one.

Revision

1 Sentence 1: **Good customer service is part of our <u>job, whether we</u> work directly with customers or not.**

Which is the best way to write the underlined portion of this sentence? If the original is the best way, choose option (1).

(1) job, whether we
(2) job we
(3) job whether we
(4) job, and we
(5) job; whether we

Revision

2 Sentence 2: **Our company exists because of our <u>customers, we must</u> provide excellent customer service to keep their business.**

Which is the best way to write the underlined portion of this sentence? If the original is the best way, choose option (1).

(1) customers, we must
(2) customers we must
(3) customers, must
(4) customers, however, we must
(5) customers, so we must

Correction

3 Sentence 8: **Third, listen carefully a customer has a complaint.**

Which correction should be made to sentence 8?

(1) insert <u>when</u> after <u>carefully</u>
(2) insert a comma after <u>carefully</u>
(3) insert <u>yet</u> after <u>carefully</u>
(4) insert <u>so</u> after <u>carefully</u>
(5) no correction is necessary

Revision

4 Sentence 11: **Remember, it's easy to lose a <u>customer, it's</u> much harder to get a new one.**

Which is the best way to write the underlined portion of this sentence? If the original is the best way, choose option (1).

(1) customer, it's
(2) customer; it's
(3) customer it's
(4) customer, however, it's
(5) customer, so it's

4

Subordination

Subordinate Clauses

A clause is a group of words including a subject and a verb. An independent clause expresses a complete thought and can stand alone. A **dependent or subordinate clause** does not express a complete thought and cannot stand alone. A subordinate clause needs to be joined to an independent clause.

Example:

> Every spring, we go on a picnic at the state park **once the weather is nice**.

The subordinate clause *once the weather is nice* is joined to an independent clause.

Example:

> We always leave early **so that we can enjoy the spring weather**.

The subordinate clause *so that we can enjoy the spring weather* is joined to an independent clause.

Subordinating Conjunctions

These subordinating conjunctions introduce subordinate clauses:

Time	Reason or Effect	Concession	Place	Condition	Manner

after
as
before
once
since
when
until
whenever
while
	as
	because
	since
	so that
	in order
	  that
		although
		even
		  though
		though
		while
			where
			wherever
				even if
				if
				in case
				unless
				until
					as if
					as though

Examples:

> Tomorrow we are going to go on a picnic **unless** it rains.
> We are going to go to the state park **because** it has nice hiking trails.
> We'll find a nice picnic spot **where** we can relax and eat.
> We'll bring charcoal **so that** we can barbeque hot dogs and hamburgers.
> **After** we eat lunch, we'll go on a long hike in the forest.
> **Although** we like to hike, we won't walk more than two miles.
> We'll stay at the park **until** it gets dark.
> You're invited to come with us **if** you want.

A **dependent or subordinate clause** has a subject and a verb but is not a complete thought and cannot stand alone. A subordinate clause needs to be joined to an independent clause.

Tip

Use a comma when a subordinate clause is first in the sentence. Do not use a comma when the subordinate clause is at the end of the sentence.

Examples:

We'll go on a picnic unless it rains. (no comma)
Unless it rains, we'll go on a picnic. (comma)

GED Readiness

Questions 1 through 4 refer to the following information. Circle the number of the one best answer to each item.

HOW TO GET ON A TV GAME SHOW

(1) It seems that every day, people are winning big prizes on TV game shows. (2) How can you get a chance to win prizes on your favorite game show? (3) On some shows, contestants are selected from the audience the day of the show. (4) On other shows, contestants are selected months in advance. (5) For example, on the popular show *The Price Is Right*, contestants are picked from the audience. (6) You run to the front of the studio. (7) Your name is called. (8) Of course, before the show is taped, you will need to fill out forms in case you are selected and win a prize. (9) On the more selective shows, you will need to take a test. (10) That's the case on a show like *Jeopardy*. (11) People have to take a written test and then wait unless they are called for a screen test.

Construction Shift

❶ Sentences 3 and 4: **On some shows, contestants are selected from the audience the day of the show. On other shows, contestants are selected months in advance.**

The most effective combination of sentences 3 and 4 would include which group of words?

① the day of the show when on other shows
② the day of the show, when on other shows
③ the day of the show while on other shows
④ the day of the show where on other shows
⑤ the day of the show since on other shows

Construction Shift

❷ Sentences 6 and 7: **You run to the front of the studio. Your name is called.**

Which is the most effective combination of sentences 6 and 7?

① You run to the front of the studio, and your name is called.
② You run to the front of the studio your name is called.
③ You run to the front of the studio, your name is called.
④ You run to the front of the studio when your name is called.
⑤ You run to the front of the studio, when your name is called.

Correction

❸ Sentence 8: **Of course, before the show is taped, you will need to fill out forms in case you are selected and win a prize.**

Which correction should be made to sentence 8?

① replace before with until
② replace before with while
③ remove the comma after taped
④ replace in case with because
⑤ no correction is necessary

Correction

❹ Sentence 11: **People have to take a written test and then wait unless they are called for a screen test.**

Which correction should be made to sentence 11?

① insert a comma after wait
② replace unless with until
③ replace unless with when
④ replace unless with after
⑤ replace unless with although

5 Misplaced and Dangling Modifiers

Misplaced Modifiers

A modifier is a word or phrase that describes another word or phrase. A **misplaced modifier** is not placed near the word or phrase it describes. The reader cannot tell what is being described.

Examples:

Jin saw an auto accident looking out the window.

According to the way the sentence is written, an auto accident was looking out the window, not Jin.

Mrs. Johnson is a tall woman with blond hair weighing 170 pounds.

According to the sentence, Mrs. Johnson's hair weighs 170 pounds.

Correcting a Misplaced Modifier

To fix a misplaced modifier, move the modifier closer to the noun or phrase it modifies. Sometimes you may need to reword the modifier.

Examples:

Looking out the window, Jin saw an accident.

Mrs. Johnson is a tall, **170-pound** woman with blond hair.

Dangling Modifiers

A **dangling modifier** has no word to modify in the sentence.

Examples:

Waiting for the elevator, the fire alarm went off.

Who was waiting for the elevator? According to the sentence, the fire alarm.

Doing the laundry, the buttons came off the new shirt.

Who was doing the laundry? According to the sentence, the buttons.

Correcting a Dangling Modifier

To fix a dangling modifier, revise the sentence so that the modifier has a noun or phrase to describe.

Examples:

Waiting for the elevator, **Evelyn heard** the fire alarm go off.

While Max was doing the laundry, the buttons came off the new shirt.

A **misplaced modifier** is a modifier that is not placed near the word it modifies.

A **dangling modifier** occurs when the sentence lacks a word for the modifier to describe.

Tip

To correct a misplaced or dangling modifier, figure out which word should be modified. Then revise the sentence to make the relationship clear.

GED Readiness

Questions 1 through 5 refer to the following information. Circle the number of the **one best answer** to each item.

THE LOST DOG

(1) Marcus barely avoided a freak traffic accident last week. (2) Driving home from work, a dog ran across the highway in front of his car. (3) Marcus braked and veered to the right to avoid the dog sharply. (4) Confused, the dog turned and ran back into the path of Marcus's car. (5) This time Marcus stopped. (6) Then the dog limped to the side of the road. (7) Realizing that the dog was hurt, Marcus pulled off the highway and approached the dog completely. (8) Marcus gathered the dog up, took it home, and called the dog's owner. (9) Picking up the dog at Marcus's house, the dog was glad to see his owner.

Revision

1 Sentence 2: **Driving home from work, a dog ran across the highway in front of his car.**

Which is the best way to rewrite the underlined portion of this sentence? If the original is the best, choose option (1).

① work, a dog ran
② work a dog ran
③ work, Marcus saw a dog run
④ work, Marcus ran
⑤ work ran

Correction

2 Sentence 3: **Marcus braked and veered to the right to avoid the dog sharply.**

Which correction should be made to sentence 3?

① move sharply to the beginning of the sentence
② move sharply to follow veered
③ change sharply to sharp
④ change sharply to sharper
⑤ no correction is necessary

Correction

3 Sentence 4: **Confused, the dog turned and ran back into the path of Marcus's car.**

Which correction should be made to sentence 4?

① remove the comma after Confused
② remove Confused
③ move Confused to preceed path
④ move Confused to follow Marcus's
⑤ no correction is necessary

Correction

4 Sentence 7: **Realizing that the dog was hurt, Marcus pulled off the highway and approached the dog completely.**

Which correction should be made to sentence 7?

① Move Realizing that the dog was hurt, to the end of the sentence.
② remove the comma after hurt
③ insert a comma after highway
④ move completely to follow highway
⑤ no correction is necessary

Construction Shift

5 Sentence 9: **Picking up the dog at Marcus's house, the dog was glad to see his owner.**

Which is the most effective revision of sentence 9?

① Picking up the dog at Marcus's house, Marcus was glad to see the owner.
② Picking up the dog at Marcus's house, the dog knew that the owner was glad to see him.
③ When the owner picked up the dog at Marcus's house, the dog was glad to see him.
④ Picking up the dog at Marcus's house, the dog was glad to see Marcus.
⑤ Picking up the dog at Marcus's house, Marcus was glad to see the owner.

Parallel Structure

A sentence can contain two or more nouns, verbs, adverbs, phrases, or clauses joined by a conjunction (such as *and* or *or*). Words joined by a conjunction should always be in the same grammatical form. This is called **parallel structure.**

Examples:

> On weekday mornings, Joni **gets up** early, **exercises**, and **leaves** for work by 7:00 A.M. (verbs)

> Getting up so early every day requires **focus** and **discipline**. (nouns)

Correcting Faulty Parallel Structure

When words or phrases joined by a conjunction are not in the same grammatical form, the sentence has faulty parallel structure. Sentences with faulty parallelism are hard to read.

Example:

> On Monday mornings, **Joni gets up** early, **exercises**, and **she leaves** for work by 7:00 A.M.

The sentence has a subject and verb *(Joni gets up)*, then a verb *(exercise)*, then a subject and verb *(she leaves)*. To correct this sentence, use one subject with three verbs, or use three sets of subjects and verbs.

> On Monday mornings, **Joni gets up** early, **exercises**, and **leaves** for work by 7:00 A.M. (one subject with three verbs)

> On Monday mornings, **Joni gets up** early, **she exercises**, and **she leaves** for work by 7:00 A.M. (three sets of subjects and verbs)

Example:

> Getting up so early every day requires **focus** and **being disciplined**.

The sentence has a noun *(focus)* and an *-ing* form *(being disciplined)*. To correct this sentence, use two nouns or two *-ing* forms.

> Getting up so early every day requires **focus** and **discipline**. (two nouns)

> Getting up so early every day requires **being focused** and **being disciplined**. (two *-ing* forms)

Example:

> It's not fun **to clean** the bathroom and **doing** the laundry.

The sentence has an infinitive *(to clean)* and an *-ing* form *(doing)*. To correct this sentence, use two infinitives or two *-ing* forms

> It's not fun **to clean** the bathroom and **do** the laundry. (two infinitives)

> It's not fun **cleaning** the bathroom and **doing** the laundry. (two *-ing* forms)

> A sentence has **parallel structure** when the items joined by a conjunction are in the same grammatical form. Parallel structure makes a sentence easy to read.

Tip

To figure out whether a sentence is in parallel structure, look at the items joined by *and* or *or*. The items should be in the same grammatical form.

GED Readiness

ORGANIZING YOUR CLOSETS

(1) Keeping your closets clean and in an organized state is not easy. (2) In fact, there are now closet consultants, experts who will tell you how to clean and organizing your closets. (3) Usually, a closet consultant will tell you to start by going through everything in your closet. (4) First, get rid of any clothes that are too small or very large. (5) Donate everything you don't want or need to charity. (6) Then organize your clothes into groups and hang them together. (7) Having an organized closet will help you find the right outfit for a night on the town or to spend a day at the park.

Correction

① Sentence 1: **Keeping your closets clean and in an organized state is not easy.**

Which correction should be made to sentence 1?

① change <u>Keeping</u> to <u>Keep</u>
② change <u>clean</u> to <u>cleaned</u>
③ replace <u>in an organized state</u> with <u>organized</u>
④ replace <u>in an organized state</u> with <u>organization</u>
⑤ no correction is necessary

Correction

② Sentence 2: **In fact, there are now closet consultants, experts who will tell you how to clean and organizing your closets.**

Which correction should be made to sentence 2?

① change <u>will tell</u> to <u>telling</u>
② insert <u>how to</u> before <u>organizing</u>
③ change <u>organizing</u> to <u>organize</u>
④ change <u>organizing</u> to <u>organizes</u>
⑤ no correction is necessary

Correction

③ Sentence 4: **First, get rid of any clothes that are too small or very large.**

Which correction should be made to sentence 4?

① change <u>get</u> to <u>getting</u>
② replace <u>too small</u> with <u>smaller</u>
③ insert <u>too</u> before <u>very</u>
④ replace <u>very</u> with <u>too</u>
⑤ no correction is necessary

Revision

④ Sentence 5: **Donate everything you <u>don't want or need</u> to charity.**

Which is the best way to rewrite the underlined portion of the sentence? If the original is the best way, choose option (1).

① don't want or need
② don't to want or need
③ don't to want or to need
④ don't want or needing
⑤ don't wanting or needing

Correction

⑤ Sentence 7: **Having an organized closet will help you find the right outfit for a night on the town or to spend a day at the park.**

Which correction should be made to sentence 7?

① insert <u>to</u> after <u>you</u>
② insert <u>spending</u> after <u>for</u>
③ insert <u>the right outfit</u> after <u>or</u>
④ remove <u>to spend</u>
⑤ no correction is necessary

Subject–Verb Agreement

Nouns and pronouns can be singular or plural. Present-tense verbs can be singular or plural, too. Look at the chart:

Singular	Plural
I **am** You **are** He, She, It **is**	We **are** You **are** They **are**
I **have** You **have** He, She, It **has**	We **have** You **have** They **have**
I **like** You **like** He, She, It **likes**	We **like** You **like** They **like**

Notice that the singular verbs that go with *he*, *she*, and *it* always end in *–s* or *–es*.

Examples:

- He **is**
- She **has**
- It **likes**

When you write, subjects and verbs should agree.

- Singular subjects should have singular verbs:
  <u>Miguel</u> <u>has</u> worked for this company for a long time.
  <u>He</u> <u>is</u> a good employee.

- Plural subjects should have plural verbs:
  <u>They</u> <u>have</u> worked for this company for a long time.
  <u>Miguel and Sonya</u> <u>are</u> good employees.

It can be hard to tell whether certain subjects are singular or plural. Some words seem plural, but they are singular. For example:

- *Group* can refer to a group of people or things. But *group* takes a singular verb.
  This <u>**group**</u> of employees <u>**is**</u> getting a bonus.

- *Each* refers to several people but takes a singular verb.
  <u>**Each**</u> of the employees <u>**is**</u> getting a bonus for good attendance.

Singular Words: each, either, neither, no one, nothing, nobody, everyone, everything, everybody
Plural Words: several, few, both, many
Singular or Plural: some, most, any, none, all

When the subject has two parts joined by *or* or *nor*, the verb agrees with the word nearest to it.

Examples:

The coach or the players **are** getting the prize.
Neither the players nor the coach **is** getting the prize.

Subjects and present-tense verbs should agree in number. A singular subject should have a singular verb. A plural subject should have a plural verb.

Tip

To figure out whether words like *some* and *all* are singular or plural, check the sentences that follow.

Examples:
Some employees are getting a bonus.

Some money is being distributed to employees as bonuses.

GED Readiness

Questions 1 through 4 refer to the following information. Circle the number of the <u>one best answer</u> to each item.

Modern and Contemporary Art Museum

Visitor Information

(1) The Modern and Contemporary Art Museum have offered an inviting setting for the community to experience works of art for over 50 years.

Hours

(2) The museum is open from 10 A.M. to 5 P.M. seven days a week. (3) We are closed on Thanksgiving Day, Christmas Day, and New Year's Day.

Admission

(4) Admission to the museum is free on Tuesdays. (5) On other days, admission is by donation. (6) Suggested admission is $7.00 for adults. (7) Suggested admission for seniors is $3.00. (8) Suggested admission for children is $3.00. (9) Children under five are always free. (10) Visitors may pay more or less than the suggested donation, but all is required to pay something.

School Groups

(11) School groups are invited to visit the museum on school days. (12) A trained guide always help teachers plan their visits.

Correction

1 Sentence 1: **The Modern and Contemporary Art Museum have offered an inviting setting for the community to experience works of art for over 50 years.**

Which correction should be made to sentence 1?

1. remove <u>have</u>
2. replace <u>have</u> with <u>is</u>
3. change <u>have</u> to <u>has</u>
4. change <u>have</u> to <u>had</u>
5. no correction is necessary

Construction Shift

2 Sentences 7 and 8: **Suggested admission for seniors is $3.00. Suggested admission for children is $3.00.**

Which is the most effective combination of sentences 7 and 8?

1. Suggested admission is $3.00 for seniors and children.
2. Suggested admission are $3.00 for seniors and children.
3. Suggested admission for seniors is $3.00 suggested admission for children is $3.00.
4. Suggested admission for seniors is $3.00, suggested admission for children is $3.00.
5. Suggested admission for seniors is $3.00 and for children.

Correction

3 Sentence 10: **Visitors may pay more or less than the suggested donation, but all is required to pay something.**

Which correction should be made to sentence 10?

1. change <u>may pay</u> to <u>pays</u>
2. change <u>may pay</u> to <u>have paid</u>
3. change <u>is</u> to <u>are</u>
4. change <u>is</u> to <u>have</u>
5. no correction is necessary

Revision

4 Sentence 12: **A trained guide always <u>help</u> teachers plan their visits.**

Which is the best way to write the underlined portion of this sentence? If the original is the best way, choose option (1).

1. help
2. helps
3. helping
4. has helped
5. are helped

Agreement with Interrupting Structures

Sometimes a word or a phrase comes between the subject and the verb. In this case, it can be confusing to determine the subject, which leads to subject-verb agreement errors.

Examples:

- **Incorrect:** Repairing car engines require special skills.
  Problem: *Require* agrees with *engines,* which is not the subject of the sentence.

- **Incorrect:** Replacement parts for your car is on order.
  Problem: *Is* agrees with *car,* which is not the subject of the sentence.

- **Incorrect:** The mechanic who is repairing the cars are almost done.
  Problem: *Are* agrees with *cars,* which is not the subject of the sentence.

- **Incorrect:** The mechanic, one of the company's most skillful workers, usually figure out the problem immediately.
  Problem: *Figure* agrees with *workers,* which is not the subject of the sentence.

Finding and Fixing Agreement Problems with Interrupting Structures

To find and fix agreement problems caused by interrupting structures, you first need to find the real subject of the verb. Then you need to make sure that the verb agrees with that subject.

Examples:

- **Correct:** <u>Repairing</u> car engines <u>requires</u> special skills.
  Requires now agrees with its subject, *repairing,* which is singular.

- **Correct:** <u>Replacement parts</u> for your car <u>are</u> on order.
  Are now agrees with its subject, *replacement parts,* which is plural.

- **Correct:** The <u>mechanic</u> who is repairing the cars <u>is</u> almost done.
  Is now agrees with its subject, *mechanic,* which is singular.

- **Correct:** The <u>mechanic</u>, one of the company's most skillful workers, usually <u>figures</u> out the problem immediately.
  Figures now agrees with its subject, *mechanic,* which is singular.

A word, phrase, or clause may come between a subject and a verb. This can make it difficult to figure out the real subject of the sentence.

Tip

To figure out the actual subject of a sentence, delete any phrases or clauses that come between the subject and the verb. Then make sure the verb and subject agree.

Examples:

The car ~~that the mechanics fixed~~ now works perfectly.

The replacement parts ~~for the car~~ were very expensive.

GED Readiness

Questions 1 through 5 refer to the following information. Circle the number of the <u>one best answer</u> to each item.

COMPUTERS FOR BEGINNERS

(1) Have you always wanted to learn how to use a computer? (2) Learning to use computers are easy in this one-day class at City Community College. (3) Students in this class learns how to start a computer and use basic software. (4) Using computers to send e-mails are also a topic. (5) Our instructor, David Bell, a trainer for several area companies, have experience helping beginners become successful computer users. (6) This course prepares learners for our six-week computer course, *Internet Basics*. (7) Students wanting to learn keyboarding skills can take *Keyboarding for Beginners*, another six-week course.

Correction

1 Sentence 2: **Learning to use computers are easy in this one-day class at City Community College.**

Which correction should be made to sentence 2?

1. replace <u>computers</u> with <u>a computer</u>
2. change <u>are</u> to <u>be</u>
3. change <u>are</u> to <u>is</u>
4. change <u>are</u> to <u>has been</u>
5. no correction is necessary

Correction

2 Sentence 3: **Students in this class learns how to start a computer and use basic software.**

Which correction should be made to sentence 3?

1. change <u>learns</u> to <u>will learn</u>
2. change <u>learns</u> to <u>learned</u>
3. change <u>start</u> to <u>starts</u>
4. change <u>use</u> to <u>uses</u>
5. no correction is necessary

Revision

3 Sentence 4: <u>Using computers to send e-mails are</u> also a topic.

Which is the best way to write the underlined portion of this sentence? If the original is the best way, choose option (1).

1. Using computers to send e-mails are
2. Using a computer to send e-mails are
3. Using a computer to send an e-mail are
4. Using computers to send e-mails is
5. Using computers to send an e-mail are

Correction

4 Sentence 5: **Our instructor, David Bell, a trainer for several area companies, have experience helping beginners become successful computer users.**

Which correction should be made to sentence 5?

1. insert <u>is</u> after <u>Bell</u>
2. change <u>have</u> to <u>has</u>
3. change have to is
4. change <u>become</u> to <u>becomes</u>
5. no correction is necessary

Correction

5 Sentence 7: **Students wanting to learn keyboarding skills can take *Keyboarding for Beginners*, another six-week course.**

Which correction should be made to sentence 7?

1. insert <u>are</u> after <u>Students</u>
2. insert <u>is</u> after <u>Students</u>
3. change <u>can take</u> to <u>is taking</u>
4. insert <u>which are</u> before <u>another</u>
5. no correction is necessary

Agreement with Inverted Structures

Usually the subject comes before the verb in a sentence. But sometimes, subjects and verbs are inverted—the verb comes before the subject. When subjects and verbs are inverted, it can be easy to make a subject-verb agreement error.

- Questions
  Incorrect: Does Mr. Williams and his son want to buy a new SUV?
  Problem: *Does* agrees with *Mr. Williams,* which is not the entire subject of the sentence.

- Sentences that begin with *There* or *Here*
  Incorrect: Here are the SUV they want to buy.
  Incorrect: There is several reasons they want to buy a new SUV.
  Problem: *Here* and *There* are not the subjects of the sentences. The verbs should not agree with them.

- Sentences that begin with an introductory phrase
  Incorrect: In their garage is two classic cars.
  Problem: *Is* agrees with *garage,* which is not the subject of the sentence.

Finding and Fixing Agreement Problems with Inverted Structures

- *Here* and *there* are not the subject of a sentence. For sentences that begin with *here* and *there,* find the subject in the sentence. Make sure the verb agrees with that subject.

- For questions or sentences with an introductory phrase, change the word order so that the subject comes first. Then make sure the subject and verb agree.

Examples:

- **Correct:** <u>Do</u> <u>Mr. Williams and his son</u> <u>want</u> to buy a new SUV?
  (Change the word order to: *Mr. Williams and his son* **do** *want to buy a new SUV.*)

- **Correct:** Here <u>is</u> the <u>SUV</u> they want to buy.
  (*Here* is not the subject. The subject is *SUV.*)

- **Correct:** There <u>are</u> <u>several reasons</u> they want to buy a new SUV.
  (*There* is not the subject. The subject is *several reasons.*)

- **Correct:** In their garage <u>are</u> two classic <u>cars</u>.
  (Change the word order to: *Two classic cars* **are** *in their garage.*)

Several kinds of sentences can have inverted order:
- questions
- sentences that begin with *here* or *there*
- sentences that begin with an introductory phrase

Tip
To find the subject of a sentence with inverted order, check each noun in the sentence until you find a noun that makes sense as the subject of the verb.

GED Readiness

Questions 1 through 5 refer to the following information. Circle the number of the <u>one best answer</u> to each item.

(1) Do you and your family want to have a fun family vacation? (2) Look no further than your nearest state or national park! (3) There is many reasons to vacation in a state or national park. (4) First, most state parks have excellent camping facilities. (5) Second, the state and national park systems offer a wide variety of sights. (6) Yellowstone National Park, for example, has geysers, such as the famous Old Faithful, that frequently spew water into the air. (7) At Grand Canyon National Park are one of the most amazing sights in the world, the Grand Canyon. (8) Third, the park system, which includes hundreds of parks in all 50 states and Puerto Rico, offer plenty of activities. (9) So for your next family vacation, consider our state and national parks.

Correction

1 Sentence 1: **Do you and your family want to have a fun family vacation?**

Which correction should be made to sentence 1?

① change <u>Do</u> to <u>Does</u>
② replace <u>Do</u> with <u>Are</u>
③ change <u>want</u> to <u>wants</u>
④ change <u>have</u> to <u>has</u>
⑤ no correction is needed

Correction

2 Sentence 3: **There is many reasons to vacation in a state or national park.**

Which correction should be made to sentence 3?

① remove <u>is</u>
② change <u>is</u> to <u>are</u>
③ insert <u>is</u> after <u>or</u>
④ insert <u>are</u> after <u>or</u>
⑤ no correction is necessary

Correction

3 Sentence 6: **Yellowstone National Park, for example, has geysers, such as the famous Old Faithful, that frequently spew water into the air.**

Which correction should be made to sentence 6?

① change <u>has</u> to <u>have</u>
② change <u>has</u> to <u>are</u>
③ change <u>has</u> to <u>is</u>
④ change <u>spew</u> to <u>spews</u>
⑤ no correction is necessary

Correction

4 Sentence 7: **At Grand Canyon National Park are one of the most amazing sights in the world, the Grand Canyon.**

Which correction should be made to sentence 7?

① change <u>are</u> to <u>is</u>
② change <u>are</u> to <u>has</u>
③ change <u>are</u> to <u>have</u>
④ insert <u>is</u> after <u>sights</u>
⑤ insert <u>are</u> after <u>sights</u>

Correction

5 Sentence 8: **Third, the park system, which includes hundreds of parks in all 50 states and Puerto Rico, offer plenty of activities.**

Which correction should be made to sentence 8?

① change <u>includes</u> to <u>include</u>
② change <u>includes</u> to <u>including</u>
③ change <u>offer</u> to <u>offers</u>
④ change <u>offer</u> to <u>offered</u>
⑤ no correction is necessary

Correct Verb Forms

A sentence should have a complete subject and a complete verb. Certain verb forms, such as present participles and past participles, cannot stand on their own. They need to have a helping verb, such as a form of *be (am, is, are, was, were)* or *have (has, had)*.

Here are some present and past participles that use helping verbs:

Tense or Structure	Example
Present Progressive Tense	She **is cleaning** the living room.
Past Progressive Tense	He **was doing** the laundry when the phone rang.
Present Perfect Tense	She **has lived** here since 1999.
Past Perfect Tense	She **had washed** the car just before the rain started.
Passive voice	The man **was bit** by the dog.

Correcting Verb Form Errors

To correct verb form errors, make sure that every present and past participle has a form of *be* or *have* with it when it is the main verb in the sentence.

Examples:

> **Incorrect:** Maria's dishwasher is not working, so she **done** the dishes by hand every night this week.

> **Correct:** Maria's dishwasher is not working, so she **has done** the dishes by hand every night this week.

> **Incorrect:** Maria **getting** tired of washing the dishes every night.

> **Correct:** Maria **is getting** tired of washing the dishes every night.

A gerund (an -ing verb used as a noun) doesn't need a form of *have* or *be*.

Example:

> Smoking **is** a bad habit.

A present participle used as an adjective doesn't need a form of *have* or *be*.

Example:

> He **read** a fascinating book.

A sentence should have a complete subject and a complete verb. Present participles and past participles cannot stand on their own. They need to have a helping verb, such as a form of *be* or *have*.

GED Readiness

Questions 1 through 5 refer to the following information. Circle the number of the <u>one best answer</u> to each item.

> To: All Employees
> From: David Salinas, Data Services Manager
>
> (1) We have having several problems with data loss on the company's personal computers. (2) In some cases, workers losing a day or more of work because their computer's hard drive crashed. (3) One department lost a database of 10,000 customer names, addresses, and phone numbers. (4) To stop these losses, the company requesting that employees back up important files on a separate floppy disk. (5) If you working on a file over a period of several days, back up the file regularly.

Revision

1 Sentence 1: **We <u>have having</u> several problems with data loss on the company's personal computers.**

Which is the best way to write the underlined portion of this sentence? If the original is the best way, choose option (1).

1. have having
2. had having
3. has having
4. are having
5. are had

Correction

2 Sentence 2: **In some cases, workers losing a day or more of work because their computer's hard drive crashed.**

Which correction should be made to sentence 2?

1. change <u>losing</u> to <u>has lost</u>
2. change <u>losing</u> to <u>had losing</u>
3. change <u>losing</u> to <u>are losing</u>
4. change <u>crashed</u> to <u>has crashed</u>
5. changed <u>crashed</u> to <u>crashing</u>

Revision

3 Sentence 3: **One department <u>lost</u> a database of 10,000 customer names, addresses, and phone numbers.**

Which is the best way to write the underlined portion of this sentence? If the original is the best way, choose option (1).

1. lost
2. have lost
3. had lost
4. are losing
5. losing

Correction

4 Sentence 4: **To stop these losses, the company requesting that employees back up important files on a separate floppy disk.**

Which correction should be made to sentence 4?

1. change <u>stop</u> to <u>have stopped</u>
2. change <u>requesting</u> to <u>requests</u>
3. change <u>back up</u> to <u>had backed up</u>
4. change <u>back up</u> to <u>are backing up</u>
5. no correction is necessary

Revision

5 Sentence 5: **If you <u>working</u> on a file over a period of several days, back up the file regularly.**

Which is the best way to write the underlined portion of this sentence? If the original is the best way, choose option (1).

1. working
2. are working
3. worked
4. had worked
5. were worked

Using Word Clues to Figure Out Verb Tense

The form of a verb shows person—singular or plural. The form of a verb also shows the time it refers to—past, present or future. This is called **verb tense.**

- **Past:** I went to bed late last night.

- **Present:** I feel really sleepy today.

- **Future:** I will try to get a better night's sleep tonight.

Word Clues in the Sentence

Usually, the words in a sentence will help you figure out the tense of the verb. An adverb such as *tomorrow,* for instance, will help you figure out that the sentence is about the future. Or, a verb in the simple past tense may tell you that other verbs in the sentence should also be in the past tense.

Examples:
 Yesterday, I **started** work at 5:00 A.M.
 I **left** home at 4:30 in the morning and **got** to work at 4:55.

Word Clues in the Paragraph

Sometimes, the clue to the tense of a verb will be in the other sentences in the paragraph. For example, if a paragraph is about something that happened in the past, all of the sentences in the paragraph should be in the past tense.

Example:
 Yesterday morning was Saturday, so I **slept** late. Then I **got** up and **cooked** my wife breakfast. I **made** her favorite—fresh orange juice, whole-wheat pancakes with real maple syrup, and a cup of hot coffee. It **was** a beautiful spring morning, so we **worked** in our front yard and garden most of the day.

In this example, only one adverb phrase, *yesterday morning,* tells the time the action took place. But all of the verbs in the paragraph are in the simple past tense.

A verb can show the time of the action: past, present, or future. This is called the **tense** of the verb.

Tip

To figure out the tense of a verb, look at the words in the sentence. The adverbs and other verbs can help you figure out the correct tense of the verb. If you can't figure out the tense from the words in the sentence, look at the verbs and adverbs in the rest of the paragraph.

GED Readiness

Questions 1 through 5 refer to the following information. Circle the number of the <u>one best answer</u> to each item.

---

(1) Collecting baseball cards was one of the most popular hobbies today. (2) But what is the history of baseball cards?

(3) The first baseball cards were produced in about 1869. (4) These original cards are not sold with gum or any other product. (5) The front of each card had a picture of a baseball player, and the back had an advertisement. (6) In the 1880s, tobacco companies began to include cards with their products. (7) The companies produced over 2,000 kinds of cards, and occasionally collectors still found new cards from that time today.

(8) Tobacco companies stopped making baseball cards during World War 1, but then gum and candy companies began making them. (9) Today, many adults have collections of baseball cards that they start when they were children, and many more continue to collect them.

Revision

❶ Sentence 1: **Collecting baseball cards <u>was</u> one of the most popular hobbies today.**

Which is the best way to write the underlined portion of this sentence? If the original is the best way, choose option (1).

① was   ④ is
② has been   ⑤ will be
③ are

Revision

❷ Sentence 4: **These original cards <u>are</u> not sold with gum or any other product.**

Which is the best way to write the underlined portion of this sentence? If the original is the best way, choose option (1).

① are   ④ have been
② was   ⑤ will be
③ were

Revision

❸ Sentence 5: **The front of each card had a picture of a baseball player, and the back <u>had</u> an advertisement.**

Which is the best way to write the underlined portion of this sentence? If the original is the best way, choose option (1).

① had   ④ is having
② has   ⑤ will have
③ have

Correction

❹ Sentence 7: **The companies produced over 2,000 kinds of cards, and occasionally collectors still found new cards from that time today.**

Which correction should be made to sentence 7?

① change <u>produced</u> to <u>produce</u>
② change <u>produced</u> to <u>have produced</u>
③ change <u>found</u> to <u>find</u>
④ change <u>found</u> to <u>had found</u>
⑤ no corrcction is necessary

Correction

❺ Sentence 9: **Today, many adults have collections of baseball cards that they start when they were children, and many more continue to collect them.**

Which correction should be made to sentence 9?

① change <u>have</u> to <u>had</u>
② change <u>have</u> to <u>having</u>
③ change <u>start</u> to <u>started</u>
④ change <u>continue</u> to <u>continued</u>
⑤ no correction is necessary

Sequence of Verb Tense

Using the Same Tense

Usually, all of the verbs in a sentence are in the same tense. For example, all of the verbs will be in the present progressive or in the simple past.

Examples:

- Magdalena and I **cooked** dinner, and everyone **ate** at 7:30.
  (Two actions took place in the past.)

- Renata **is studying**, and Carlos **is cleaning** the house.
  (Two actions are taking place in the present.)

Changing Tenses

However, in some cases, the verbs in a sentence may be in different tenses in order to show that the actions happened at different times.

Examples:

- I **am** certain that John **pressed** the wrong button.
  (The speaker is certain now that John made a mistake in the past.)

- If the bus **is** late, I **won't** get to work on time.
  (If the bus is late now, something will happen later in the future—the speaker will be late to work.)

- Magellan **proved** that the earth **is** round by sailing around it.
  (Magellan's action in the past demonstrated something that is always true.)

- While we **were waiting** for the bus, it **started** to rain.
  (An action that took place over time, waiting for the bus, was interrupted by the start of another action, the start of a rainstorm.)

- She **was washing** the dishes when the phone **rang**.
  (An action that took place over time, washing the dishes, was interrupted by the start of another action, the ringing of the phone.)

- Marcus **realized** that he **had made** a mistake.
  (A past action, *had made a mistake,* occurred before another action—realizing the mistake.)

Usually, all of the verbs in a sentence are in the same tense. But sometimes we use different tenses to show actions that happened at different times. This is called **sequence of tense**.

Tip

When the verbs in a sentence are in different tenses, decide whether the actions logically took place at different times. Then make any necessary corrections.

Example:

Yesterday he **decided** that he **will go** to Tahiti on vacation next month.
(The sentence is correct. Yesterday he made a decision about his future plans for next month.)

GED Readiness

Questions 1 through 5 refer to the following newspaper article. Circle the number of the <u>one best answer</u> to each item.

(1) At last Saturday's concert, the Parkville Chorus showed that it had been one of the best musical groups in our city. (2) The Parkville Chorus sang 20 popular songs, and a smaller group, The Clip Notes, entertained with barbershop quartet favorites. (3) The concert started at 7:30 on the main stage of the Pickwick Theater, and it was lasting until 10:00 at night. (4) The performance was so energetic that while the chorus were singing, most of the audience was tapping their feet along with the music. (5) At the end of the concert, the chorus announced that their next performance had been at 7:30 on Saturday, April 30.

Revision

1 Sentence 1: **At last Saturday's concert, the Parkville Chorus <u>showed that it had been</u> one of the best musical groups in our city.**

Which is the best way to write the underlined portion of this sentence? If the original is the best way, choose option (1).

1. showed that it had been
2. showed that it is
3. shows that it be
4. is showing that it is
5. will show that it will be

Correction

2 Sentence 2: **The Parkville Chorus sang 20 popular songs, and a smaller group, The Clip Notes, entertained with barbershop quartet favorites.**

Which correction should be made to sentence 2?

1. change <u>sang</u> to <u>sung</u>
2. change <u>sang</u> to <u>was singing</u>
3. change <u>entertained</u> to <u>were entertaining</u>
4. change <u>entertained</u> to <u>will entertain</u>
5. no correction is necessary

Correction

3 Sentence 3: **The concert started at 7:30 on the main stage of the Pickwick Theater, and it was lasting until 10:00 at night.**

Which correction should be made to sentence 3?

1. change <u>started</u> to <u>was starting</u>
2. change <u>started</u> to <u>will start</u>
3. change <u>was lasting</u> to <u>lasted</u>
4. change <u>was lasting</u> to <u>will last</u>
5. no correction is necessary

Correction

4 Sentence 4: **The performance was so energetic that while the chorus were singing, most of the audience was tapping their feet along with the music.**

Which correction should be made to sentence 4?

1. change <u>were</u> to <u>was</u>
2. change <u>were singing</u> to <u>had sung</u>
3. remove <u>were</u>
4. change <u>was tapping</u> to <u>tapped</u>
5. remove <u>was</u> before <u>tapping</u>

Correction

5 Sentence 5: **At the end of the concert, the chorus announced that their next performance had been at 7:30 on Saturday, April 30.**

Which correction should be made to sentence 5?

1. change <u>announced</u> to <u>was announcing</u>
2. change <u>announced</u> to <u>will announce</u>
3. remove <u>had</u>
4. change <u>had been</u> to <u>were</u>
5. change <u>had been</u> to <u>will be</u>

13 Subject and Object Pronouns

A pronoun is a word that takes the place of a noun. Two kinds of pronouns are **subject pronouns** and **object pronouns**.

Subject pronouns take the place of the subject of a sentence.

- **Ron** is a nice person.
  He is a nice person.

Object pronouns take the place of the object of the verb.

- Frank read **the book** from cover to cover.
  Frank read **it** from cover to cover.

Pronouns that follow a preposition (such as *for, to,* or *of*) are also object pronouns.

- Betsy bought the birthday present for **Maria**.
  Betsy bought the birthday present for **her**.

This chart shows the forms of subject and object pronouns.

Subject Pronouns	Object Pronouns
I	me
you	you
he, she, it	him, her, it
we	us
they	them

Here are some common subject and object pronoun errors and ways to correct them.

Examples:

- **Incorrect:** Phil and **me** saw a great movie last night.
  Correct: Phil and **I** saw a great movie last night.
  (The pronoun is the subject of the sentence, so it should be the subject pronoun *I.*)

- **Incorrect:** I met Jennifer and **she** at the party last night.
  Correct: I met Jennifer and **her** at the party last night.
  (The pronoun is the object of the verb *met,* so it should be the object pronoun *her.*)

- **Incorrect:** Please keep this a secret between you and **I.**
  Correct: Please keep this a secret between you and **me.**
  (The pronoun is the object of the preposition *between,* so it should be the object pronoun *me.*)

A **subject pronoun** is a pronoun that takes the place of a noun that is the subject of a sentence.

Example:

He is a very nice person.

An **object pronoun** is a pronoun that takes the place of a noun that is the object of a verb or a preposition.

Examples:

I met **him** last week. (object of the verb)
I set an e-mail to **them** yesterday. (object of the preposition)

Tip

To figure out whether to use a subject or an object pronoun, find the verb in the sentence. Then decide whether the pronoun is the subject or the object of the verb. If the pronoun follows a preposition, use an object pronoun.

GED Readiness

Questions 1 through 5 refer to the following information. Circle the number of the one best answer to each item.

(1) Identity theft is a growing problem. (2) Lawanda Roberson, for example, was a recent victim of identity theft. (3) Thieves accessed her checking and savings accounts and emptied them. (4) Her husband and her spent six months and over $500 of their own money to get everything back. (5) Identity theft can happen to you or I.

(6) What can we do to stop it from happening to us? (7) First, you should never throw away any paper that has your name, address, or Social Security number on it. (8) Second, do not leave your mail in the mailbox for extended periods of time. (9) Finally, if you use the Internet for banking, should keep your passwords secret and change them frequently.

Correction

1 Sentence 3: **Thieves accessed her checking and savings accounts and emptied them.**

Which correction should be made to sentence 3?

(1) insert them before emptied
(2) replace them with her
(3) replace them with they
(4) replace them with it
(5) no correction is necessary

Revision

2 Sentence 4: **Her husband and her spent six months and over $500 of their own money to get everything back.**

Which is the best way to write the underlined portion of this sentence? If the original is the best way, choose option (1).

(1) Her husband and her
(2) Her and her husband
(3) Them
(4) She and her husband
(5) She and it

Revision

3 Sentence 5: **Identity theft can happen to you or I.**

Which is the best way to write the underlined portion of this sentence? If the original is the best way, choose option (1).

(1) you or I
(2) they or us
(3) you or me
(4) they or we
(5) we

Correction

4 Sentence 6: **What can we do to stop it from happening to us?**

Which correction should be made to sentence 6?

(1) replace we with us
(2) replace we with them
(3) replace it with them
(4) replace us with we
(5) no correction is necessary

Correction

5 Sentence 9: **Finally, if you use the Internet for banking, should keep your passwords secret and change them frequently.**

Which correction should be made to sentence 9?

(1) replace you with they
(2) insert you before should
(3) insert we before should
(4) change them to they
(5) no correction is necessary

14 Possessive Pronouns

Possessive pronouns show the ownership or possession of something. Possessive pronouns take the place of possessive nouns.

Examples:

- This is **Francisco's** book.
  This is **his** book.

- Someone took **Diane's and Jim's** chairs from their desks.
  Someone took **their** chairs from their desks.

- Those chairs are **Jim's and Diane's**.
  Those chairs are **theirs**.

There are two kinds of possessive words:

- **Possessive pronouns** come before a noun.

Examples:

Walker always eats **his** lunch at 12:30.
Mr. and Mrs. Washington love **their** new car.
Let's try to finish **our** work by 5:00.

- **Emphatic possessive pronouns** occur alone, usually at the end of a sentence.

Examples:

Is this briefcase **yours** or **his**?
That problem is **yours**, not **ours**!
After I make the final payment, the car will be completely **mine**.

Here are the possessive and emphatic possessive pronouns:

Possessive Pronouns	Emphatic Possessives
my	mine
your	yours
his	his
her	hers
it	its
our	ours
their	theirs

Possessive pronouns do not use apostrophes, but possessive nouns do.

Examples:

Riley's bicycle has a flat tire. (possessive noun)
That bicycle is **Riley's**. (possessive noun)

His bicycle has a flat tire. (possessive pronoun)
The dog chased **its** tail. (possessive pronoun)

Possessive pronouns show who a noun belongs to. Possessive pronouns come before nouns.

An **emphatic possessive pronoun** shows possession but stands alone.

Example:
The kitten is **hers**.

Tip

When a pronoun comes before a noun, always use a possessive pronoun.

Example:
She loves **her** new kitten.

GED Readiness

To: All Employees
From: Bill Roberts, Operations

(1) All employees need to have his company ID cards with them at all times while at work. (2) Office employees can either wear their cards around their necks or clip them to their clothes. (3) Employees in the warehouse should keep them in their pockets.

(4) If you leave the building without your card, the security guard must call your manager before you can reenter the building. (5) Do not try to enter the building using a company ID that is not you. (6) An employee can be dismissed for using an ID that is not him or hers.

Correction

1 Sentence 1: **All employees need to have his company ID cards with them at all times while at work.**

Which correction should be made to sentence 1?

(1) replace <u>All employees</u> with <u>Your</u>
(2) replace <u>All employees</u> with <u>Yours</u>
(3) replace <u>his</u> with <u>their</u>
(4) replace <u>them</u> with <u>their</u>
(5) insert <u>their</u> after <u>while</u>

Correction

2 Sentence 3: **Employees in the warehouse should keep them in their pockets.**

Which correction should be made to sentence 3?

(1) replace <u>them</u> with <u>their</u>
(2) replace <u>their</u> with <u>them</u>
(3) replace <u>their</u> with <u>his</u>
(4) replace <u>their</u> with <u>theirs</u>
(5) no correction is necessary

Revision

3 Sentence 4: **If you leave the building without <u>your card</u>, the security guard must call your manager before you can reenter the building.**

Which is the best way to write the underlined portion of this sentence? If the original is the best way, choose option (1).

(1) your card
(2) you card
(3) yours card
(4) their card
(5) his or her card

Revision

4 Sentence 5: **Do not try to enter the building using a company ID that is not <u>you</u>.**

Which is the best way to write the underlined portion of this sentence? If the original is the best way, choose option (1).

(1) you
(2) your
(3) yours
(4) his or hers
(5) theirs

Revision

5 Sentence 6: **An employee can be dismissed for using an ID that is not <u>him or hers</u>.**

Which is the best way to write the underlined portion of this sentence? If the original is the best way, choose option (1).

(1) him or hers
(2) his or her
(3) him or her
(4) he or her
(5) his or hers

15

Pronoun Agreement

Pronouns must agree with the nouns they replace. Use **singular pronouns** to replace singular nouns. Use **plural pronouns** to replace plural nouns.

Some pronouns have masculine and feminine forms: *he, she, his, him, her,* and *hers.* Use these pronouns to refer to people. Use the pronoun *it* to refer to objects or animals.

Examples:

- Joni got **her** GED last year.
  (Her agrees with the noun it replaces, *Joni,* which is feminine and singular.)

- The money that you found is not **yours**.
  (Yours agrees with the person it replaces, *you.)*

- You need to return the money to **its** owner.
  (Its agrees with the noun it replaces, *money,* which is singular.)

- At amusement parks, young children should be accompanied by **their** parents at all times.
  (Their agrees with the noun it replaces, *children,* which is plural.)

You, your, and *yours* are both singular and plural.

Examples:

- Students, here are **your** assignments.
  (Your refers to a plural noun, *students.)*

- Frank, is the car with its headlights on **yours**?
  (Yours refers to a singular noun, *Frank.)*

Here are the subject, object, possessive, and emphatic possessive pronouns:

	Subject Pronouns	Object Pronouns	Possessive Pronouns	Emphatic Possessive
Singular	I	me	my	mine
Singular or plural	you	you	your	yours
Singular, masculine	he	him	his	his
Singular, feminine	she	her	her	hers
Singular, neuter	it	it	its	its
Plural	we, they	us, them	our, their	ours, theirs

Pronouns must agree with the nouns they replace. They can be singular pronouns or plural pronouns.

The pronouns *he, him,* and *his* are masculine. Use them to replace singular, masculine nouns. The pronouns *she, her,* and *hers* are feminine. Use them to replace singular, feminine nouns.

Tip

The pronouns *you, your,* and *yours* are both singular and plural.

GED Readiness

Questions 1 through 5 refer to the following information. Circle the number of the <u>one best answer</u> to each item.

(1) A good friend of yours is getting married. (2) You want to give the bride and groom a gift, but you don't know what to get the bride and groom. (3) These ideas can help you find the perfect gift.

(4) If the couple registers at a store, finding a gift for them is easy. (5) You just choose them from a list of items that the couple selected. (6) If the couple is not registered, then ask someone close to her for advice. (7) Usually, the maid of honor is a good friend of the bride and groom, so they may have some ideas for you.

(8) You should make sure your name is inside the package. (9) That way, the couple will know it is from them and will be able to thank you.

Revision

1 Sentence 2: **You want to give the bride and groom a gift, but you don't know what to get <u>the bride and groom</u>.**

Which is the best way to write the underlined portion of this sentence? If the original is the best way, choose option (1).

(1) the bride and groom
(2) it
(3) him and she
(4) them
(5) us

Correction

2 Sentence 5: **You just choose them from a list of items that the couple selected.**

Which correction should be made to sentence 5?

(1) replace <u>You</u> with <u>We</u>
(2) replace <u>them</u> with <u>it</u>
(3) replace <u>them</u> with <u>him</u>
(4) replace <u>items</u> with <u>them</u>
(5) replace <u>the couple</u> with <u>they</u>

Revision

3 Sentence 6: **If the couple is not registered, then ask someone close to <u>her</u> for advice.**

Which is the best way to write the underlined portion of this sentence? If the original is the best way, choose option (1).

(1) her
(2) hers
(3) them
(4) they
(5) their

Correction

4 Sentence 7: **Usually, the maid of honor is a good friend of the bride and groom, so they may have some ideas for you.**

Which correction should be made to sentence 7?

(1) replace <u>the maid of honor</u> with <u>he</u>
(2) replace <u>they</u> with <u>it</u>
(3) replace <u>they</u> with <u>she</u>
(4) replace <u>you</u> with <u>her</u>
(5) replace <u>you</u> with <u>them</u>

Correction

5 Sentence 9: **That way, the couple will know it is from them and will be able to thank you.**

Which correction should be made to sentence 9?

(1) replace <u>it is</u> with <u>they are</u>
(2) replace <u>from them</u> with <u>you</u>
(3) replace <u>from them</u> with <u>theirs</u>
(4) replace <u>from them</u> with <u>yours</u>
(5) replace <u>you</u> with <u>yours</u>

Reflexive and Indefinite Pronouns

A **reflexive pronoun** is a pronoun that refers to the same noun as the subject of the sentence. A reflexive pronoun should agree with that noun or pronoun.

An **indefinite pronoun** is a pronoun that refers to an unknown or unspecified noun. An indefinite pronoun can be singular or plural.

Tip

When an object and subject pronoun refer to the same person or thing, you need to use a reflexive pronoun.

Reflexive Pronouns

A **reflexive pronoun** is an object pronoun that refers to the same noun as the subject of the sentence. A reflexive pronoun should agree with that noun or pronoun.

Examples:
- **Marta** cut **herself** chopping the onions.
  (The reflexive pronoun *herself* refers to the noun, *Marta*.)

- **We** laughed **ourselves** silly watching that old Laurel and Hardy movie.
  (The reflexive pronoun *ourselves* refers to the pronoun *we*.)

- She made a mistake, but then **she** corrected **herself**.
  (The reflexive pronoun *herself* refers to the pronoun *she*.)

Here are the reflexive pronouns:

Singular Reflexive Pronouns	Plural Reflexive Pronouns
myself	ourselves
yourself	yourselves
himself, herself, itself	themselves

Indefinite Pronouns

An **indefinite pronoun** is a pronoun that takes the place of an unspecified or unknown noun. Indefinite pronouns can be singular or plural.

Examples:
- Does **anyone** know the answer to this question?
- Many students applied for scholarships, and **several** got them.

Here are the most common indefinite pronouns:

Always Singular	Always Plural	Singular or Plural
another, anybody, anyone, anything, each, either, everybody, everyone, everything, nobody, no one, neither, nothing, one, somebody, someone, something	both, few, many, others, several	all, any, more, most, none, some

GED Readiness

Questions 1 through 5 refer to the following information. Circle the number of the one best answer to each item.

EVERYONE STILL LOVES LUCY

(1) *I Love Lucy* is one of the biggest success stories of television. (2) Almost no one has heard of the loveable redhead Lucy and her Cuban bandleader husband, Ricky. (3) The show premiered on October 15, 1951, and is still on the air today. (4) The show has been seen in almost every country around the world. (5) Why is the show so popular? (6) First, the show is really funny. (7) In one famous episode, Lucy stuffed themselves with chocolate in order to avoid losing her job at a candy factory. (8) But, more importantly, experts say that we can see us in the program. (9) Each episode focused on real problems that everyone face. (10) That's the real reason why we all love Lucy.

Correction

1 Sentence 1: *I Love Lucy* **is one of the biggest success stories of television.**

Which correction should be made to sentence 1?

1. change is to are
2. replace one with some
3. replace one with each
4. replace one with something
5. no correction is necessary

Correction

2 Sentence 2: **Almost no one has heard of the loveable redhead Lucy and her Cuban bandleader husband, Ricky.**

Which is the best way to write the underlined portion of this sentence? If the original is the best way, choose option (1).

1. no one
2. someone
3. everyone
4. everything
5. many

Correction

3 Sentence 7: **In one famous episode, Lucy stuffed themselves with chocolate in order to avoid losing her job at a candy factory.**

Which correction should be made to sentence 7?

1. replace themselves with herself
2. replace themselves with itself
3. insert herself after losing
4. replace her with herself
5. no correction is necessary

Correction

4 Sentence 8: **But, more importantly, experts say that we can see us in the program.**

Which correction should be made to sentence 8?

1. replace we with they
2. replace us with oneself
3. replace us with ourselves
4. replace us with everyone
5. no correction is necessary

Correction

5 Sentence 9: **Each episode focused on real problems that everyone face.**

Which correction should be made to sentence 9?

1. remove Each
2. replace everyone with oneself
3. replace everyone with anyone
4. change face to faces
5. change face to facing

17 Avoiding Pronoun Shift

If you refer to a noun with the pronouns *he* or *she*, all of the pronouns should be forms related to *he (him, his)* or *she (her, hers)*, as called for by the sentence.

Example:

- You should remind **her** that **she** has a dentist's appointment on Tuesday.
  (*She* and *her* are both singular and feminine.)

If the noun is plural, all of the pronouns that refer to that noun should be plural.

Example:

- At the airport, **we** checked our luggage and boarded **our** flight.

A common error is to change the number of the pronouns (singular or plural) or to change the person of the pronouns (from *you* to *one* or from *you* to *we*). To correct a **pronoun shift**, make sure that the pronouns that refer to the same noun match in number and person.

Examples:

- **Incorrect:** After **you** pick up the food from the kitchen, **one** brings it to the customers. (The pronoun *you* in the first clause changes person to *one* in the second clause.)
  Correct: After **you** pick up the food from the kitchen, **you** bring it to the customers.

- **Incorrect:** When **you** do aerobics, **we** need to avoid hurting **ourselves**.
  (The pronoun *you* in the first clause changes person to *we* and *ourselves* in the second clause.)
  Correct: When **we** do aerobics, **we** need to avoid hurting **ourselves**.

- **Incorrect:** If a customer breaks **something**, the customer will have to pay for **them**.
  (The singular indefinite pronoun *something* in the first clause changes to the plural *them* in the second clause.)
  Correct: If a customer breaks **something**, the customer will have to pay for **it**.

People often use the pronouns *they* or *them* to avoid the awkward phrase *he or she*. This causes a pronoun error.

Example:

- **Incorrect:** If an **employee** is hurt on the job, **they** should report to the company nurse.
  (The plural noun *they* incorrectly replaces the singular noun *employee*.)
  Correct: If an **employee** is hurt on the job, **he or she** should report to the company nurse.

A **pronoun shift** occurs when the number or person of pronouns is changed when referring to the same person or thing.

Tip

To avoid pronoun shifts, compare the pronouns in the sentence. Do the pronouns refer to the same person or thing? If so, they should be in the same person and number.

GED Readiness

Questions 1 through 4 refer to the following letter. Circle the number of the <u>one best answer</u> to each item.

Ryan-Park Home Theater
Your local source for home entertainment

Dear Customers,

(1) We are proud to announce that after 49 years in downtown Parkville, Ryan-Park Home Theater is moving from our original location to their new, larger location in Parkville Mall. (2) Our new store will have more room to show the state-of-the art widescreen TVs and home theater systems that we specialize in. (3) To reward you, our valued customers, we are having a special moving sale from May 2 to May 22. (4) During this time, you can get 20 percent off all purchases of in-stock merchandise if one orders by May 20. (5) All of our loyal customers are invited to our Grand Opening celebration May 21 at the Parkville Mall at 7:00. (6) You can win free DVDs, CDs, DVD players, or a complete home theater system. (7) If a name is called but that person is not present, they cannot win. (8) Our store has been serving Parkville families like theirs for almost 50 years, and we hope to continue to do so from our new location for 50 more years.

Correction

❶ Sentence 1: **We are proud to announce that after 49 years in downtown Parkville, Ryan-Park Home Theater is moving from our original location to their new, larger location in Parkville Mall.**

Which correction should be made to sentence 1?

① replace <u>We</u> with <u>They</u>
② replace <u>our</u> with <u>their</u>
③ replace <u>our</u> with <u>its</u>
④ replace <u>their</u> with <u>our</u>
⑤ replace <u>their</u> with <u>its</u>

Correction

❷ Sentence 4: **During this time, you can get 20 percent off all purchases of in-stock merchandise if one orders by May 20.**

Which correction should be made to sentence 4?

① replace <u>you</u> with <u>they</u>
② replace <u>you</u> with <u>we</u>
③ replace <u>one orders</u> with <u>you order</u>
④ replace <u>one orders</u> with <u>they order</u>
⑤ no correction is necessary

Correction

❸ Sentence 7: **If a name is called but that person is not present, they cannot win.**

Which correction should be made to sentence 7?

① replace <u>a</u> with <u>your</u>
② replace <u>a</u> with <u>someone's</u>
③ replace <u>that person is</u> with <u>you are</u>
④ replace <u>that person is</u> with <u>they are</u>
⑤ replace <u>they</u> with <u>he or she</u>

Correction

❹ Sentence 8: **Our store has been serving Parkville families like theirs for almost 50 years, and we hope to continue to do so from our new location for 50 more years.**

Which correction should be made to sentence 8?

① replace <u>Our</u> with <u>My</u>
② replace <u>theirs</u> with <u>yours</u>
③ replace <u>we hope</u> with <u>one hopes</u>
④ replace <u>our</u> with <u>its</u>
⑤ replace <u>our</u> with <u>their</u>

Capitalization

When you write, you should capitalize the first letters of these words:

- The first word of a sentence
  The truck just pulled up to the loading dock.

- The pronoun *I*
  My boss told me that **I** am a good worker.

- Proper nouns (names of a specific person, place, group, or thing)
  Phil and **M**arie think that **L**ake **T**ahoe is one of the most scenic spots in the **U**nited **S**tates.

- Proper adjectives (adjectives that come from proper nouns)
  I think that **M**oroccan cooking is delicious.

- People's titles (such as **doctor** or **aunt**), when they come directly before the person's name
  He was checked by **D**r. Ida Steinberg, but she couldn't find anything wrong.
  I visited my **A**unt Phyllis yesterday.

- The names of days of the week, months of the year, and holidays
  The bank will be closed on **M**artin **L**uther **K**ing, **J**r. **D**ay, **M**onday, **J**anuary 21.

Do not capitalize:

- Names of seasons
  I can't wait for **w**inter to be over!

- Directional words (such as **north**) unless they refer to parts of the country
  We are going **s**outh for the winter.
  The **S**outh lost the Civil War.

- Subjects in school (such as **math**), unless they refer to specific courses (such as **Math 1**)
  We had a great **m**ath teacher for **A**lgebra 1.

- People's titles (such as **doctor** or **aunt**), when they are not next to a name
  We took my **g**randmother to the **d**octor's office.

> Capitalize specific nouns, such as **D**octor **J**ones or **C**hristmas.
> Do not capitalize general nouns, such as **s**ummer or **h**oliday.

GED Readiness

Questions 1 through 5 refer to the following letter. Circle the number of the <u>one best answer</u> to each item.

Dear Ms. Gray,

(1) I am writing to you to apply for the position of Office Assistant at Heartland Printing Company. (2) I read about this opening in the Sunday, May 8, edition of the *Daily News*. (3) For the last three years, I have been a clerk for Dr. Mary Wells. (4) In this position, I answered phones, ordered supplies, and handled all patient billing. (5) I am looking for a new job because the Doctor is retiring at the end of this month. (6) Prior to this position, I was a clerk in the purchasing office of Capitol Electric in springfield.

(7) My education includes graduation from High School, where I studied office occupations and keyboarding and took Accounting 1.

Correction

1 Sentence 1: **I am writing to you to apply for the position of Office Assistant at Heartland Printing Company.**

Which correction should be made to sentence 1?

(1) change <u>you</u> to <u>You</u>
(2) change <u>Office Assistant</u> to <u>office assistant</u>
(3) change <u>Printing Company</u> to <u>printing company</u>
(4) change <u>Company</u> to <u>company</u>
(5) no correction is necessary

Correction

2 Sentence 2: **I read about this opening in the Sunday, May 8, edition of the *Daily News*.**

Which correction should be made to sentence 2?

(1) change <u>Sunday</u> to <u>sunday</u>
(2) change <u>May</u> to <u>may</u>
(3) change <u>edition</u> to <u>Edition</u>
(4) change *<u>Daily News</u>* to *<u>daily news</u>*
(5) no correction is necessary

Correction

3 Sentence 5: **I am looking for a new job because the Doctor is retiring at the end of this month.**

Which correction should be made to sentence 5?

(1) change <u>new job</u> to <u>New Job</u>
(2) change <u>Doctor</u> to <u>doctor</u>
(3) change <u>end</u> to <u>End</u>
(4) change <u>month</u> to <u>Month</u>
(5) no correction is necessary

Correction

4 Sentence 6: **Prior to this position, I was a clerk in the purchasing office of Capitol Electric in springfield.**

Which correction should be made to sentence 6?

(1) change <u>clerk</u> to <u>Clerk</u>
(2) change <u>purchasing office</u> to <u>Purchasing Office</u>
(3) change <u>Capitol Electric</u> to <u>capitol electric</u>
(4) change <u>springfield</u> to <u>Springfield</u>
(5) no correction is necessary

Correction

5 Sentence 7: **My education includes graduation from High School, where I studied office occupations and keyboarding and took Accounting 1.**

Which correction should be made to sentence 7?

(1) change <u>graduation</u> to <u>Graduation</u>
(2) change <u>High School</u> to <u>high school</u>
(3) change <u>office occupations</u> to <u>Office Occupations</u>
(4) change <u>keyboarding</u> to <u>Keyboarding</u>
(5) change <u>Accounting</u> to <u>accounting</u>

19

Commas in a Series

When you write lists of three or more items (such as nouns, verbs, or phrases) joined by *and* or *or*, use commas between the items in the list.

Examples:

- Pedro, Pablo, or Maria can help you. (three nouns)

- Today, I cleaned the supply room, planted flowers along the front walkway, and cut the grass. (four verb phrases)

- This recipe for chicken salad calls for cooked chicken, artichokes, sun-dried tomatoes, celery, onion, and mayonnaise. (six nouns)

The items in the list should be in the same grammatical form: all nouns, all verbs, and so on.

Example:

Incorrect: Mexican cooking is often hot, spicy, and tastes delicious. (two adjectives and a verb phrase)

Correct: Mexican cooking is often hot, spicy, and delicious. (three adjectives)

Use a comma before *and* or *or* and between each of the items in a list of three or more. Do not put a comma after the last item.

Example:

Incorrect: Do you want sugar, honey, or lemon, in your tea? (comma after the last item)

Correct: Do you want sugar, honey, or lemon in your tea? (three nouns in a list with commas)

When you write lists of only two items joined by *and* or *or*, do not use a comma.

Examples:

- Pedro and Maria are early for work every day.

- Tomorrow I will either mow the lawn or fix the front door.

When a list of items is joined by *and* or *or* between each of the items, do not use a comma.

Examples:

- We don't have any onions or celery or parsley in the fridge.

- My dogs sits and begs and heels on command.

Tip

On the GED Test, the comma before *and* is not tested. However, the other commas in these sentences can be tested on the GED.

GED Readiness

Questions 1 through 4 refer to the following information. Circle the number of the <u>one best answer</u> to each item.

(1) Do you like cereal? (2) Do you crave granola corn flakes raisin bran or oatmeal at different times of the day? (3) If so, downtown's newest and most unusual restaurant, the Cereal Bowl, might be for you. (4) This fun spot is a great place for a bowl of cereal morning, noon, or night. (5) The Cereal Bowl has a selection of hundreds of hot and cold cereals. (6) You can top off your cereal with whole milk, low-fat milk, or fat-free milk. (7) What if your oatmeal isn't sweet enough? (8) You can add sweeteners such as sugar, brown sugar, honey, or molasses. (9) You can also add raisins, nuts, strawberries, bananas, blueberries to your cereal. (10) Are you in a hurry but can't stop for a bowl of cereal? (11) In that case, you might want to grab a milk and a cereal bar. (12) You can also get a bag of granola, order a breakfast tortilla, a cup of yogurt, or get a donut to go. (13) The Cereal Bowl is not just for breakfast. (14) It's open from 6:00 in the morning until 9:00 at night.

Revision

1 Sentence 2: **Do you crave <u>granola corn flakes raisin bran or oatmeal</u> at different times of the day?**

Which is the best way to write the underlined portion of this sentence? If the original is the best way, choose option (1).

(1) granola corn flakes raisin bran or oatmeal
(2) granola, corn, flakes, raisin, bran, or, oatmeal
(3) granola, corn flakes, raisin bran, or oatmeal
(4) granola, corn, flakes, raisin, bran, or oatmeal
(5) granola, corn flakes, raisin, bran, or oatmeal,

Revision

2 Sentence 5: **The Cereal Bowl has a selection <u>of hundreds of hot and cold cereals</u>.**

Which is the best way to write the underlined portion of this sentence? If the original is the best way, choose option (1).

(1) of hundreds of hot and cold cereals
(2) of hundreds, of hot, and cold cereals
(3) of hundreds of hot, and cold cereals
(4) of hundreds of hot, and, cold cereals
(5) of hundreds of hot, and cold, cereals

Correction

3 Sentence 9: **You can also add raisins, nuts, strawberries, bananas, blueberries to your cereal.**

Which correction should be made to sentence 9?

(1) replace <u>raisins, nuts</u> with <u>raisins and nuts</u>
(2) insert a comma after <u>add</u>
(3) insert <u>but</u> after <u>bananas</u>
(4) insert <u>or</u> after <u>bananas</u>
(5) add a comma after <u>blueberries</u>

Correction

4 Sentence 12: **You can also get a bag of granola, order a breakfast tortilla, a cup of yogurt, or get a donut to go.**

Which correction should be made to sentence 12?

(1) remove <u>order</u>
(2) insert <u>buy</u> before <u>a cup</u>
(3) remove the comma after <u>tortilla</u>
(4) insert a comma after <u>donut</u>
(5) no correction is necessary

20

Commas Joining Independent Clauses

Independent Clauses

A clause is a group of words with a complete subject and verb. An **independent clause** is a complete thought that can stand alone as a sentence.

Examples:

- Tony and Tina got married last year.
  (*Tony and Tina* are the subject, *got married* is the verb)

- This year they bought a house.
  (*They* is the subject, *bought* is the verb.)

Joining Independent Clauses

When joining two independent clauses with *and, but,* or *or,* always use a comma.

Examples:
- Tony and Tina got married last year, **and** this year they bought a house.

- This summer, my son will go to summer school, **or** he will find a summer job.

- I fixed the car, **but** I didn't wash it.

Joining Predicates

Do not use a comma to join two predicates into a compound predicate with *and* or *or.*

Examples:
- This summer, my <u>son</u> <u>will go to summer school</u> **or** <u>find a summer job</u>.

- <u>Diane</u> <u>bought a new dress</u> **and** <u>went to the movies</u>.

Use commas to join three or more predicates with *and, but,* or *or.*

Examples:
- <u>We</u> <u>bought some flowers at the nursery</u>, <u>planted them</u>, **and** <u>watered them</u>.

- <u>Jeff</u> <u>walks</u>, <u>takes the bus</u>, **or** <u>rides the subway to work</u>.

An **independent clause** is a complete thought that can stand alone as a sentence. When joining two independent clauses with *and, but,* or *or,* always use a comma. Do not use a comma to join two predicates.

Tip

To figure out if you are joining clauses or predicates, look for the subjects. If they are clauses, each clause will have a subject. If they are predicates, there will be only one subject.

Examples:

<u>John</u> <u>works</u> in New York but <u>lives</u> in New Jersey. (one subject; no comma)

<u>John</u> <u>works</u> in New York, but <u>his wife</u> <u>works</u> in New Jersey. (two subjects; use a comma)

GED Readiness

Questions 1 through 5 refer to the following information. Circle the number of the <u>one best answer</u> to each item.

(1) You may have a lot of old clothes that your children outgrew, or maybe you have household items and collectables that you no longer need. (2) You want to sell them but you don't want to have a garage sale. (3) You can try an Internet auction.

(4) There are several places on the Internet where you can sell used items online. (5) You just go to the site, fill out a form, and upload pictures of your items. (6) At the end of the auction, you simply examine the bids and the customer with the highest bid gets the item. (7) The customer sends you a payment using a credit card or an online payment system. (8) You ship the customer his or her purchase. (9) You will soon find out that buying and selling things on the Internet is easy and fun.

Correction

1 Sentence 1: **You may have a lot of old clothes that your children outgrew, or maybe you have household items and collectables that you no longer need.**

Which correction should be made to sentence 1?

(1) remove the comma after <u>outgrew</u>
(2) insert a comma after <u>or</u>
(3) insert commas after <u>household</u> and <u>items</u>
(4) insert a comma after <u>items</u>
(5) no correction is necessary

Revision

2 Sentence 2: **You want to sell <u>them but you</u> don't want to have a garage sale.**

Which is the best way to write the underlined portion of this sentence? If the original is the best way, choose option (1).

(1) them but you
(2) them, but you
(3) them you
(4) them, you
(5) them, but, you

Correction

3 Sentence 6: **At the end of the auction, you simply examine the bids and the customer with the highest bid gets the item.**

Which correction should be made to sentence 6?

(1) remove the comma after <u>auction</u>
(2) insert a comma after <u>bids</u>
(3) remove <u>and</u>
(4) replace <u>and</u> with <u>or</u>
(5) no correction is necessary

Construction Shift

4 Sentences 7 and 8: **The customer sends you a payment using a credit card or an online payment system. You ship the customer his or her purchase.**

The most effective combination of sentences 7 and 8 would include which group of words?

(1) online payment system, you ship
(2) online payment system you ship
(3) online payment system, and you ship
(4) online payment system, but you ship
(5) online payment system and ships

Correction

5 Sentence 9: **You will soon find out that buying and selling things on the Internet is easy and fun.**

Which correction should be made to sentence 9?

(1) insert a comma after <u>buying</u>
(2) insert a comma after <u>things</u>
(3) insert a comma after <u>Internet</u>
(4) insert a comma after <u>easy</u>
(5) no correction is necessary

Commas Joining Subordinate Clauses

Subordinate, or Dependent, Clauses

An independent clause is a complete thought that can stand alone as a sentence. A **subordinate or dependent clause** is not a complete thought and cannot stand alone as a sentence. Join a subordinate clause with an independent clause to make a sentence that makes sense.

Examples:

- We won't go on a picnic.
  (An independent clause—a complete thought that can stand alone)

- If it rains tomorrow.
  (A subordinate clause—not a complete thought and cannot stand alone)

- We won't go on a picnic if it rains tomorrow.
  (Subordinate clause joined with an independent clause)

A subordinating conjunction always begins a dependent clause. Some common conjunctions are *after, because, since, when, while, unless, if,* and *until.* A complete list of subordinating conjunctions is in Skill 4.

Joining Independent and Dependent Clauses

When you join independent and dependent clauses, a comma is sometimes needed. How do you decide when to use a comma? It depends on which clause is first.

- Use a comma when the dependent clause is first in the sentence.

Example:

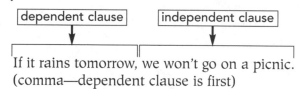

If it rains tomorrow, we won't go on a picnic.
(comma—dependent clause is first)

- A comma is not needed when the independent clause is first in the sentence.

Example:

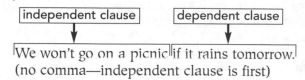

We won't go on a picnic if it rains tomorrow.
(no comma—independent clause is first)

A **subordinate or dependent clause** is not a complete thought and cannot stand alone as a sentence. To fix it, join the subordinate clause with an independent clause.

Tip

To figure out whether a comma is needed when joining independent and dependent clauses, look for the subordinating conjunction. If it's at the beginning of the sentence, a comma is needed at the end of the clause. If it's in the middle of the sentence, a comma is not needed.

GED Readiness

Questions 1 through 5 refer to the following information. Circle the number of the <u>one best answer</u> to each item.

(1) Although all adult citizens can vote, voter turnout has been low in recent elections. (2) Voter participation will continue to decrease, unless we take action and reverse this trend. (3) There are many reasons why people don't vote. (4) For example, many citizens can't vote because they are not registered. (5) People are registered to vote but often do not exercise this vital right. (6) Many citizens fail to vote. (7) They think that voting is time-consuming.

(8) The government needs to do more to encourage people to vote. (9) Before each election, the city should hold registration drives. (10) In addition, people should get time off from work they can vote.

Correction

1 Sentence 1: **Although all adult citizens can vote, voter turnout has been low in recent elections.**

Which correction should be made to sentence 1?

(1) insert a comma after <u>Although</u>
(2) remove the comma after <u>vote</u>
(3) insert <u>and</u> before <u>voter</u>
(4) insert a comma before <u>turnout</u>
(5) no correction is necessary

Correction

2 Sentence 2: **Voter participation will continue to decrease, unless we take action and reverse this trend.**

Which correction should be made to sentence 2?

(1) insert a comma after <u>participation</u>
(2) remove the comma after <u>decrease</u>
(3) remove <u>unless</u>
(4) insert a comma after <u>action</u>
(5) no correction is necessary

Construction Shift

3 Sentence 5: **People are registered to vote but often do not exercise this vital right.**

If you rewrote sentence 5 beginning with <u>Even though people are registered</u> the next words should be

(1) to vote but often do not
(2) to vote, they often do not
(3) to vote they often do not
(4) to vote often do not
(5) to vote, but they often do not

Construction Shift

4 Sentences 6 and 7: **Many citizens fail to vote. They think that voting is time-consuming.**

Which is the most effective combination of sentences 6 and 7?

(1) Many citizens fail to vote they think that voting is time-consuming.
(2) Many citizens fail to vote, they think that voting is time-consuming.
(3) Many citizens fail to vote because they think that voting is time-consuming.
(4) Many citizens fail to vote, because they think that voting is time-consuming.
(5) Many citizens fail to vote although they think that voting is time-consuming.

Correction

5 Sentence 10: **In addition, people should get time off from work they can vote.**

Which correction should be made to sentence 10?

(1) remove the comma after <u>addition</u>
(2) insert a comma after <u>work</u>
(3) insert a comma and <u>so that</u> after <u>work</u>
(4) insert <u>so that</u> after <u>work</u>
(5) no correction is necessary

Commas After Introductory Prepositional Phrases

A **prepositional phrase** consists of a preposition and its object (the noun or pronoun that follows the preposition). Common prepositions include *on, at, for, in, with, without, before, after, to, during,* and *by*.

Examples:
- on the right
- at work
- for lunch
- in June
- with Anna's help
- after work
- during the movie

When a prepositional phrase begins a sentence, it is usually followed by a comma.

Examples:
- **On the right**, you can see one of the most famous buildings in our city.
- **At work**, Francisco sells car insurance.
- **For lunch**, I ate a fresh salad.
- **In June**, I will take the GED test.
- **With Anna's help**, I was able to repair the computer.
- **After work**, we are having a baby shower for Mrs. Papovich.
- **During the movie**, the people sitting in front of me kept talking.

Do not use a comma when the prepositional phrase comes later in the sentence.

Examples:
- You can see one of the most famous buildings in our city **on the right**.
- Francisco sells car insurance **at work**.
- I ate a fresh salad **for lunch**.
- I will take the GED test **in June**.
- I was able to repair the computer **with Anna's help**.
- We are having a baby shower for Mrs. Papovich **after work**.
- The people sitting in front of me kept talking **during the movie**.

Tip

When a **prepositional phrase** begins a sentence, it is followed by a comma. Do not use a comma when the prepositional phrase comes later in the sentence.

GED Readiness

Questions 1 through 4 refer to the following information. Circle the number of the <u>one best answer</u> to each item.

ARTS COMPLEX ANNOUNCES GRAND OPENING

(1) The Madison Performing Arts Complex, Grandville's brand-new theater complex, is having its grand opening on May 14. (2) With two auditoriums the complex has seats for 1,800 people in its main auditorium. (3) A second, smaller theater in the lower level seats 350 people. (4) The auditorium can be used for plays, pop and classical concerts, and ballets. (5) In downtown Grandville the beautiful white stone building with large windows looks out onto the large plaza on Main Street. (6) Inside the auditorium, large murals on each side of the stage depict scenes from the history of Grandville. (7) Madison Arts Complex also has a great new restaurant, the Madison Café. (8) Before or after a concert or play enjoy a meal, a snack, or a delicious dessert. (9) On Saturday, May 14 residents can take a tour of the complex. (10) Later in May, residents can attend the first performance in the theater, *A Raisin in the Sun*.

Correction

1 Sentence 2: **With two auditoriums the complex has seats for 1,800 people in its main auditorium.**

Which correction should be made to sentence 2?

(1) insert a comma after <u>auditoriums</u>
(2) replace <u>complex</u> with <u>Complex</u>
(3) insert a comma after <u>complex</u>
(4) insert a comma after <u>people</u>
(5) no correction is necessary

Correction

2 Sentence 5: **In downtown Grandville the beautiful white stone building with large windows looks out onto the large plaza on Main Street.**

Which correction should be made to sentence 5?

(1) insert a comma after <u>Grandville</u>
(2) insert a comma after <u>building</u>
(3) insert commas after <u>windows</u>
(4) insert a comma after <u>out</u>
(5) insert a comma after <u>plaza</u>

Correction

3 Sentence 8: **Before or after a concert or play enjoy a meal, a snack, or a delicious dessert.**

Which correction should be made to sentence 8?

(1) insert a comma after <u>Before</u>
(2) insert a comma after <u>concert</u>
(3) insert a comma after <u>play</u>
(4) remove the comma after <u>meal</u>
(5) remove the comma after <u>snack</u>

Correction

4 Sentence 9: **On Saturday, May 14 residents can take a tour of the complex.**

Which correction should be made to sentence 9?

(1) remove the comma after <u>Saturday</u>
(2) insert a comma after <u>14</u>
(3) insert a comma after <u>residents</u>
(4) insert a comma after <u>tour</u>
(5) no correction is necessary

Comma Details

Use commas with introductory phrases, appositives, interrupting expressions, and words in direct address.

Tip

Be careful not to confuse an appositive with a list of two items with *or*.

- A list of two different items joined by *or* does not have commas.

Example:

- Were you trained to give artificial respiration or the Heimlich maneuver? *(Artificial respiration* and *Heimlich maneuver* are items in a list joined by *or*. Commas are not needed.)

Introductory Phrases

You already know to use a comma after an introductory prepositional phrase. You should also use a comma after other introductory phrases.

Examples:

In the garden, he planted several kinds of vegetables. (introductory prepositional phrase)

Carefully, the driver backed the truck into the loading dock entrance. (introductory adverb)

Unfortunately for Liz, she slipped and hurt her ankle. (introductory adverb phrase)

Appositives

An **appositive** is a word or phrase that re-names a noun using different words. Use commas to separate appositives from the rest of the sentence.

Examples:

My neighbor, **Mrs. Green**, is 98 years old.

My car, **a sporty red convertible**, is the envy of my friends.

Interrupting Expressions

An adverb or a transition word or phrase can interrupt a sentence. Set off these expressions with commas.

Examples:

Mrs. Williamson, **unfortunately**, lost her car keys at the picnic. (adverb)

She found her keys later, **however**, in the parking lot. (transition word)

There are many things to do in this town. We could, **for example**, go to the movies. (transition phrase)

Direct Address

Use a comma when a word or phrase directly addresses someone.

Examples:

Mrs. Smith, may I offer a suggestion?

Ben, please put the casserole in the oven at 5:00.

Related Skills: 19, 20, and 21

GED Readiness

Questions 1 through 4 refer to the following information. Circle the number of the <u>one best answer</u> to each item.

---

(1) Getting a credit card is an important financial step for anyone. (2) However finding a credit card that offers a good deal is also important.

(3) When you look for a credit card, you should examine two key numbers: the annual fee and the annual percentage rate. (4) The annual fee is the amount you have to pay each year to keep the card. (5) The annual percentage rate, or APR, is the interest rate you pay each month.

(6) If you plan on paying your balance each month, then you should look for a card with a low annual fee. (7) Typically, annual fees range from $29 to $50, but some premium plastic, such as gold credit cards may cost more. (8) Additionally, if you plan to pay your bill in full each month, you should ensure that the card offers a grace period. (9) The grace period, usually 30 days, is the time you have to pay the charges before interest starts.

(10) In contrast, if you will carry a balance each month, you should look for a low APR. (11) Saving even one or two percent in interest can mean hundreds of dollars over the course of a year if you carry a balance.

Correction

1 Sentence 2: **However finding a credit card that offers a good deal is also important.**

Which correction should be made to sentence 2?

(1) insert a comma after <u>However</u>
(2) insert commas after <u>card</u> and <u>deal</u>
(3) insert a comma after <u>deal</u>
(4) insert commas after <u>is</u> and <u>also</u>
(5) no correction is necessary

Correction

2 Sentence 5: **The annual percentage rate, or APR, is the interest rate you pay each month.**

Which correction should be made to sentence 5?

(1) insert a comma after <u>annual</u>
(2) insert commas after <u>annual</u> and <u>percentage</u>
(3) remove the comma after <u>percentage rate</u>
(4) remove the comma after <u>APR</u>
(5) no correction is necessary

Correction

3 Sentence 7: **Typically, annual fees range from $29 to $50, but some premium plastic, such as gold credit cards may cost more.**

Which correction should be made to sentence 7?

(1) remove the comma after <u>Typically</u>
(2) remove the comma after <u>$50</u>
(3) remove the comma after <u>plastic</u>
(4) insert a comma after <u>gold</u>
(5) insert a comma after <u>cards</u>

Correction

4 Sentence 9: **The grace period, usually 30 days, is the time you have to pay the charges before interest starts.**

Which correction should be made to sentence 9?

(1) remove the comma after <u>period</u>
(2) remove the comma after <u>days</u>
(3) insert a comma after <u>have</u>
(4) insert a comma after <u>charges</u>
(5) no correction is necessary

Avoiding Excess Commas

Sometimes writers use extra commas accidentally. In fact, the comma is the most misused punctuation mark. Here are some frequent comma errors:

Avoid Commas with Compound Predicates

A compound predicate is two predicates joined by a word like *and* or *or*. A comma is not needed between the predicates.

> **Incorrect:** A player took a hard fall, and broke his wrist. (compound predicate: *took a hard fall* and *broke his wrist*)
> **Correct:** A player took a hard fall and broke his wrist.

Avoid Commas that Join a Dependent and an Independent Clause

When the independent clause comes first in the sentence, a comma is not needed between that clause and the dependent clause.

> **Incorrect:** He moved to California, because he could get a better job there. (independent clause: *He moved to California;* dependent clause: *because he could get a better job there*)
> **Correct:** He moved to California because he could get a better job there.

Avoid Commas in Lists of Two Items

Lists of two items joined by *and* or *or* do not need commas.

> **Incorrect:** Mark, and Lindsey went to the supermarket, and bought groceries. (two subjects: *Mark* and *Lindsey;* two predicates: *went to the supermarket* and *bought groceries*)
> **Correct:** Mark and Lindsey went to the supermarket and bought groceries.

Avoid Commas After *And* or *Or*

Commas are not needed after *and* or *or* when they are used to join lists of items.

> **Incorrect:** This salad contains lettuce, onion, tomatoes, green pepper, and, grated carrot.
> **Correct:** This salad contains lettuce, onion, tomatoes, green pepper, and grated carrot.

Avoid Commas Between a Subject and a Verb

A comma is not needed between the subject and the verb of a sentence.

> **Incorrect:** Running for an hour, is an important part of his routine. (subject: *running for an hour;* verb: *is*)
> **Correct:** Running for an hour is an important part of his routine.

Tip

Unnecessary commas are a common error. To avoid unnecessary commas, only use a comma when it is required by a rule or when it is needed for clarity.

GED Readiness

Questions 1 through 5 refer to the following information. Circle the number of the <u>one best answer</u> to each item.

---

(1) Today, many parents worry that their children spend too much time watching TV, and playing video games. (2) What can you do to encourage a more active lifestyle? (3) First, consider sports. (4) Your son or daughter, might like to participate in an organized sport, such as after-school soccer. (5) Second, encourage your child to develop interests in new crafts or hobbies. (6) Your child might be interested in dancing, or collecting coins and stamps. (7) In many places community centers offer classes for kids on interesting subjects, such as acting and magic. (8) If your child is interested he or she might want to learn to play a musical instrument.

Correction

1 Sentence 1: **Today, many parents worry that their children spend too much time watching TV, and playing video games.**

Which correction should be made to sentence 1?

① remove the comma after <u>Today</u>
② insert a comma after <u>parents</u>
③ insert a comma after <u>children</u>
④ remove the comma after <u>TV</u>
⑤ insert a comma between <u>and</u> and <u>playing</u>

Correction

2 Sentence 4: **Your son or daughter, might like to participate in an organized sport, such as after-school soccer.**

Which correction should be made to sentence 4?

① remove the comma after <u>daughter</u>
② insert a comma after <u>participate</u>
③ remove the comma after <u>sport</u>
④ insert a comma after <u>school</u>
⑤ no correction is necessary

Correction

3 Sentence 6: **Your child might be interested in dancing, or collecting coins and stamps.**

Which correction should be made to sentence 6?

① insert a comma after <u>in</u>
② remove the comma after <u>dancing</u>
③ insert a comma after <u>collecting</u>
④ insert a comma after <u>coins</u>
⑤ no correction is necessary

Correction

4 Sentence 7: **In many places community centers offer classes for kids on interesting subjects, such as acting and magic.**

Which correction should be made to sentence 7?

① insert a comma after <u>places</u>
② insert a comma after <u>centers</u>
③ remove the comma after <u>subjects</u>
④ insert a comma after <u>acting</u>
⑤ insert a comma after <u>and</u>

Correction

5 Sentence 8: **If your child is interested he or she might want to learn to play a musical instrument.**

Which correction should be made to sentence 8?

① add a comma after <u>interested</u>
② insert a comma after <u>he</u>
③ insert a comma after <u>she</u>
④ insert a comma after <u>musical</u>
⑤ no correction is necessary

Using Apostrophes

Possessives

Possessive nouns show who owns or possesses another noun.

Add an apostrophe and an *s* (*'s*) to singular and plural nouns that do not end in -*s*.

Examples:
> This is Martha**'s** book. (singular noun)
> The women**'s** restroom is down the hall on the left. (plural noun)

The possessive pronoun *its* does not use an apostrophe. Only the contraction *it's (it is)* uses an apostrophe.

Examples:
> The dog's feeding dish is in the kitchen, and **its** bed is in the hall. (possessive pronoun)
> **It's** time to feed the dog. (contraction)

Add an apostrophe after plural possessive nouns ending in –*s*.

> The twins**'** bedroom is at the end of the hall.
> The classe**s'** new teacher is Miss Applebee.

Contractions

Contractions are words that are shortened by combining two words and leaving out letters.

To write a contraction, put the apostrophe in the place where letters were omitted.

Example:
> His bus **wasn't** on time this morning. (combines *was* and *not*; the apostrophe is where the letter *o* was omitted from *not*)

Many contractions are formed with

- a subject pronoun and a verb
- a verb and *not*

Subject Pronoun and a Verb		Verb and *Not*	
she's = she is *or* has	he'll = he will	couldn't = could not	isn't = is not
I'd = I would	I'm = I am	can't = cannot	wasn't = was not
they're = they are	they'd = they had *or* would	shouldn't = should not	
you're = you are			

Possessive nouns and possessive pronouns show who owns something.

Contractions are a shortened form of two words written together, such as a subject pronoun and a verb or a verb and *not*.

Tip

To figure out whether *its* needs an apostrophe, try saying *it is* in place of *its*. If you can say *it is*, use an apostrophe. If you cannot say *it is*, then do not use an apostrophe.

Tip

In contractions, use the apostrophe to show the letters that were omitted.
it is = it's

GED Readiness

---

(1) The Friends of Lakeview will have it's next regular meeting on Monday, May 23 at 7:30 P.M. (2) The meeting will take place in Wallace O. Williams High Schools community room. (3) The meeting's agenda includes planning Lakeview's annual fair. (4) Also on the agenda is a discussion of the cities plan for its annual back-to-school parade. (5) Finally, well' be joined by Bernie Hansen, a representative from the local branch of Commerce Bank, who will update us on the construction of the bank's new branch. (6) Were going to postpone the tour of the new school auditorium until June's meeting.

Correction

1 Sentence 1: **The Friends of Lakeview will have it's next regular meeting on Monday, May 23, at 7:30 P.M.**

Which correction should be made to sentence 1?

(1) replace <u>Friends</u> with <u>Friend's</u>
(2) replace <u>Friends</u> with <u>Friends'</u>
(3) replace <u>it's</u> with <u>its</u>
(4) replace <u>it's</u> with <u>its'</u>
(5) no correction is necessary

Correction

2 Sentence 2: **The meeting will take place in Wallace O. Williams High Schools community room.**

Which correction should be made to sentence 2?

(1) replace <u>Williams</u> with <u>William's</u>
(2) replace <u>Williams</u> with <u>Williams'</u>
(3) replace <u>Schools</u> with <u>Schools'</u>
(4) replace <u>Schools</u> with <u>School's</u>
(5) no correction is necessary

Correction

3 Sentence 4: **Also on the agenda is a discussion of the cities plan for its annual back-to-school parade.**

Which correction should be made to sentence 4?

(1) replace <u>cities</u> with <u>cities'</u>
(2) replace <u>cities</u> with <u>city's</u>
(3) replace <u>cities</u> with <u>citys'</u>
(4) replace <u>its</u> with <u>it's</u>
(5) no correction is necessary

Correction

4 Sentence 5: **Finally, well' be joined by Bernie Hansen, a representative from the local branch of Commerce Bank, who will update us on the construction of the bank's new branch.**

Which correction should be made to sentence 5?

(1) replace <u>well'</u> with <u>well</u>
(2) replace <u>well'</u> with <u>we'll</u>
(3) replace <u>bank's</u> with <u>banks</u>
(4) replace <u>bank's</u> with <u>banks'</u>
(5) no correction is necessary

Correction

5 Sentence 6: **Were going to postpone the tour of the new school auditorium until June's meeting.**

Which correction should be made to sentence 6?

(1) replace <u>Were</u> with <u>We're</u>
(2) replace <u>Were</u> with <u>W'ere</u>
(3) replace <u>June's</u> with <u>Junes'</u>
(4) replace <u>June's</u> with <u>Junes</u>
(5) no correction is necessary

Homonyms

Homonyms are two or more words with the same (or similar) pronunciation but different spellings and meanings. Writing the wrong homonym is very confusing to the reader. Here are some common homonyms:

- **axe** (tool for chopping wood); **acts** (actions; performs in)

    He sharpened his **axe** before he began chopping wood.
    Marcella **acts** in commercials and plays.

- **affect** (to change something); **effect** (a result)

    Working as a rock and roll singer has **affected** her hearing.
    One of the **effects** of more education is higher income.

- **brake** (device for stopping a car); **break** (to make into pieces)

    His car's **brakes** failed, and he hit another car.
    He dropped a coffee mug, but it didn't **break**.

- **our** (possessive pronoun); **hour** (60 minutes)

    We love **our** new car.
    The train was an **hour** late.

- **it's** (contraction of *it is*); **its** (possessive pronoun)

    Where is the remote control? **It's** missing.
    My car won't start. **Its** battery is dead.

- **knew** (past tense of *know*); **new** (latest)

    I **knew** that Marcia wasn't telling the truth.
    I just bought a **new** car.

- **right** (correct; direction); **write** (put words on paper)

    He gave all the **right** answers and passed the test.
    Please **write** your answers in pencil on this answer sheet.

- **there** (a certain place); **their** (possessive pronoun); **they're** (contraction of *they are*)

    I looked all over the kitchen, but I can't find my keys **there**.
    Nancy and Sally bring **their** lunches to work every day.
    Frank and Kevin said **they're** going to the zoo.

- **wear** (have on clothes); **where** (a place)

    He likes to **wear** brand new designer jeans every day.
    Do you know **where** Mr. Lawrence is?

- **weather** (climate conditions); **whether** (if)

    I hope that the **weather** is nice for our picnic.
    Do you know **whether** or not Sue is working late tonight?

Homonyms are words that sound the same but have different meanings and spellings.

Tip

To use the right homonym, compare the meanings. Then use the spelling for that meaning.

GED Readiness

Questions 1 through 5 refer to the following information. Circle the number of the <u>one best answer</u> to each item.

(1) You want a great knew personal music player. (2) How can you buy the right won? (3) You can get a portable CD player or a portable radio. (4) You can also get the latest invention, an MP3 player. (5) An MP3 player plays special music files called MP3s. (6) You can buy and download MP3 songs from the Internet and then listen to them on your player. (7) When choosing a good MP3 player, look for a large memory. (8) Sum people have put their whole music libraries on their players. (9) Also look for good sound. (10) You wouldn't want the music to sound week when you play it back. (11) Finally, the player should have a plug for an extra headset. (12) There is no telling when you will want to share your music with a friend.

Correction

1 Sentence 1: **You want a great knew personal music player.**

Which correction should be made to sentence 1?

1. replace <u>great</u> with <u>grate</u>
2. replace <u>knew</u> with <u>new</u>
3. replace <u>personal</u> with <u>personnel</u>
4. replace <u>player</u> with <u>Player</u>
5. no correction is necessary

Correction

2 Sentence 2: **How can you buy the right won?**

Which correction should be made to sentence 2?

1. replace <u>you</u> with <u>You</u>
2. replace <u>buy</u> with <u>by</u>
3. replace <u>right</u> with <u>write</u>
4. replace <u>won</u> with <u>one</u>
5. no correction is necessary

Correction

3 Sentence 8: **Sum people have put their whole music libraries on their players.**

Which correction should be made to sentence 8?

1. replace <u>Sum</u> with <u>Some</u>
2. replace <u>their</u> with <u>there</u>
3. replace <u>their</u> with <u>they're</u>
4. replace <u>whole</u> with <u>hole</u>
5. no correction is necessary

Correction

4 Sentence 10: **You wouldn't want the music to sound week when you play it back.**

Which correction should be made to sentence 10?

1. replace <u>wouldn't</u> with <u>woodn't</u>
2. replace <u>wouldn't</u> with <u>would'nt</u>
3. replace <u>to</u> with <u>too</u>
4. replace <u>to</u> with <u>two</u>
5. replace <u>week</u> with <u>weak</u>

Correction

5 Sentence 12: **There is no telling when you will want to share your music with a friend.**

Which correction should be made to sentence 12?

1. replace <u>There</u> with <u>They're</u>
2. replace <u>There</u> with <u>Their</u>
3. replace <u>to</u> with <u>two</u>
4. replace <u>to</u> with <u>too</u>
5. no correction is necessary

27 Topic Sentences and Paragraphs

A **paragraph** is a group of sentences related to a specific subject. A good paragraph has several body sentences that give details that support the main idea of the paragraph.

The main idea is stated in the paragraph's **topic sentence**. The topic sentence

- states the main idea of the paragraph
- is general enough to introduce the more specific body sentences
- is usually the first sentence in the paragraph

Example:

| topic sentence |

Many experts do not agree on where the roller coaster was invented. Some experts say that the first roller coaster was invented in Russia in the 1700s. They say that the Russians built large slides covered with ice. People, including royalty, would go down the slides in large sleds. Later, wheels were added to the sleds so that people could ride all year round. Other experts, however, say that the first roller coasters were invented in France. They say that in 1817, the world's first two roller coasters were constructed outside of Paris. However, the roller coasters' name—"Russian Mountain," in English—seemed to give credit to the Russians, adding to the confusion. Therefore, the true history of the invention of the roller coaster will have to remain a mystery.

In this paragraph, the topic sentence, "Many experts do not agree on where the roller coaster was invented," states the main idea of the paragraph. The topic sentence introduces the body sentences of the paragraph, which present the two different theories of where roller coasters were invented.

GED test items may ask you to

- choose the best way to revise a topic sentence
- move a topic sentence to the correct place in the paragraph
- select the correct topic sentence to insert into the paragraph

---

The **topic sentence** of a paragraph states the paragraph's main idea. A good topic sentence should be general enough to introduce all of the specific details in the body sentences. Usually, a topic sentence is the first sentence in the paragraph.

Tip

The GED asks about topic sentences in several ways. Test items may ask you to revise a topic sentence, choose the best topic sentence to insert, or move the topic sentence to the proper place.

Whenever an item asks about the first sentence of a paragraph, try to decide if the question is about topic sentences. If so, then look for the best topic sentence for the paragraph.

GED Readiness

Questions 1 through 4 refer to the following information. Circle the number of the one best answer to each item.

A

(1) Merry-go-rounds are interesting machines. (2) In the 12th century, Arab horseback riders would test their skills by throwing and catching clay balls as they rode their horses. (3) European riders learned this custom and practiced their skills riding wooden horses suspended from a large wooden wheel—the first merry-go-round. (4) Eventually, merry-go-rounds became popular with French children and were later exported to the United States.

B

(5) Merry-go-rounds were installed throughout the United States in public parks, amusement parks, and traveling fairs. (6) Manufacturers competed with one another to build elaborate, colorful merry-go-rounds. (7) In fact, the period from about 1860 to 1930 was called the "Golden Age" of the merry-go-round because of the many beautiful rides created during this time. (8) In the United States, merry-go-rounds became popular forms of entertainment.

C

(9) Experts estimate that of the 7,000 merry-go-rounds built during the Golden Age, only about 300 are left. (10) People still enjoy the surviving devices at fairs and amusement parks. (11) Others collect horses from these masterpieces.

Revision

1 Sentence 1: **Merry-go-rounds are interesting machines.**

Which is the most effective rewrite of sentence 1?

(1) The first merry-go-round was invented over 700 years ago.
(2) The merry-go-round was an important invention.
(3) Merry-go-rounds are fun and entertaining.
(4) The merry-go-round has a long, surprising history.
(5) Merry-go-rounds are fun entertainment for children.

Revision

2 Sentence 7: **In fact, the period from about 1860 to 1930 was called the "Golden Age" of the merry-go-round because of the many beautiful rides created during this time.**

Which revision should be made to the placement of sentence 7?

(1) move sentence 7 to the end of paragraph A
(2) move sentence 7 to the beginning of paragraph B
(3) move sentence 7 to follow sentence 5
(4) move sentence 7 to the end of paragraph B
(5) no correction is necessary

Revision

3 Sentence 8: **In the United States, merry-go-rounds became popular forms of entertainment.**

Which revision should be made to the placement of sentence 8?

(1) move sentence 8 to the end of paragraph A
(2) move sentence 8 to the beginning of paragraph B
(3) move sentence 8 to follow sentence 6
(4) move sentence 8 to the beginning of paragraph C
(5) no correction is necessary

Construction Shift

4 Which sentence would be most effective if inserted at the beginning of paragraph C?

(1) No one can ride on merry-go-rounds any more.
(2) People still love merry-go-rounds today.
(3) Today, people collect parts from old merry-go-rounds.
(4) These beloved machines are now less and less common.
(5) Merry-go-rounds are fun to ride in summer.

Unity and Coherence

The sentences after the topic sentence are called **body sentences**. A good paragraph should have several body sentences which

- are specific
- are in a logical order
- support the main idea of the paragraph

When all of the body sentences support the main idea of the paragraph, the paragraph has **unity**. When the sentences are in a logical order, the paragraph has **coherence**.

Example:

A good paragraph should be **unified** (all of the sentences should support the main idea of the paragraph) and **coherent** (the sentences are in a logical order).

City Transit Lines' new Electronic Fare Card may be for you! This new service lets you purchase and store value on your card using the Internet or convenient pay stations at subway stops and bus stations. With the new Fare Card, you no longer have to fumble for exact change or stand in long lines to pay your fare. Simply store value on your card using cash or a credit card. Your fare will be automatically deducted when you board a bus or enter a subway station. To get a new Electronic Fare Card, go to any bus or subway station, or visit City Bus Lines' new website.

Tip

If a test item asks you to move or remove a sentence, decide first whether you need to move the sentence to another place in the same paragraph, move it to another paragraph, or remove it completely. Then look for the option that matches your answer.

In this paragraph, all of the sentences are about the main idea, the new payment system, so the paragraph has unity. The sentences are in logical order, so the paragraph has coherence.

Questions on the GED may ask you to remove or rewrite sentences in order to improve the unity of the paragraph.

Example:

(1) City Transit Lines' new Electronic Fare Card system has been a resounding success. (2) Since the program began one month ago, over 70 percent of fares are being paid with the new cards. (3) Lines at subway stations, which used to be 10 commuters long during rush hour, are now almost non-existent. (4) Bus and subway riders agree that the new cards save time and money. (5) Riders also feel that the subway stations need to be cleaner, and that trains should run all night on the airport line.

What is the main idea of the paragraph? Which sentence does not belong?

The main idea of the paragraph is the success of the new payment system. Sentence (5), which is about cleaner stations and extended schedules, is not related to this topic.

Related Skills: 29 and 38

GED Readiness

Questions 1 through 4 refer to the following announcement. Circle the number of the <u>one best answer</u> to each item.

Ⓐ

(1) The Green Street Subway Station will be closed from January 2 to March 29 for repairs and renovation. (2) During this time, a number of improvements will be made to the track and station. (3) The track between Green Street and Flynn Street will be repaired. (4) New turnstiles and fare card vending machines will be installed. (5) A new newsstand will open, and a space will be created for a new gourmet coffee shop. (6) Many people hope that Corrine's Coffee will open in that space because it's their favorite coffee shop.

Ⓑ

(7) While the station is closed, passengers may use the Brown Street and Flynn Street stations or they can ride free buses to and from Green Street Station. (8) People who drive or walk to work will not be affected.

Ⓒ

(9) The improvements to the Green Street Subway Station are only part of City Transit Lines' progress. (10) Five new bus lines will be launched on January 2. (11) This summer, extra buses will be added to route 146, Beach Express. (12) Finally, a new exit will give passengers direct access from Green Street Station to the new Skyline Tower Mall.

Construction Shift

❶ Sentence 3: **The track between Green Street and Flynn Street will be repaired.**

Which revision should be made to the placement of sentence 3?

① move sentence 3 to the beginning of paragraph A
② move sentence 3 to the beginning of paragraph B
③ move sentence 3 to follow sentence 10
④ remove sentence 3
⑤ no correction is necessary

Construction Shift

❷ Sentence 6: **Many people hope that Corrine's Coffee will open in that space because it's their favorite coffee shop.**

Which revision should be made to the placement of sentence 6?

① move sentence 6 to follow sentence 3
② move sentence 6 to the end of paragraph B
③ move sentence 6 to follow sentence 10
④ move sentence 6 to follow sentence 12
⑤ remove sentence 6

Construction Shift

❸ Sentence 8: **People who drive or walk to work will not be affected.**

Which revision should be made to the placement of sentence 8?

① move sentence 8 to the end of paragraph A
② move sentence 8 to the beginning of paragraph B
③ move sentence 8 to the beginning of paragraph C
④ move sentence 8 to follow sentence 9
⑤ remove sentence 8

Construction Shift

❹ Sentence 12: **Finally, a new exit will give passengers direct access from Green Street Station to the new Skyline Tower Mall.**

Which revision should be made to the placement of sentence 12?

① move sentence 12 to follow sentence 5
② move sentence 12 to the beginning of paragraph B
③ move sentence 12 to the end of paragraph B
④ remove sentence 12
⑤ no correction is necessary

Joining and Dividing Paragraphs

Dividing Paragraphs

A good paragraph should have **unity**—all of the sentences should support the main idea of the paragraph. When you write, you should make sure that each paragraph addresses only one main idea. If the paragraph addresses two main ideas, then you should divide it into two paragraphs.

Example:

> Parking rules are changing in the Buena Park neighborhood. Starting July 1, new parking regulations will go into effect, banning parked trucks on neighborhood streets overnight. All trucks and vans need to be parked in off-street parking lots or garages. Trash collection regulations are also changing. Effective July 1, trash collection day will switch from Wednesday to Thursday. Furthermore, we will be switching to a blue-bag recycling program. Put all metal, glass, and paper recyclables in blue trash bags available at all supermarkets.

This paragraph addresses two main ideas: parking and trash collection, so it should be divided into two paragraphs. Begin the second paragraph with the sentence, "Trash collection regulations are also changing."

Joining Paragraphs

Sometimes two paragraphs contain information on the same main idea. In this case, the paragraphs should be joined.

Example:

> Street cleaning in the Buena Park neighborhood takes place on the first Tuesday of every month. On that day, parking is banned on the north and west sides of the street from 8:00 to noon.
>
> From noon until 5:00 P.M. every day, parking is banned on the south and west sides of the street. If your car is parked illegally during any of these times, it will be ticketed and towed.

Both of the paragraphs are about the new street cleaning rules, so the paragraphs should be joined.

Tip

When joining or dividing paragraphs, find the main idea of the paragraph(s). If a paragraph has two main ideas, divide it. If two paragraphs have the same main idea, join them.

Related Skills: 28 and 38

GED Readiness

Questions 1 through 4 refer to the following memo. Circle the number of the <u>one best answer</u> to each item.

To: All Employees
From: Tony Chaitin, Payroll

A

(1) Beginning January 1, our company will offer an exciting new service: direct deposit of payroll checks to your bank account. (2) This memo details the advantages of direct deposit and tells you how to sign up. (3) Management is still discussing the increase of insurance benefits.

B

(4) Direct deposit will help employees in several ways. (5) First, you will no longer have to go to the bank or wait in line to deposit your check. (6) If you are sick or on vacation, your pay will go directly into your account.

C

(7) In addition, you will no longer have to wait for your check to clear. (8) With the new system, funds will be available at 2:01 A.M. on payday.

D

(9) To sign up, simply complete the attached form. (10) You will need to know the name and address of your bank, your account number, and the routing number of your bank. (11) The form shows where to find these numbers on a blank check. (12) Simply return the form to Human Resources. (13) The procedure for changing or stopping your direct deposit is also easy. (14) If you want to change banks or accounts, simply complete a new copy of the direct deposit form. (15) If you want to stop direct deposit, check the appropriate box on the form and turn it in. (16) Direct deposit will stop and you will begin to get traditional checks again.

E

(17) You will continue to get a printed pay stub each payday. (18) Your check stub will show your total hours worked, gross pay, withholding for taxes, Social Security, and employee deductions for insurance and other benefits. (19) The stub will also show contributions to your retirement plan. (20) You can also get a form to sign up for the retirement plan from Human Resources.

Construction Shift

1 Which revision would improve the effectiveness of the memo?

  (1) remove paragraph A
  (2) join paragraphs A and B
  (3) remove sentence 1
  (4) remove sentence 2
  (5) remove sentence 3

Construction Shift

2 Which revision would improve the effectiveness of the memo?

  (1) remove paragraph B
  (2) remove paragraph C
  (3) join paragraphs B and C
  (4) join paragraphs C and D
  (5) no correction is necessary

Construction Shift

3 Which revision would improve the effectiveness of the memo?

Begin a new paragraph with

  (1) sentence 12
  (2) sentence 13
  (3) sentence 14
  (4) sentence 15
  (5) sentence 16

Construction Shift

4 Which revision would improve the effectiveness of the memo?

  (1) remove paragraph E
  (2) remove sentence 18
  (3) remove sentence 19
  (4) remove sentence 20
  (5) no correction is necessary

Transitions Within Paragraphs

When a paragraph is **coherent**, all of the sentences are in a logical order. To show the relationship among the ideas in the sentences, use **transitions**—words such as *however, for example,* and *in contrast.* These words make it easier for the reader to understand the relationship of the ideas in the paragraph.

Examples:

- **No transition:** He went to the supermarket. He forgot to buy milk.
  With transition: He went to the supermarket. **However,** he forgot to buy milk.

- **No transition:** She's very careful about her diet. She tries to eat foods low in fat and cholesterol.
  With transition: She's very careful about her diet. **For example,** she tries to eat foods low in fat and cholesterol.

- **No transition:** Janice loves to swim for exercise. Her husband would rather play basketball with his friends.
  With transition: Janice loves to swim for exercise. **In contrast,** her husband would rather play basketball with his friends.

You can also use transitions when you join sentences with semicolons.

Example:

Janice loves to swim for exercise; **in contrast,** her husband would rather play basketball with his friends.

Here are some common transitions:

Add an idea: also, in addition, moreover, furthermore

Give a contrasting idea: however, in contrast

Give an example: for example, for instance

Say the result: as a result, as a consequence, consequently, therefore

Give a reason: for that reason

State a conclusion: to conclude, in conclusion

Summarize: to sum up, in summary

Order: first, second, third, next, last, finally

Another way to show the relationship between sentences is to join them using a subordinating conjunction (See Skill 4).

Example:

Rhonda worked very hard. She didn't get a promotion.
Although Rhonda worked very hard, she didn't get a promotion.

Use **transitions** to add an idea, show contrast among ideas, introduce an example, or introduce a result.

Tip

Read the sentences before you add a transition. Then choose the transition that shows the relationship between the two sentences.

GED Readiness

Questions 1 through 4 refer to the following information. Circle the number of the <u>one best answer</u> to each item.

(1) Family reunions are fun occasions for relatives to get together. (2) To have a successful reunion, select a date and location. (3) Make all of the necessary arrangements. (4) Plan exciting activities for everyone.

(5) Often, good times for reunions are the summer months. (6) You also might plan based upon your family's schedules. (7) If a relative who lives in Canada will be visiting at a certain time, that might be a good time to have the reunion.

(8) For the reunion itself, plan interesting activities for everyone who will be coming, including children, teens, adults, and seniors. (9) Create a play space or nursery if there will be many small children. (10) You might hire a babysitter. (11) Have everyone work together to prepare or update a family tree. (12) People at the reunion will get a better understanding of the family and its history.

Construction Shift

1 Sentences 2, 3, and 4: **To have a successful reunion, select a date and location. Make all of the necessary arrangements. Plan exciting activities for everyone.**

The most effective combination of sentences 2, 3, and 4 would include which group of words?

① location, make all of the necessary arrangements, and plan fun activities for everyone.
② location, make all of the necessary arrangements, and, in contrast, plan fun activities for everyone.
③ location, make all of the necessary arrangements, and, for example, plan fun activities for everyone.
④ location, make all of the necessary arrangements, and, therefore, plan fun activities for everyone.
⑤ location, make all of the necessary arrangements, and, as a result, plan fun activities for everyone.

Correction

2 Sentence 7: **If a good relative who lives in Canada will be visiting at a certain time, that might be a good time to have the reunion.**

Which is the best way to write the underlined portion of this sentence? If the original is the best way, choose option (1).

① If
② If, however,
③ If, to conclude,
④ If, in addition,
⑤ If, for example,

Correction

3 Sentence 10: **You might hire a babysitter.**

Which correction should be made to sentence 10?

① replace <u>You</u> with <u>For example, you</u>
② replace <u>You</u> with <u>First, you</u>
③ insert <u>also</u> after <u>You</u>
④ replace <u>might</u> with <u>mite</u>
⑤ replace <u>babybsitter</u> with <u>babysitter, furthermore</u>

Revision

4 Sentence 12: **<u>People</u> at the reunion will get a better understanding of the family and its history.**

Which is the best way to write the underlined portion of this sentence? If the original is the best way, choose option (1).

① People
② First, people
③ Last, people
④ As a result, people
⑤ For example, people

31

What Is an Essay?

The GED Essay

An important part of the GED test is the **essay**. According to the **GED Essay Scoring Guide**, in an effective essay, the "reader understands and easily follows the writer's expression of ideas."

In addition, a good essay fully develops its ideas with "specific and relevant details and examples." In order to do this, a GED essay needs to be several paragraphs long—usually five. In this section, you will begin by examining sentences and one-paragraph essays. Then you will move to three- and five-paragraph essays. By the end of this section, you will be ready to write an effective GED essay.

What Is an Essay?

An essay is more than a group of sentences. An essay

- is on a specific subject
- has organized ideas
- has a definite beginning, middle, and end
- is written in complete sentences and paragraphs
- has good spelling, grammar, and punctuation

Example:

Topic

What is your favorite free-time activity?

In your essay, state your favorite free-time activity. Give reasons to explain your choice. Use your personal observations, experience, and knowledge to support your essay.

My favorite free-time activity is watching movies. I love watching movies because I can escape into new worlds. I like many different kinds of films. For example, I love exciting action movies with car chases and explosions. But I also like detective films and romances. However, comedies are my favorite. Whether it's a classic Laurel and Hardy film from the 1930s or the latest hit from Hollywood, I'll be laughing and enjoying myself. Movies are a fun form of entertainment that give me hours of pleasure.

Why Is This an Essay?

- ☑ It's on a specific subject: a favorite activity, the movies.
- ☑ The ideas are organized. The writer tells why he or she likes movies and mentions his or her favorite movies.
- ☑ It has a beginning, a middle, and an end. The writer states the topic, gives details, and ends with a conclusion.
- ☑ It's written in complete sentences in one paragraph.
- ☑ It has good spelling, grammar, and punctuation.

An **essay** is a written composition on a specific subject. The ideas in an essay are organized and have a beginning, middle, and end.

The **GED Essay Scoring Guide** is used by raters to evaluate GED essays. A complete copy of the Scoring Guide is on page x.

Tip

The best way to learn to write an essay is by writing essays. In this section of *Top 50 Writing Skills for GED Success*, you will write 19 essays.

You should have a special notebook in which you write and keep your essays. This symbol lets you know that you will be writing in your notebook.

GED Readiness

Check Your Knowledge

Is it an essay? Write _yes_ or _no_ on the lines.

_____ ① a list of things to buy at the supermarket

_____ ② a newspaper editorial

_____ ③ a company newsletter

_____ ④ a letter to your U.S. senator expressing your opinion on a subject

_____ ⑤ a book on the history of war in Iraq

_____ ⑥ an e-mail to a friend inviting her to the movies

_____ ⑦ a notice explaining changes to your company's insurance plans

_____ ⑧ a paragraph about your grandfather's life for a book on your family history

Practice

Three writers wrote one-paragraph essays on this GED topic: What's your most memorable free-time event? Review their work. Did they write good essays? Check the boxes.

❶ Last year, went to the Superbowl. It was really exciting because it's an important football game, and I love football. We saw and did many things:
Went to the SUPERBOWL!!!
Got autographs from three famous football players
Had fun at a big party before the game
Our team scored three times. We won! HOORAY!!! I hope our team wins next year, too. Now I want to go to the superbowl everyear. I also want to go to the world Series, but my favorite team never wins. That's the Chicago Cubs.

☐ It's on a specific subject.
☐ The ideas are organized.
☐ It has a beginning, a middle, and an end.
☐ It's written in complete sentences in one paragraph.
☐ It has good spelling, grammar, and punctuation.

❷ A few years ago, a special concert took place in our city. Over 25 famous singers performed. I got to see Madonna, Prince, U2, Sting, and Elton John. The concert lasted from 4:00 in the afternoon until midnight, and all of the money went to help fight hunger in poor countries. My favorite part of the concert was the end. For the last song, all of the performers sang together. The audience held hands and sang, too. The concert was a great way to help others and have fun at the same time.

☐ It's on a specific subject.
☐ The ideas are organized.
☐ It has a beginning, a middle, and an end.
☐ It's written in complete sentences in one paragraph.
☐ It has good spelling, grammar, and punctuation.

❸ My most memorable free-time event was taking our children to Disneyworld. When they were finally old enough, my wife and I announced that we were going to Disneyworld as soon as school was out. We were all thrilled with the Disney resort, and we loved riding the monorail. Space Mountain and Pirates of the Caribbean were our favorite rides, so we enjoyed them several times. When it was time to head home, we agreed that this was our best vacation ever.

☐ It's on a specific subject.
☐ The ideas are organized.
☐ It has a beginning, a middle, and an end.
☐ It's written in complete sentences in one paragraph.
☐ It has good spelling, grammar, and punctuation.

Write

Name some topics you want to write about.

① _____

② _____

③ _____

④ _____

32 Understanding the Topic

As you learned in Skill 31, an essay is written on a specific subject. When you take the GED, you will find out the topic by reading the **writing prompt.** According to the GED Essay Scoring Guide, an effective GED essay "presents a clearly focused main idea that addresses the prompt." A GED writing prompt has two parts:

- question
- instructions

Example:

Topic

Why do you want to get your GED? ← Question

Instructions → In your essay, explain why you have decided get your GED. Give reasons to explain your decision. Use your personal observations, experience, and knowledge to support your essay.

The **question** gives you a clear idea of the topic your essay should address. The topic of this essay is why you want to get your GED. The **instructions** indicate the type of information your essay should contain. In this case, your essay should provide the reasons behind your goal. GED writing prompts might ask you to

- describe someone or something
- tell what happened
- give reasons to explain something
- tell how to do something

The prompt also tells you that you do not need special knowledge to write a good essay. The instructions always tell you to "use your personal observations, experience, and knowledge." But what if you don't know anything about the topic? For example, a writing prompt might ask you to name your favorite sport. However, you hate all sports. In that case, write an essay giving reasons why you don't like sports.

Read this writing prompt. Write *question* next to the question and *instructions* next to the instructions. What is the topic? What kind of information does the topic ask for?

Topic

What's the most important experience of your life?

In your essay, state your most important experience. Tell what happened and explain why that experience was so important. Use your personal observations, experience, and knowledge to support your essay.

> The **writing prompt** states the topic your essay should address. An effective GED essay should "present a clearly focused main idea that addresses the prompt."

> **Tip**
>
> When you take the GED or a GED practice test, read the writing prompt first. Then answer the multiple-choice questions. That way, items for the essay may come to you as you work on the multiple-choice items. When 45 minutes are left, begin the essay. Then the topic will already be familiar to you.

GED Readiness

Check Your Knowledge

Read the statements. Write *true* or *false* on the lines.

_____ ① A good GED essay does not have to address the topic.

_____ ② The topic is the subject of your essay.

_____ ③ You never have to give reasons when you write a GED essay.

_____ ④ You don't need special knowledge to write a good GED essay.

_____ ⑤ If you don't know much about the topic in the writing prompt, you can write about another topic.

_____ ⑥ A GED writing prompt has a question and instructions.

_____ ⑦ In some GED essays, you will describe someone or something.

_____ ⑧ An effective GED essay needs to have a main idea.

Practice

Read the GED writing prompts. Write the topic on the line. Then explain how you will answer. Should your essay describe, tell what happened, give reasons, or tell how to do something?

Topic

Is it important to vote?

In your essay, state whether you think it's important to vote. Give reasons to back up your opinion. Use your personal observations, experience, and knowledge to support your essay.

❶ Topic: _____

How you will answer: _____

Topic

Everyone has a favorite food.

In your essay, describe one or two of your favorite foods. What are they like? Use your personal observations, experience, and knowledge to support your essay.

❷ Topic: _____

How you will answer: _____

Topic

Everyone has an exceptionally good day from time to time.

In your essay, name a recent good day. Tell what happened and explain why that day was so good. Use your personal observations, experience, and knowledge to support your essay.

❸ Topic: _____

How you will answer: _____

Write

Look at the topics you wrote on page 81. How would you answer them? Would you describe, tell what happened, tell how to do something, or give reasons? Write the answers on the lines below.

① _____

② _____

③ _____

④ _____

33

Brainstorming

To write a good GED essay, you need to have plenty of good ideas about the topic. According to the GED Essay Scoring Guide, an effective GED essay has "specific and relevant details and examples." You will need to have enough ideas for a four- or five-paragraph essay. In order to have enough ideas, it's a good idea to spend a few minutes gathering ideas before you start to write. One good way to gather ideas quickly is **brainstorming**. When you brainstorm, you write a list of as many ideas as possible as quickly as you can. Follow these guidelines to brainstorm effectively:

- Write in words and phrases, not sentences, to save time.
- Don't worry about spelling, capitalization, or punctuation.
- Focus on gathering as many ideas as you can.

Example:

Topic

Most people have a best friend.

In your essay, identify your best friend. Explain why that person is your best friend. What are the person's qualities and traits that make him or her such a good friend? Use your personal observations, experience, and knowledge to support your essay.

Here is the list Juan created when he brainstormed:

Best friend—Miguel Rodriguez

friendly
has same values—hard work, honesty
likes the same sports—swimming, playing soccer
likes the same weekend activities—watching soccer, dancing
likes the same soccer team, go to games together
helps me—last week gave me bus fare when I lost my wallet, gives me
   a ride to work every morning
good relationship with my family—he and my parents like each other

Review Juan's list of ideas. Add one or two ideas of your own to the list.

_____

_____

_____

Brainstorming is a way to gather ideas for an essay. When you brainstorm, write many ideas as quickly as possible. Write a list of words and phrases. Don't worry about spelling or other mistakes. Just get your ideas down on paper so you can use them when you write your essay.

Tip

After you brainstorm, review your idea list. Make sure that all of the ideas are related to the essay topic.

Related Skills: 28 and 29

GED Readiness

Check Your Knowledge

These people are writing GED essays. Are they brainstorming correctly? Write *yes* or *no* on the line.

_____ ① Frank is checking each word in his electronic dictionary.

_____ ② Pearl is writing her ideas in a list.

_____ ③ Jeff is taking 45 minutes to complete his list.

_____ ④ José is really worried about correct grammar while writing his list.

_____ ⑤ Margie is writing in complete sentences.

_____ ⑥ Tom finished his list in six minutes.

Practice

❶ **Read the GED essay topic. Brainstorm a list of ideas.**

> ### Topic
>
> What are the characteristics of a good parent?
>
> In your essay, identify the characteristics of a good parent. Why are these characteristics important? Use your personal observations, experience, and knowledge to support your essay.

_____

_____

_____

_____

_____

_____

❷ **Review your brainstormed list. Did you brainstorm well? Check the boxes.**

☐ I wrote my ideas in a list.
☐ I wrote quickly.
☐ I wrote in words and phrases.
☐ I didn't worry about spelling, capitalization, or punctuation.

Write

Read the GED essay topic. Brainstorm a list of ideas.

> ### Topic
>
> Each of us is influenced by many people. Who was your biggest influence?
>
> In your essay, identify the person who influenced you the most. How did the person influence you? Why did the person influence you so strongly? Use your personal observations, experience, and knowledge to support your essay.

_____

_____

_____

_____

_____

_____

_____

_____

_____

_____

34

Complete Sentences

According to the GED Essay Scoring Guide, a good GED essay "consistently controls sentence structure." In a good GED essay, all of the sentences are complete. A **complete sentence**

- has a subject and a verb
- expresses a complete thought and can stand alone
- begins with a capital letter and ends with a period

Examples:

<u>William</u> <u>bought</u> a new car.

- *William* is the subject and *bought* is the verb.
- The sentence expresses a complete thought and can stand alone.
- It begins with a capital letter and ends with a period.

<u>His old car</u> <u>hadn't been running</u> well.

- *His old car* is the subject and *hadn't been running* is the verb.
- The sentence expresses a complete thought and can stand alone.
- It begins with a capital letter and ends with a period.

Writing Complete Sentences

Example:

Look at Maria's idea list below. The ideas are for an essay on the topic, "What makes a good neighbor?" One of the ideas is crossed off. Which one? Why?

Maria also wrote a sentence about each of the items in the list. Look at the idea list and sentences.

> A **complete sentence** has a subject and a verb, is a complete thought, and can stand alone. A complete sentence begins with a capital letter and ends with a period.

> **Tip**
>
> Are your sentences complete? To check, underline each <u>subject</u> once and the <u>verb</u> twice. Be sure each sentence makes sense alone. Then check for capital letters and periods.

great neighbor—Carla Chen
quiet
keeps home clean and nice
shovels sidewalks in winter
cuts grass in summer
friendly and polite
beautiful flowers and bushes
~~other neighbors have a mean dog~~
_____
_____
_____

I have a great neighbor, Carla Chen.
Her family is quiet.
She keeps her home clean and nice.
Her sons shovel the sidewalks in winter.
Her sons cut the grass in summer.
Her family is friendly and polite.
She has beautiful flowers and bushes.
_____
_____

Add another idea to the list. Then write a complete sentence.

GED Readiness

Check Your Knowledge

Trini wrote sentences about the topic on page 86, too. Underline the <u>subject</u> once and the <u>verb</u> twice.

① I have a great neighbor, Carmen Mendoza.

② Carmen is very friendly.

③ Sometimes we spend hours talking.

④ Her home is always beautiful.

⑤ She has beautiful flowers in her garden.

⑥ She's very helpful.

⑦ Carmen always checks on our oldest neighbor, Ms. Espinoza.

⑧ Carmen babysits for me when I have to work late.

Practice

❶ Review the list of ideas you wrote on page 85. Write a sentence for each item on the list.

_____
_____
_____
_____
_____
_____
_____
_____
_____

❷ Review the sentences you wrote. Check the boxes.

☐ Each sentence has a subject.
☐ Each sentence has a verb.
☐ Each sentence expresses a complete thought.
☐ Each sentence begins with a capital letter.
☐ Each sentence ends with a period.

Write

❶ Read the GED essay topic below. Brainstorm a list of ideas.

Topic

What are the characteristics of a good boss?

In your essay, describe the characteristics of a good boss. Why is it important to have a good boss? Use your personal observations, experience, and knowledge to support your essay.

_____
_____
_____
_____
_____
_____
_____
_____
_____

❷ Review your list of ideas. Cross off any ideas that are not related to the main idea of your essay.

Parts of the Paragraph

The Paragraph

An essay can consist of one paragraph or several. A **paragraph**

- is a group of sentences on a specific subject
- has a **topic sentence** (which gives the main idea of the paragraph), several **body sentences** (which give details and examples about the main idea), and a **concluding sentence** (which sums up the paragraph)
- begins on a new line and is indented at the beginning (begins slightly farther to the right of the margin than the other lines)

According to the GED Essay Scoring Guide, an effective essay

- presents a clearly focused main idea
- establishes a clear and logical order
- has specific and relevant details and examples

Example:

> ### Topic
>
> Explain a decision you made that has changed your life.
>
> In your essay tell what your decision was and explain how it has changed your life. Use your personal observations, experience, and knowledge to support your essay.

Here is an idea list that Linda created:

> have a healthier life
> exercise more
> quit smoking
> stop eating fatty foods
> cut down on sweets
> will feel better
> lose weight (lost 20 pounds)

Using her idea list, Linda wrote the following essay:

Indent | Topic Sentence

A few years ago, I took some steps to have a healthier lifestyle. First, I was smoking a pack of cigarettes a day, so I quit smoking. In addition, I stopped eating fatty foods and tried to eat more fresh fruit and vegetables. I also cut down on sweets. Finally, I started exercising more. Now I go for a long walk every morning before work. So far, I've lost 20 pounds, my blood pressure is down, and I feel great.

Body Sentence

Concluding Sentence

A **paragraph** is a group of sentences on a specific topic. It has a beginning, middle, and end, and the first line is indented.

The **topic sentence** is usually the first sentence of a paragraph. The topic sentence is general and states the main idea of the paragraph.

Tip

A good paragraph should have a topic sentence that expresses its main idea and several body sentences to back up the main idea.

Related Skill: 27

The Topic Sentence

An effective paragraph usually begins with a topic sentence. The **topic sentence** is a general statement that contains the main idea of the paragraph.

A good way to write your topic sentence is to look at the writing prompt and your idea list. Use them to write a general statement about the topic of your essay.

Here is the topic sentence Linda wrote. Notice that her topic sentence is a direct response to the topic given: "a decision you made that has changed your life."

> A few years ago, I took some steps to have a healthier lifestyle.

The Body Sentences

Body sentences give examples and details about the main idea of the essay. The body sentences are more specific than the topic sentence.

Here are the body sentences Linda wrote. Notice that she gives five examples or details about the healthier lifestyle she has adopted (quit smoking, stopped eating fatty foods, eat more fruit and vegetables, eat less sweets, and exercise more).

> First, I was smoking a pack of cigarettes a day, so I quit smoking. In addition, I stopped eating fatty foods and tried to eat more fresh fruit and vegetables. I also cut down on sweets. Finally, I started exercising more. Now I go for a long walk every morning before work.

The **body sentences** are specific. They back up the topic sentences.

The Concluding Sentence

An effective paragraph ends with a **concluding sentence**. It sums up the information in the body.

Linda concluded her paragraph this way. This sentence is the conclusion, or the result, of her move toward a healthier lifestyle.

> So far, I've lost 20 pounds, my blood pressure is down, and I feel great.

The **concluding sentence** sums up the information in the body sentences.

GED Readiness

Check Your Knowledge

Read the paragraph and answer the questions.

> A healthful meal should be low in fat and contain plenty of fresh, natural ingredients. For example, last night I served my family chicken tacos. The tacos were filled with spicy chicken and plenty of lettuce, tomatoes, and chopped onions. In addition, I served some refried beans and some Mexican rice. For dessert, we had fresh grapes. My husband and kids loved everything, and I was happy because everything was good for them.

❶ What is the main idea of the paragraph?

_____

_____

_____

❷ What is the topic sentence? Underline it.

❸ How many details support the main idea?

_____

❹ Write two of the supporting details on the lines.

① _____

_____

_____

② _____

_____

_____

❺ What is the concluding sentence? Underline it.

Practice

❶ **Put the sentences below in order. Write *TS* next to the topic sentence. Write *CS* next to the concluding sentence. Then number the body sentences from *B1* to *B3*.**

_____ Still others enjoy treating themselves to a favorite food such as a pizza or a burger and fries.

_____ If we watch our diets, we don't have to eat sensible foods all the time— sometimes we can splurge on a favorite food.

_____ Some people really enjoy chocolate as a splurge.

_____ So even if you are watching your diet, leave some room for an occasional treat.

_____ Other people enjoy salty snacks, such as potato chips or tortilla chips.

❷ **In your notebook, write the sentences above in order in the form of a paragraph.**

❸ **Review the list of ideas you wrote in Skill 34 on page 87. Use your list to write a paragraph in your notebook. Make sure that your paragraph has a topic sentence that states the main idea. Also, be sure that each of the body sentences supports the main idea, and that you have a strong concluding sentence.**

Write

1 Read the GED essay topic, and brainstorm a list of ideas.

Topic

Everyone has a favorite way to exercise.

What is your favorite way to exercise?
Use your personal observations, experience, and knowledge to support your essay.

_____

_____

_____

_____

_____

_____

_____

_____

_____

_____

_____

_____

_____

_____

2 Review your idea list. Make sure all of the ideas are related to the essay topic. Cross off ideas that are not related. If your list seems short, add more ideas to the list.

3 Use your idea list to write a paragraph in your notebook. Make sure you have a topic sentence, body sentences, and a concluding sentence.

4 Review your paragraph and check the boxes.

My paragraph

☐ begins on a new line
☐ has an indentation at the beginning (begins slightly farther to the right of the margin than the other lines)
☐ is on a specific topic
☐ has a topic sentence
☐ has several body sentences to support the topic sentence
☐ has a concluding sentence

36

Description

Many GED writing prompts will ask you to describe something. When you describe, you tell what something is like. A GED writing prompt might ask you to describe a person, place, thing, or feeling. You may see these clue words in the writing prompt:

describe   define   characteristics   traits

According to the GED Essay Scoring Guide, an effective GED essay has "a clear and logical organization." After you brainstorm ideas for an essay, organize the ideas. A good way to organize your ideas is by numbering them in order. Here are some of the ways to order the ideas in a **descriptive essay:**

- most to least important or least to most important
- top to bottom or bottom to top
- smallest to largest or largest to smallest

Example:

Look at the writing prompt. What words tell you that this essay involves description? Circle them.

Topic

What are the characteristics of a good neighborhood?

In your essay, describe the characteristics of a good neighborhood. Use your personal observations, experience, and knowledge to support your essay.

Here is Susan's idea list. She has numbered her ideas in the order of least important to most important to her. Then Susan has used her idea list to write a one-paragraph essay.

4. stores and a supermarket nearby
1. clean—not a lot of trash in the streets
5. quiet
2. plenty of parking
6. safe—feel secure when leave the house, never worry about kids
3. near a bus stop—kids take the bus to school

    I'm lucky because I live in a good neighborhood. I never find litter on the street. There is plenty of parking, which is important because I have a car. We live near a bus stop so my kids can take the bus to school. Our neighborhood has stores and a supermarket nearby. It is always peaceful and quiet. Above all, I always feel secure when I leave the house, and I never have to worry about my kids. I'm glad I found a home in my neighborhood, and I hope I never have to move away.

Tip

When you describe, use verbs such as *is, are, looks like, sounds like, seems like, feels,* and the simple present tense *(have, has).*

GED Readiness

Check Your Knowledge

Read the essay topics below. Are they asking you to describe something? Write *yes* or *no* on the lines.

    ① What's the most exciting experience of your life?

    ② State the characteristics of a good friend.

    ③ Why don't people wear seat belts?

    ④ Describe the person who influenced you the most in your life.

_____ ⑤ You had a terrible day yesterday. What happened?

_____ ⑥ How have you changed as a person in the past few years?

    ⑦ What is your favorite food?

    ⑧ What did you do on your last day off?

Practice

Look at this list of ideas for a descriptive essay on favorite foods. Number the ideas in order. Then use the list to write a one-paragraph descriptive essay in your notebook. Make sure the paragraph has a topic sentence, several body sentences, and a concluding sentence.

    Favorite food is salad

    Ripe red tomatoes

    Chopped onions

_____ Top it off with blue cheese dressing

_____ Like to eat salad for lunch or dinner

_____ Sometimes eat it for lunch and dinner

_____ Always add special ingredients—nuts, cheese, fresh vegetables

    Fresh lettuce

Write

❶ Read the GED writing prompt. Use it to brainstorm a list of ideas.

Topic

What is your favorite dessert?

In your essay, describe what the food tastes like and why you like it so much. Use your personal observations, experience, and knowledge to support your essay.

_____

_____

_____

_____

_____

_____

_____

_____

_____

_____

_____

_____

❷ Organize your list by numbering your ideas. Then use your list to write a one-paragraph essay in your notebook. Make sure your paragraph has a topic sentence, several body sentences, and a concluding sentence.

Word Choice

When you write an essay, you want to use specific, descriptive words that will make your writing come alive for the reader. The GED Essay Scoring Guide says that an effective GED essay has "varied and precise word choice." How can you make sure that your essay meets this requirement? After you write your essay, review your **word choice**. Follow these suggestions:

- Nouns: A noun is a person, place, or a thing. Use nouns that refer to specific examples and individuals.
  She ate **dessert.**   She ate a **chocolate-macadamia cookie.**

- Verbs: The verb states the action of the sentence. Use action verbs that convey the precise meaning of what you want to say.
  She **ate** the cookie.   She **gobbled up** the cookie.

- Adjectives and Adverbs: Adjectives describe nouns. Adverbs describe verbs and adjectives. Use precise, colorful adjectives and adverbs to make your descriptions specific and detailed.

  She ate a **good** cookie.
  She ate a **rich and chewy** cookie.

  She gobbled up a cookie **quickly.**
  She gobbled up a cookie **in two seconds flat.**

Look at the difference when all of the changes are put together:

> **Original sentence:** She ate dessert.
> **Revised sentence:** She gobbled up a rich and chewy chocolate-macadamia cookie in two seconds flat.

A good time to check your word choice is after you finish writing your essay. Take a few minutes to read your essay. In the real GED test, you don't have time to write two drafts, so just cross off and add words.

Example:

Read the paragraph. Look at how Renata improved the word choice.

> a refreshing cup of   tastes
> My favorite drink is green tea. A cup of it is̶ good any time of day.
>   r health Health
> Doctors say that green tea is good for you. Experts also say that people
>
> who drink green tea live longer than people who d̶o̶n̶'̶t̶ ̶d̶r̶i̶n̶k̶ ̶i̶t̶.
>   drink black tea or coffee
> But the best part of drinking green tea is the taste—it is very good.

Look at the last sentence. Can you improve the word choice?

Related Skill: 5

GED Readiness

Check Your Knowledge

Read the sentences below. Improve the word choice by using specific nouns and verbs along with colorful adjectives and adverbs. Write your revised sentences on the lines.

① Mr. Chun made a nice sandwich for lunch.

_____

② The fresh air smells good.

_____

③ She drove to the store quickly.

_____

④ He read an interesting book.

_____

⑤ I need a new shirt for winter.

_____

⑥ It's raining hard right now.

_____

⑦ Going to the movies is fun.

_____

⑧ His kitchen is a mess.

_____

Practice

Review the essay you wrote in your notebook for Skill 36. Pay attention to your word choice. Cross off and add words to improve the word choice. Check the boxes below.

- ☐ Uses specific nouns and verbs
- ☐ Uses colorful adjectives and adverbs
- ☐ Has a topic sentence, several body sentences, and a concluding sentence

Write

❶ Read the GED writing prompt. Brainstorm a list of ideas on the lines below. Then write a paragraph in your notebook.

Topic

What is your favorite place?

In your essay, describe your favorite place. Tell what the place looks like and why you like it so much. Use your personal observations, experience, and knowledge to support your essay.

_____
_____
_____
_____
_____
_____
_____
_____
_____
_____

❷ Review your paragraph. Cross off and add words to improve the word choice. Check the boxes below.

- ☐ Uses specific nouns and verbs
- ☐ Uses colorful adjectives and adverbs
- ☐ Has a topic sentence, several body sentences, and a concluding sentence

38 Support and Relevance

According to the GED Essay Scoring Guide, an effective GED essay has "specific and relevant details and examples." The body sentences should have plenty of ideas that **support** the main idea expressed in the topic sentence. All of the ideas should be **relevant**: they should be related to the main idea. But sometimes, unrelated or irrelevant ideas can get into your idea list or essay. There are several ways to avoid this problem:

- After you brainstorm, review your idea list. Make sure all of the ideas are about the main idea. Cross off any idea that isn't relevant. Then make sure you have enough ideas for an essay.
- After you finish writing your essay, review your work. Check that all of the sentences are about the main idea. Cross off any sentence that isn't relevant. Then make sure that you have enough ideas. Add ideas to your essay, if necessary.

Example:

Read Tim's idea list for an essay on favorite pets.

My cat Ellen	
clean	rich, dark brown fur
friendly	beautiful purr
quiet	afraid of strangers
greets me when I come home from work	~~dogs annoy me~~

One of the ideas in the list was not relevant, so Tim crossed it off. Add another idea to the list that is relevant.

Now read Mary's one-paragraph essay about her favorite pet.

> My dog Coco is my best friend. She is a light gray mutt. She loves to play with her toys and with our other dogs. But Coco is also a good guard dog. If a stranger comes near our house, she will bark to warn us. But if you know Coco, she is friendly and loyal. She always waits by the door for my children to come home from school. I am home alone a lot during the day, but I never feel lonely because Coco keeps me company. ~~I usually stay busy cooking and cleaning until it's time to go to work.~~ We have two other dogs, but Coco is my favorite.

One of the sentences in the paragraph was not relevant, so Mary crossed it off. Add another sentence that is relevant.

_____

_____

An idea that is **relevant** tells about the main idea of your essay. In a good GED essay, all of the ideas should be relevant.

Tip

Always review your idea list to make sure the ideas are relevant. After you write your essay, review it to make sure all the ideas are still relevant.

GED Readiness

Check Your Knowledge

Read the idea lists below. The main idea is underlined. Cross off the ideas that are not relevant to the main idea. Then add another idea that is relevant.

① <u>Fish are great pets.</u>
colorful and exotic
easy to care for
fun to watch
don't make noise or disturb people
can get sick and die easily

_____

② <u>Dogs have many roles.</u>
watch dogs
some dogs are very lazy
help blind people
care for animals—sheep dogs
provide friendship for people

_____

③ <u>Exotic pets can cause problems.</u>
alligators can get large
snakes can escape
lizards are hard to care for
ferrets can bite
dogs are very friendly

_____

④ <u>My parrot is an unusual pet.</u>
beautiful green color
cats like to catch birds
likes to fly around the house
tries to escape from her cage
she can talk

_____

Practice

Review the essay you wrote in your notebook for Skill 37. Are all of the sentences relevant? Cross off any irrelevant sentences. Then add one more sentence that is relevant.

Write

❶ Read the GED essay topic. Brainstorm a list of ideas.

Topic

Imagine that you could have any pet you wanted. What would be your ideal pet?

In your essay, describe your ideal pet. Use specific details and examples to back up your ideas.

_____
_____
_____
_____
_____
_____
_____
_____
_____
_____

❷ Review your idea list. Cross off any ideas that are not relevant. Then use your idea list to write a paragraph in your notebook.

❸ Review your paragraph, and check the boxes. Add or cross off words to improve your essay.

☐ All of the ideas are relevant.
☐ The ideas are in the correct order.
☐ The paragraph has a topic sentence, body sentences, and a concluding sentence.

According to the GED Essay Scoring Guide, an effective GED essay should have "a clear and logical organization." **Narration** is one way to organize an essay. Narration tells what happened in the past. When you narrate, your ideas are in **chronological order**. (Chronological order means arranged in the order of time.) History books, newspaper articles, and stories use chronological order.

Often, certain words in the writing prompt will tell you that your essay will use narration:

tell	say what happened	event	past

Example:
Read the GED essay topic. What words tell you that it involves narration? Circle them. Then read the one-paragraph essay that Jill wrote about this topic.

Narration tells what happened in the past. When you narrate, use chronological order—order your ideas by time.

Tip
When you write in chronological order, use words like *first, second, next, after that,* and *finally* to make the order of the events clear.

Topic

We often have good or bad days.

What day stands out in your mind as particularly good? In your essay, say what happened that made it so good. Use specific details and examples to back up your ideas.

Last week, I had a great day. First, the weather was good and traffic was light, so I was early for work. I decided to have a relaxing cup of coffee at my favorite café before work. When I got to work, my boss called me into her office. I was afraid I was in trouble. But then she told me that the assistant manager had quit and offered me the job! I was so excited I thought I was going to cry. I got a raise and have better hours, too. At lunch time, I decided to go out to eat with my friend Marlene to celebrate. On our way to the restaurant I found a $20 bill on the ground. I split the money with Marlene. Finally, after work, I told my husband about my great day. He was really surprised, but then he had another surprise for me: He asked me if I wanted to go to Hawaii for our wedding anniversary. What a great day!

Jill wants to add one more idea to the essay. Where does it go? Draw a line.

When I got back from lunch, I had a call on my voicemail. It was my youngest son saying that he got an "A" on his math test. I felt so happy because he'd been struggling with math.

GED Readiness

Check Your Knowledge

1 These sentences are from a paragraph about a bad day. Put the sentences in chronological order by numbering them from 1 to 8.

_____ I had to work through lunch.

_____ Then the bus was late.

_____ First, when I got up, I stepped on my glasses and broke them.

_____ I had to pay my landlord $25 to come over and let me in my apartment.

_____ After that, I had to repair them with tape.

_____ I had a terrible day yesterday.

_____ When I got to work, my boss yelled at me for being late.

_____ When I got home after work, I found out I'd lost my keys.

2 In your notebook, rewrite the sentences in the form of a paragraph. Add a concluding sentence.

Practice

1 Read the GED essay topic. Brainstorm a list of ideas for a one-paragraph essay.

Topic

Describe your idea of a perfect day.

Where would you go? What would you do? In your essay, tell what would happen to make it perfect. Use specific details and examples to back up your ideas.

_____

_____

_____

_____

2 Review your idea list. Make sure all of the ideas are related to the main idea. Cross off any irrelevant ideas and then put your ideas in chronological order. Do you have enough ideas? Add some ideas if necessary.

Write

1 Use your list above to write a paragraph in your notebook.

2 Review your paragraph and check the boxes. Add or cross off words and sentences to improve your writing.

☐ The ideas are all relevant.

☐ The ideas are in chronological order.

☐ The paragraph has a topic sentence, several body sentences, and a concluding sentence.

☐ The sentences have specific nouns and verbs and colorful adjectives and adverbs.

How-To

As you have learned, an effective GED essay should have "a clear and logical organization." One way to order your ideas is according to the steps in a process. This is called a "how-to" essay.

How-to essays tell readers how to make or do something. Many kinds of writing are organized in this way.

- an article on how to frost wedding cakes
- instructions for changing the oil in your car
- directions for using a computer
- driving directions to someone's home

These words in the writing prompt signal that you will write a how-to essay:

    steps   process   how   make

Example:

Read the GED essay topic. Circle the words that tell you to write a how-to essay. Then read the one-paragraph essay that Raphael wrote.

Topic

Everyone has a skill that he or she is particularly good at. It might be cooking, building, sewing, or something else.

In your essay, tell how to do something that you are good at. Give all the steps in the process in order. Use your personal observations, experience, and knowledge to support your essay.

I am an expert at baking homemade bread. The first step is to gather all of the ingredients: flour, water, yeast, sugar, and salt. Dissolve the yeast in a little water. Combine the flour, sugar, and salt in a large mixing bowl. Then add in the yeast mixture and more water. Mix the ingredients into a smooth dough. Then turn the dough out onto the counter and knead it for about 20 minutes. Then let it rise two times in a warm location. Next, form it into a loaf, put it in a loaf pan, and let it rise again. After that, bake it for about 50 minutes. Take it from the oven and remove it from the pan. Then enjoy your delicious, homemade bread.

Raphael forgot to include the idea below. Draw a line to where it goes in the essay.

Let the bread cool completely before cutting it.

A **how-to** essay tells us the steps in a process.

Tip

When you write a how-to essay, brainstorm all of the steps. Then number them in order. When you write, use words like *first, second, next, after that,* and *finally* to make the order of the steps clear.

GED Readiness

Check Your Knowledge

1. These sentences are from a paragraph about using a new cell phone. Put the sentences in order by numbering them from 1 to 7.

_____ After the word "Ready" appears, dial the number you want to call.

_____ When you are finished using the phone, hold down the red on-off button until you hear another musical chime.

_____ When the phone turns on, you will hear a short musical chime.

_____ Turn on the phone by holding down the red on-off button.

_____ Watch the display panel for the word "Ready" to appear.

_____ When you are finished talking, press the red on-off button again.

_____ Press the Talk button after you dial.

2. In your notebook, rewrite the sentences in the form of a paragraph.

Practice

1. Read the GED essay topic below. Circle the words that indicate you should write a how-to essay. Then brainstorm a list of ideas for a one-paragraph essay.

Topic

What is your favorite breakfast? How do you make it?

In your essay, give the steps for making your favorite breakfast. Give all the steps of the process in order. Use your personal observations, experience, and knowledge to support your essay.

2. Review your idea list. Make sure the ideas are in the correct order. Number them in order starting with 1. Check that they are all related to the main idea.

Write

1. Use your list to write a paragraph in your notebook.

2. Review your paragraph and check the boxes. Add or cross off words and ideas to improve your writing.

   □ All of the ideas are relevant.
   □ The ideas are in the correct order.
   □ All important ideas are included.
   □ The paragraph has a topic sentence, several body sentences, and a concluding sentence.
   □ The sentences have specific nouns and verbs and colorful adjectives and adverbs.

41

Giving Reasons

Many GED writing prompts ask you to **give reasons** to explain an opinion, belief, or action. Many kinds of writing involve giving reasons:

- a newspaper editorial on reasons the government should take a certain action
- a magazine article on reasons people need to get more exercise
- an e-mail to your boss giving the reason for your request for a day off

Certain words in a GED writing prompt signal that your essay should give reasons:

| explain | why | tell why |
| give reasons | because | how |

When you give reasons, you usually organize your ideas in order of importance. You can order your ideas:

- from least important to most important, or
- from most important to least important

When you **give reasons**, you explain the thinking behind an opinion, belief, or action.

Tip

When you write an essay giving reasons, use words like *first*, *second*, *next*, *finally*, and *most importantly* to show the order of importance of your ideas.

Example:

Read the GED writing prompt. What words indicate that the writer should give reasons? Circle them. Then look at the paragraph Namby wrote. Circle the words that introduce each reason he gives.

Topic

People have many different reasons for wanting a GED certificate. Why do you want to get your GED?

In your essay, give reasons for wanting a GED certificate. How will getting a GED change your life? Use your personal observations, experience, and knowledge to support your essay.

There are many reasons why I want to get a GED certificate. First, I know that in order to get a promotion at my job, I have to have a high school diploma or a GED. I want to become an assistant manager some day, and a GED will help me. Second, I want to have a GED in case this company moves or closes. With a GED, it will be much easier for me to get another job. Most importantly, I want to get a GED to set an example for my kids. My son is having trouble in school. I don't want him to drop out. If he knows I am working hard to get my GED, maybe he will stay in school.

GED Readiness

Check Your Knowledge

Read the GED writing prompts. Circle the words that indicate that your essay should give reasons.

Topic

Do you like large families or small families? Why?

In your essay, state whether you think large families or small families are better. Then give reasons to explain your choice. Use your personal observations, experience, and knowledge to support your essay.

Topic

Many people prefer to live in a big city. Others like to live in a small town.

Where would you rather live, a big city or a small town? Why? What are the advantages of your choice? Give specific reasons and examples. Use your personal observations, experience, and knowledge to support your essay.

Topic

Many people enjoy living in a house with a yard. Others enjoy the convenience of living in an apartment.

Where would you rather live, in a house or an apartment? Why? What are the advantages of your choice? Give specific reasons and examples. Use your personal observations, experience, and knowledge to support your essay.

Practice

1 Choose one of the topics from *Check Your Knowledge*. Brainstorm a list of ideas for a one-paragraph essay.

_____

_____

_____

_____

_____

_____

_____

_____

2 Check and organize your list.

- ☐ Are all of the ideas relevant? Cross off any irrelevant ideas.
- ☐ Do you have enough ideas? Add ideas if necessary.
- ☐ Are your ideas in the right order? Number them in order of importance.

Write

1 In your notebook, write a one-paragraph essay using your idea list from above.

2 After you write your essay, review it. Check the boxes below. Make any needed corrections on your first draft. Add or cross off words or sentences.

- ☐ All of the ideas are relevant.
- ☐ The ideas are in the correct order.
- ☐ The paragraph has a topic sentence, body sentences, and a concluding sentence.

Checking the Organization

As you have seen before, an effective GED essay "establishes a clear and logical organization." Here are ways to organize different types of essays:

- **Description**—describing something. Possible ways to organize a description are by importance (least important to most important), by size (smallest to largest), or by location.
- **Narration**—telling what happened. Usually, you use chronological order for narration: you tell the events in the order they happened.
- **How-to**—telling how to do something. When you use how-to order, you tell the steps in a process in the order you do them.
- **Giving Reasons**—giving reasons for something. Usually, you state your reasons in order of importance.

Follow these steps so your essay will have clear, logical **organization**:

❶ After you brainstorm, organize the ideas in your idea list. One good way is to number them in order.

❷ After you write your GED essay, check the organization of your sentences. Make sure you followed your plan. If necessary, reorder your ideas, add ideas, or cross off ideas.

Example:

Martha wrote this idea list and one-paragraph essay about her favorite room. When she reviewed her essay, she realized that two sentences were in the wrong place. The lines show how she changed the order of the sentences.

> 5. breakfast nook   2. island sink
> 4. pots, pans, knives   3. counter space
> 1. white tiles, stove, fridge
> 6. storage space, pantry

> My kitchen is my favorite room. I painted it white and put white tiles on the floor, too. The stove and fridge are white, too, so it looks very clean. It has an island sink and lots of counter space. I have plenty of nice pots and pans, and lots of nice kitchen utensils and equipment, such as sharp knives and cutting boards. My favorite part of my kitchen is the breakfast nook. I use the breakfast nook for breakfast or to have a cup of coffee when I am reading or studying. In addition, it has plenty of storage space. There are lots of shelves and cabinets, and a nice walk-in pantry where I store food and supplies.

Organization is the order in which you present ideas. In an effective GED essay, the ideas are in an order that makes sense to the reader.

Tip

When you take the GED test, you won't have time to write two drafts of your essay. So when you check the organization, draw lines or arrows to show the correct order of the sentences.

GED Readiness

Check Your Knowledge

Read the essays below. Write *description*, *narration*, *how-to*, or *give reasons* on the line. One sentence in each paragraph is in the wrong order. Move it to the correct place by drawing a line.

❶ _____

    Cleaning the kitchen after a big meal is not difficult. First, put away all of the food. If there are leftovers, pack them in plastic containers and put them in the fridge. Then gather up all the dirty dishes. Always wash the cooking pots last. Put a squeeze of dish soap in the dishpan and fill the dishpan with hot water. First, wash and rinse the glasses. Then put the silverware in the water. Wash and rinse the plates and serving bowls. Then rinse the silverware. When all the dishes are clean, wipe the counters with a sponge and pour out the dishwater. Next, sweep the floor and you are done.

❷ _____

    Finding an apartment I could afford was not easy. In fact, it took me a month. First, I identified neighborhoods where I wanted to live. Then I checked the classified ads every Saturday morning. I saw several apartments, but they were all small or expensive, or both. Then a friend at work told me that an apartment was opening up in her building. I saw the apartment. It was small but nice, and the price was right. I moved less than three weeks later. I signed a lease right after I looked at the apartment the first time.

❸ _____

    Some people think it's strange, but my favorite room is the hall in my apartment. The hall is large and has doors into the living room, my bedroom, and my baby daughter's bedroom. My desk is in the hall. I study there when my baby is sleeping. That way, I am always nearby in case she cries or needs help. There is also a comfortable chair in the hall. At night I can work on my knitting there in the quiet while my husband and sons watch TV. I keep all of my materials for the GED on my desk.

Practice

❶ Read the GED essay topic. Will you use description, narration, or how-to? First, brainstorm a list of ideas for your essay.

Topic

Most people have a favorite place to visit. What's your favorite place?

In your essay, name your favorite place and describe what it's like. Use your personal observations, experience, and knowledge to support your essay.

_____

_____

_____

_____

_____

_____

_____

_____

❷ Organize your list. Number your ideas in order.

Write

❶ Use your idea list above to write a one-paragraph essay in your notebook.

❷ Review your essay, and check the boxes. Make any needed corrections on your first draft. Add or cross off words or sentences.

☐ All of the ideas are relevant.
☐ The ideas are in the correct order.
☐ The paragraph has a topic sentence, body sentences, and a concluding sentence.

Revising Mechanics

According to the GED Essay Scoring Guide, an effective GED essay "consistently controls sentence structure and the conventions of Edited American English." **Edited American English** is the language people use in newspapers, magazines, and business writing. It is more formal than the language people use in friendly notes, e-mails to friends, or online chat. Edited American English

- uses complete sentences
- spells words correctly
- uses correct punctuation
- uses correct grammar

For a complete review of the conventions, or rules, of Edited American English, see Skills 1–30 in this book.

Mechanics is the least important part of the GED essay, so you should check these things last:

- Each sentence is complete (has a subject and a verb).
- Each sentence starts with a capital letter and ends with a period.
- Proper nouns (such as names of people and places) and proper adjectives (adjectives made from proper nouns) are capitalized.
- The words are spelled correctly.
- The sentences are grammatically correct.

You should write your corrections directly on your first draft because during the GED test, you won't have time to write two drafts.

Example:

Look at how Robert corrected the mechanics in this one-paragraph essay. How many mistakes did he correct? Robert also forgot to add a period. Add the missing period.

Americans
I believe that all young ~~americans~~ should serve their country in some
                eighteen   they
way. When they turn ~~eigteen, he or she~~ should do either a year of
                                         can help
military service or a year of public service. Young people ~~help~~ in
hospitals, service agencies, or community organizations. This way, young
people can develop a sense of patriotism. Serving other Americans can
                                    conscious
help young people become more socially ~~consious~~ and help the
country solve its problems

Mechanics includes spelling, punctuation, and grammar.

Tip

GED candidates often worry about mechanics, but it is actually the least important part of the GED Scoring Guide. The essays that get the highest scores address the prompt, have plenty of good ideas, and are organized. Spend most of your time planning and writing your essay. When you are finished, check the organization and word choice. Check the mechanics last. Make sure all of the sentences are complete. Then check the punctuation, spelling, and capitalization.

GED Readiness

Check Your Knowledge

Each of these sentences has a problem with mechanics. Correct the errors by adding the corrections directly to the sentence.

① all young people should do a year or more of public service.

② For example, joining the Piece Corps is a great way to serve the country.

③ Might want to join the military.

④ Joining the army or the navy great ways to serve the country and see the world.

⑤ young people should get benefits' for serving the country.

⑥ One binifit could be a year of free callege education for each year of service

⑦ The biggest benefit are that young people will develop a sense of Responsibility.

⑧ Doing a year of public service benefit the Whole Country and all of its citizens.

Practice

Review the one-paragraph essay you wrote in your notebook for Skill 42. Review the mechanics and check the boxes.

- ☐ Each sentence is complete (has a subject and a verb).
- ☐ Each sentence starts with a capital letter and ends with a period.
- ☐ Proper nouns (such as names of people and places) and proper adjectives (adjectives made from proper nouns) are capitalized.
- ☐ The words are spelled correctly.
- ☐ The grammar is correct.

Write

❶ **Read the GED writing prompt below. Then brainstorm a list of ideas.**

Topic

People get to work in different ways. They can walk, drive, or take public transportation.

How do you like to get to work? Why? Explain your reasons with specific reasons and examples. Use your personal observations, experience, and knowledge to support your essay.

_____

_____

_____

_____

_____

_____

_____

_____

❷ **Use your idea list above to write a one-paragraph essay in your notebook.**

❸ **After you write your essay, review it.**

- ☐ The ideas are all relevant.
- ☐ The paragraph has a topic sentence, several body sentences, and a concluding sentence.
- ☐ The sentences have specific nouns, dynamic verbs, and colorful adjectives.
- ☐ Each sentence is complete.
- ☐ Each sentence starts with a capital letter and ends with a period.
- ☐ Proper nouns and proper adjectives are capitalized.
- ☐ The words are spelled correctly.
- ☐ The grammar is correct.

44 The Three-Paragraph Essay

Up to now, you have been writing one-paragraph essays. As you know, an effective GED essay "clearly addresses the prompt" and has "specific and relevant details and examples." Usually, one paragraph is not enough to address the prompt and give enough details and examples. An effective GED essay needs more than one paragraph.

How can you move from a one-paragraph essay to a three-paragraph essay? Imagine that you are taking your one-paragraph essay and converting sentences into paragraphs.

One-Paragraph Essay ⟶	Three-Paragraph Essay
Topic Sentence ⟶	Introductory Paragraph
Body Sentences ⟶	Body Paragraph
Concluding Sentence ⟶	Concluding Paragraph

In a three-paragraph essay, each paragraph has a specific role:

- Paragraph 1—**the introduction**—states the main idea of the essay.
- Paragraph 2—**the body**—gives details and examples to support the main idea.
- Paragraph 3—**the conclusion**—sums up the details and restates the main idea.

Example:

Notice how the introduction, body, and conclusion of the one-paragraph essay have been developed into a three-paragraph essay.

Tip

Each part of a one-paragraph essay becomes a paragraph in a three-paragraph essay.

- The topic sentence of your paragraph becomes the introductory paragraph.
- The body sentences, with more detail and a topic sentence, become the body paragraph.
- The concluding sentence becomes the concluding paragraph.

One-Paragraph Essay

One of the best ways to stay healthy is by swimming regularly. Swimming exercises every muscle in your body. It also burns calories. Finally, swimming reduces stress because it's so relaxing. For these reasons, I recommend that you try swimming.

Three-Paragraph Essay

Getting enough exercise is very important. Exercise helps you control your weight and keeps your heart healthy. One of the best exercises is swimming.

There are several reasons why swimming is a good exercise. First, swimming exercises every muscle in your body. You use your arms, legs, and shoulder and back muscles as you swim. Second, swimming burns calories which will keep your weight down. Finally, swimming is relaxing. Whether you are young or old, swimming is an enjoyable workout that won't stress you out.

As you can see, swimming builds your body, burns calories, and lowers stress. For these reasons, swimming is an excellent exercise. I recommend that you give swimming a try.

GED Readiness

Check Your Knowledge

Write *introduction, body,* or *conclusion* on the line.

① The _____ provides examples and illustrations that back up the main idea.

② The _____ summarizes the essay and states the main idea again.

③ The _____ tells readers what the essay will be about.

Practice

Read the paragraphs of the three-paragraph essay. Then write *introduction, body,* or *conclusion* before the correct paragraph.

_____

By following these simple guidelines, you will have a heart-healthy diet. This diet will also help you keep your weight down. Try it and see how much better you feel!

_____

There are several guidelines you need to follow in order to have a healthful diet. First, get plenty of whole grains. Switch to whole grain bread, pasta, and cereal. Avoid white flour. Second, get plenty of fresh fruit and vegetables every day. Have smaller servings of meat. Eat lean meat and avoid fried foods. Finally, avoid sweets.

_____

In order to stay healthy, people need to be careful about what they eat. A lot of salt, fat, and calories can cause health problems. A diet low in fat and high in whole grains, fruit, and vegetables can be very good for your health.

Write

❶ In the next three skill lessons, you will be writing introduction, body, and concluding paragraphs for a three-paragraph essay. Read the topic below and brainstorm an idea list.

Topic

Having a successful party takes lots of planning. Tell how you would plan a party.

Where would you hold the party? What would you have for food and entertainment? Give specific details and examples. Use your personal observations, experience, and knowledge to support your essay.

_____

_____

_____

_____

_____

_____

_____

_____

❷ Check and organize your list.

☐ Are all of the ideas relevant? Cross off any irrelevant ideas.

☐ Do you have enough ideas for a three-paragraph essay? Add ideas if necessary.

☐ Are your ideas in the right order? If necessary, number them in order of importance.

The Introductory Paragraph and Thesis Statement

The first paragraph of a three-paragraph essay introduces the topic of the essay. The **introductory paragraph**

- tells the reader what the essay will be about
- builds interest
- prepares the reader for the information to come in the body paragraph

Usually, the first paragraph begins with a general statement and becomes more specific. The last sentence of the introductory paragraph is very specific. It states the main idea of the essay and indicates the kind of information that will come in the body paragraph. This sentence is called the **thesis statement**. The thesis statement

- is specific
- states the main idea of the essay
- tells the reader exactly what will come in the rest of the essay

Example:

Here is the introductory paragraph of the three-paragraph essay from Skill 44 on page 108:

> Getting enough exercise is very important. Exercise helps you control your weight and keeps your heart healthy. One of the best exercises is swimming.

Which sentence is the most general? The most specific? The thesis statement is "One of the best exercises is swimming."

Now review the body paragraph of the essay. Does the thesis statement do a good job of introducing the information that appears in the body paragraph?

> There are several reasons why swimming is a good exercise. First, swimming exercises every muscle in your body. You use your arms, legs, and shoulder and back muscles as you swim. Second, swimming burns calories which will keep your weight down. Finally, swimming is relaxing. Whether you are young or old, swimming is an enjoyable workout that won't stress you out.

Each sentence in the body paragraph supports the idea in the thesis statement.

The **thesis statement** is the last sentence of the introductory paragraph. This specific sentence states the main idea of the essay. It indicates the kind of information that will come later in the body paragraph.

Tip

After you write your essay, check the thesis statement. If necessary, change it so it exactly matches the content of the body paragraph.

Related Skills: 27 and 30

GED Readiness

Check Your Knowledge

What should an introductory paragraph do? Check the boxes.

- ☐ build interest in the essay
- ☐ have a thesis statement
- ☐ tell people how long the essay will be
- ☐ be organized from general to specific
- ☐ be organized from specific to general

Practice

❶ The sentences below are the general statements for introductory paragraphs in three-paragraph essays. Write a thesis statement for each essay.

① Hobbies are a great way to have fun. Hobbies are also great ways to pass time. I have several hobbies, but collecting stamps is my favorite.

_____

_____

② Many people keep pets. People also keep many kinds of pets. There are many reasons why people like to keep pets.

_____

_____

③ Pastimes are fun ways to spend time. Most people have one or more pastimes.

_____

_____

④ We have many tasks we need to do to keep our houses clean and orderly. But we like some of them more than others. For example, some people hate ironing, but others hate cleaning the bathroom.

_____

_____

⑤ There are many makes and models of cars to choose from. Some people might want a sleek sports car. Others might want a roomy SUV for transporting a large family.

_____

_____

❷ Review your thesis statements and check the boxes. Correct your thesis statements if necessary.

- ☐ The thesis statement gives the main idea of the essay.
- ☐ The thesis statement is specific.
- ☐ The thesis statement indicates the kind of information that will come in the body paragraph.

Write

❶ Look at the list of ideas you brainstormed in Skill 44 on page 109. What will be the main idea of your three-paragraph essay? Write it on the line. Then write an introductory paragraph for your essay in your notebook.

Main Idea: _____

_____

❷ Review your introductory paragraph and check the boxes.

- ☐ The paragraph starts with general statements and becomes more specific.
- ☐ The paragraph ends with a thesis statement.
- ☐ The thesis statement gives the main idea of the essay.
- ☐ The thesis statement is specific.
- ☐ The thesis statement indicates the kind of information that will come in the body paragraph.

Writing Body Paragraphs

The **body paragraph** gives specific examples and details to support the main idea of your essay. If you take the time to gather and organize your ideas, writing the body paragraph will be easy.

A good body paragraph

- begins with a **topic sentence** which states the main idea of the paragraph
- contains specific details to support the main idea of the essay

In a three-paragraph essay, the topic sentence of the body paragraph is usually a more specific version of the thesis statement (the last sentence of the introduction).

Example:

Review the introduction and body paragraph of the essay from Skill 44.

Introduction

Getting enough exercise is very important. Exercise helps you control your weight and keeps your heart healthy. One of the best exercises is swimming.

There are several reasons that swimming is a good exercise. First, swimming exercises every muscle in your body. You use your arms, legs, and shoulder and back muscles as you swim. Second, swimming burns calories, which will keep your weight down. Finally, swimming is relaxing. Whether you are young or old, swimming is an enjoyable workout that won't stress you out.

Body Paragraph

Notice that the topic sentence is more specific than the thesis statement.

> **Thesis statement:** One of the best exercises is swimming.
> **Topic sentence:** There are several reasons that swimming is a good exercise. (more specific)

The thesis statement states the main idea of the essay, "One of the best exercises is swimming."

The topic sentence in the body paragraph is more specific than the thesis statement. The topic sentence clearly indicates that in the body paragraph, the reader will find reasons stating why swimming is good exercise.

The rest of the body paragraph contains details and examples. Review the body paragraph. How many reasons does it give? There are three reasons.

Notice the words that point out each reason: *first*, *second*, and *finally*.

The **body paragraph** is the second paragraph of a three-paragraph essay. A good body paragraph gives plenty of examples and details to support the main idea of the essay.

Tip

Begin a body paragraph with a topic sentence that tells what the body paragraph will be about.

Related Skills: 35 and 44

GED Readiness

Check Your Knowledge

1 **What do these terms mean? Write a short definition on the each line.**

① introductory paragraph: _____

_____

② body paragraph: _____

_____

③ thesis statement: _____

_____

④ topic sentence: _____

_____

2 **Where do these sentences go? Write *introduction* or *body* on the line.**

_____ ① general statements to get readers' attention

_____ ② the thesis statement

_____ ③ specific examples to support the main idea

_____ ④ the topic sentence

Practice

Read the body paragraphs. Write a topic sentence for each one.

1 _____

_____

First, mix the flour, salt, and baking soda. Then beat the egg lightly. Add the milk to the egg and mix. Add the egg and milk mixture to the dry ingredients and mix. Pour the pancake batter onto a hot griddle. Turn the pancakes when bubbles appear on the top. Serve the pancakes with warm syrup or honey.

2 _____

_____

First, camping is not an expensive vacation. Fees at most parks are just a few dollars a night. You also don't need a lot of special equipment. You just need a tent and a sleeping bag. On a camping vacation, you can really get in touch with nature. You can hike, fish, and enjoy beautiful scenery. Finally, camping is a great way to get in touch with your family. The time you spend together around the campfire or hiking in the woods will give plenty of opportunities to talk about your family's hopes and dreams.

Write

1 Review the idea list you made in Skill 44 (page 109) and the introductory paragraph you wrote in your notebook in Skill 45 (page 111). Use your idea list to write the body paragraph for your three-paragraph essay.

2 **Review your body paragraph and check the boxes.**

☐ The body paragraph begins with a topic sentence that states the main idea of the paragraph.

☐ The body paragraph contains specific details and examples that support the topic sentence.

☐ The supporting ideas are all relevant to the main idea.

Writing Concluding Paragraphs

The last paragraph of a three-paragraph essay is the **conclusion**. The purpose of the conclusion is to sum up the essay and present your final thoughts to the reader. A good final paragraph

- restates the main idea of the essay
- summarizes the information in the essay
- provides the reader with a final thought or generalization about the subject of the essay

Usually, the conclusion is organized from specific to general, moving from a restatement of the main idea to your final thought about the topic.

Example:

Introduction

Getting enough exercise is very important. Exercise helps you control your weight and keeps your heart healthy. One of the best exercises is swimming.

There are several reasons why swimming is a good exercise. First, swimming exercises every muscle in your body. You use your arms, legs, and shoulder and back muscles as you swim. Second, swimming burns calories which will keep your weight down. Finally, swimming is relaxing. Whether you are young or old, swimming is an enjoyable workout that won't stress you out.

Body Paragraph

As you can see, swimming builds your body, burns calories, and lowers stress. For these reasons, swimming is an excellent exercise for everyone. I recommend that you give swimming a try.

Conclusion

The **concluding paragraph** is the last paragraph in an essay. A concluding paragraph restates the main idea, summarizes the information in the body, and provides a final thought to the reader.

Tip

A good way to start a concluding paragraph is by summarizing the body paragraph in a single sentence. Another good way to start a concluding paragraph is by restating the thesis statement.

Each of the sentences in the concluding paragraph has a specific role:

Summarizes the information in the body: "As you can see, swimming builds your body, burns calories, and lowers stress."

Restates the main idea: "For these reasons, swimming is an excellent exercise for everyone."

Provides a final thought: "I recommend that you give swimming a try."

Related Skills: 35 and 44

GED Readiness

Check Your Knowledge

Write *introduction*, *body*, or *conclusion* on the line.

_____ ① leaves the reader with a generalization or final thought about the topic

_____ ② gives examples and details

_____ ③ starts the essay with a general statement about the topic

_____ ④ begins with a topic sentence

_____ ⑤ is organized from general to specific

_____ ⑥ restates the main idea of the essay

_____ ⑦ ends with a thesis statement

_____ ⑧ summarizes the information in the essay

_____ ⑨ is organized from specific to general

Practice

❶ Review the introductory paragraph and the body paragraph you wrote in your notebook for Skills 45 and 46. Now write the concluding paragraph for your three-paragraph essay in your notebook.

❷ Review your concluding paragraph. Check the boxes.

☐ The concluding paragraph restates the main idea of the essay.
☐ The concluding paragraph summarizes the information in the essay.
☐ The concluding paragraph is organized from specific to general.

Write

❶ In this exercise, you will write a complete three-paragraph essay. First, read the topic and brainstorm a list of ideas in your notebook. Organize your idea list and make sure that all of the ideas are relevant.

Topic

Some people believe that talking on cell phones should be banned in public places. Do you agree?

In your essay, state whether talking on cell phones should be banned in public places. Why do you think so? Give reasons to support your answer. Use your personal observations, experience, and knowledge to support your essay.

❷ Use your idea list to write a three-paragraph essay in your notebook. Make sure your essay has introductory, body, and concluding paragraphs.

❸ Review your essay and check the boxes.

The Introduction
☐ is organized from general to specific
☐ ends with a thesis statement that gives the main idea of the essay

The Body
☐ begins with a topic sentence that states the main idea of the paragraph
☐ contains specific details and examples that support the topic sentence
☐ contains only relevant ideas

The Conclusion
☐ restates the main idea of the essay
☐ summarizes the information in the essay
☐ is organized from specific to general

48

Writing Longer Essays

As you have seen, an effective GED essay "achieves coherent development with specific and relevant details and examples." Usually, a three-paragraph essay is not long enough to completely explain the details and examples of the topic. In general, an effective GED essay will have five paragraphs.

- the introductory paragraph with the thesis statement
- three body paragraphs, each with a topic sentence
- the concluding paragraph

When you brainstorm and organize ideas for a five-paragraph essay, you should put your ideas into logical groups. Each of these groups will become one of the paragraphs in your essay.

Example:

Look at how Miguel brainstormed and organized ideas for a five-paragraph essay on the topic of favorite free-time activities.

A **multi-paragraph essay** has more than one paragraph. An effective GED essay is usually five paragraphs long.

Tip

After you create your idea list, organize it into three groups, one for each of the body paragraphs of a five-paragraph essay.

Topic

What is your favorite free-time activity?

In your essay, name your favorite free-time activity and explain why you enjoy it. Use your personal observations, experience, and knowledge to support your essay.

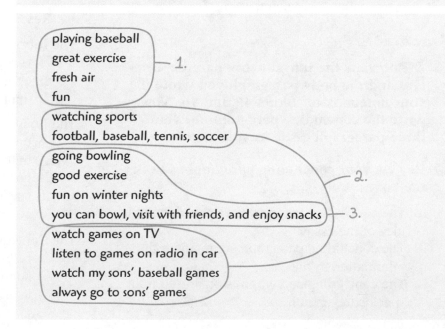

GED Readiness

Check Your Knowledge

Below is an essay on a favorite free-time activity. Read the essay and match the letter of the part of the essay with its title.

_____ Introductory paragraph

_____ Thesis statement

_____ Body paragraph 1

_____ Topic sentence 1

_____ Body paragraph 2

_____ Topic sentence 2

_____ Body paragraph 3

_____ Topic sentence 3

_____ Concluding paragraph

Ⓔ Almost everyone has some favorite free-time activities. My favorite free-time activities help me have fun and stay in shape. I like sports, so all of my free time activities involve sports. My favorite free-time activities are playing baseball, watching sports on TV, and going bowling. Ⓑ

Ⓘ I love to play baseball. I play in the young women's league at my local park. Each Saturday from June to September we play another team from the league. We get plenty of fresh air, exercise, and fun while we play. Ⓖ

Ⓕ I not only play sports, I watch sports. I love to watch football, baseball, tennis, and soccer on TV and in person. If there is a game on TV and I am at home, I am probably watching it. If I am driving, and a game is on, I will listen on the radio. I also get Ⓐ tickets to watch my local baseball team play at home. But my favorite games to watch are the ones my sons play in. My youngest two sons play Little League baseball, and my oldest son is on the high school baseball team.

Ⓓ Finally, I have another favorite sport, bowling. I am in a winter bowling league, and my friends and I go bowling every Thursday night from 7 to 9 P.M. Bowling is my favorite sport because while we play Ⓗ we can talk and enjoy our favorite foods from the snack bar!

Ⓒ As you can see, I really love watching and playing sports. I have lots of fun and always enjoy myself. I recommend that everyone play a sport of some kind.

Practice

Read the GED writing prompt and the idea list. Organize the idea list into three groups, one for each body paragraph in a five-paragraph essay.

Topic

People are always developing new skills.

Think of something you learned to do recently. What was the skill? Why did you learn it? How has learning this new skill helped you? Use your personal observations, experience, and knowledge to support your essay.

learned to drive
needed to learn because I moved to
 Los Angeles
now can drive to work
can drive kids to school, too
had to learn other new skills
pumping gas
changing a flat
in Los Angeles many people have cars
I needed to drive to work
can drive to the beach on weekends

Write

❶ 📝 Write an essay on the writing prompt above. First, brainstorm a list of your own ideas in your notebook. Organize your idea list into three groups (one for each of the body paragraphs) and make sure that all of the ideas are relevant.

❷ 📝 Use your idea list to write a five-paragraph essay in your notebook. Make sure your five-paragraph essay has an introductory paragraph, three body paragraphs, and a concluding paragraph.

49

Raising Your Score: Content and Organization

GED test takers often wonder how they can raise their scores on the GED essay test. The most important factors in scoring well on the GED essay are

- "coherent development with specific and relevant details and examples"
- "a clear and logical organization"
- "a clearly focused main idea that addresses the prompt"

Two ways to raise your score are ensuring you have plenty of supporting details and a clear organization.

Support

To ensure you have enough support in your GED essay, try these techniques as you brainstorm:

- Ask and answer the five *wh*-questions: *Who? What? When? Where? Why?* and *How?*
- Consider each of the five senses: *sight, sound, touch, taste,* and *smell.* Ask questions such as, "What does it look like? What does it sound like?"

An **idea map** is a way to gather and organize your ideas at the same time. You will save time because when you finish brainstorming, your ideas will already be organized.

Tip

After you gather ideas, always check your idea map or idea list to ensure that all the ideas are relevant to the main idea. Cross off any ideas that are not relevant.

Organization

Another way to organize your ideas is to use an **idea map** while you brainstorm. When you use an idea map, you write the main idea in the center of your paper. Then you write related ideas around the main idea. This way, you will be organizing your ideas as you gather them. Then all you need to do is ensure that your ideas are divided into three main groups: one for each of the three body paragraphs of your five-paragraph essay.

Example:

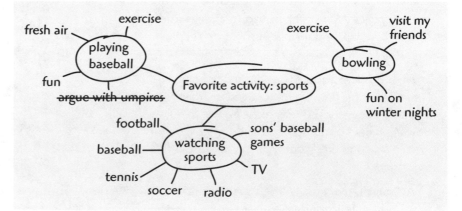

How many ideas are in the idea map? Use the *wh*-questions or the five senses to add one or two more ideas to the idea map.

GED Readiness

Check Your Knowledge

Read the GED writing prompt. Then brainstorm an idea list below or make an idea map in your notebook. Gather enough ideas for a five-paragraph essay.

Topic

Everyone wants to improve his or her life.

What improvements do you want to make to your life? Do you want a better education? A better job? More time with your family? In your essay, state the improvement you want to make and why you want to make it. Then tell how you will make the change. Use your personal observations, experience, and knowledge to support your essay.

Practice

1. Review the ideas in your idea list or map. Use the *wh*-questions or the five senses to add more ideas.

2. Review your idea list or map again. Ensure that all of the ideas are relevant. Cross off any ideas that are not relevant.

Write

1. Use your idea list or map to write a five-paragraph essay in your notebook.

2. Review your essay and check the boxes.

Check the content.

☐ Your essay has plenty of support.
☐ All of the ideas are relevant to the main idea.

Check the organization.

☐ Your ideas are in a logical order.
☐ You wrote a five-paragraph essay with an introduction, three body paragraphs, and a concluding paragraph.
☐ The introductory paragraph has a thesis statement.
☐ Each body paragraph has a topic sentence.
☐ The concluding paragraph restates the main idea and summarizes your main points.

Raising Your Score: Sentence Structure

Another way to raise your GED essay score is to use longer, more complicated sentences. Using these two sentence patterns can help raise your score:

- compound sentences
- complex sentences

Compound Sentences

A **compound sentence** consists of two independent clauses joined by a coordinating conjunction. An independent clause has a complete subject and verb and can stand alone as a sentence. A coordinating conjunction is a word such as *and* that joins the two clauses.

Coordinating Conjunctions

| and | but | or | for | nor | yet | so |

Examples:

He won the lottery. He moved to a larger house.
He won the lottery, **so** he moved to a larger house.

She sold her car. She didn't buy a new one.
She sold her car, **but** she didn't buy a new one.

Complex Sentences

A **complex sentence** consists of an independent clause and a dependent clause joined together by a subordinating conjunction. A dependent clause has a complete subject and verb but cannot stand alone as a sentence. It must be joined to an independent clause. A subordinating conjunction is a word such as *because* that joins the two clauses into a single sentence.

Subordinating Conjunctions

| although | because | before | (even) though | after |
| if | unless | when | while | since |

| independent clause | subordinating conjunction |

He bought a new house | because he won the lottery.

dependent clause

Examples:

He will buy a new house **if** he wins the lottery.
He will buy a new house **when** he wins the lottery.

A **compound sentence** consists of two independent clauses joined with a word like *and, but, or,* or *so.*

A **complex sentence** consists of an independent clause and a dependent clause joined with a word such as *if, because, when, while,* or *unless.*

Tip

Use a comma when you join **independent clauses** to form a compound sentence.

Example:

He won the lottery, so he moved to a larger house.

When you form a **complex sentence**, use a comma only if the dependent clause comes first.

Example:

I'll move to New York if I win the lottery. (no comma)

If I win the lottery, I'll move to New York. (has a comma)

GED Readiness

Check Your Knowledge

📓 Join the following sentences using the words in parentheses. Write your answers in your notebook.

1. I had a lot of fun last weekend. I got a lot of work done, too. (and)

2. On Saturday morning, I cleaned the kitchen and bathroom. I didn't vacuum. (but)

3. I was washing the dishes. The phone rang. (when)

4. My brother was calling. He wanted to go to the mall with me. (because)

5. He wanted me to go to the mall with him. He needed to buy a new suit. (since)

6. I didn't have any plans for the afternoon. I went with him to the mall. (so)

7. He didn't want to buy a suit. It was on sale. (unless)

8. We bought him a nice suit on sale. We went to a restaurant for dinner. (after)

9. On Sunday, I studied for the GED. I got ready for work on Monday. (and)

10. On Sunday night, I read a magazine. My children were doing their homework. (while)

Practice

Review the essay you wrote for Skill 49 in your notebook. Check the boxes. Make any necessary corrections by writing the changes directly on your first draft.

- ☐ Compound sentences increase the sophistication of your writing.
- ☐ Complex sentences increase the sophistication of your writing.

Write

1. 📓 Read the GED writing prompt. Then brainstorm an idea list or create an idea map. Gather enough ideas in your notebook for a five-paragraph essay.

Topic

What did you do on your last day off?

Think about your most recent day off. What did you do that day? Did you do housework? Catch up on your studies for the GED? Have fun with your friends or family? In your essay, tell what you did on your most recent day off. Use your personal observations, experience, and knowledge to support your essay.

2. Review the ideas in your idea list or map. Use the *wh*-questions or the five senses to add more ideas to your idea map. Then ensure that all the ideas are relevant. Cross off any ideas that are not related to the main idea.

3. 📓 Use your idea map to write a five-paragraph essay in your notebook.

4. Review your essay. Check the boxes. Make any corrections necessary by writing the changes directly on your first draft.

Check the mechanics.

- ☐ Each sentence is complete (has a subject and a verb).
- ☐ Each sentence starts with a capital letter and ends with a period.
- ☐ Proper nouns (such as names of people and places) and proper adjectives (adjectives made from proper nouns) are capitalized.
- ☐ The words are spelled correctly.
- ☐ The grammar is correct.

Taking the GED Test

Congratulations on completing the instruction section of this book. You are now familiar with the types of questions you will see on the GED Language Arts, Writing Test. As you ready yourself for the GED test, you may want to think about these test-taking strategies:

- Get a good night's sleep prior to the test.
- Eat breakfast before the test, especially if you are taking the test in the morning.
- Arrive at the testing center a few minutes early. If you have never been to the testing center, visit it before the day of the test so that you can find it easily.
- Grid your answers carefully, ensuring that you mark each answer in the place provided for it.
- Answer every question.
- During the test, work quickly and accurately. If you do not know the answer to a question, try to eliminate any options that do not make sense; then select the best answer from the remaining options.
- If you still cannot answer a question, or if you run out of time, guess.
- Use the scratch paper provided to plan your essay. Remember to use all of the steps in the writing process: planning, organizing, writing, and revising. See pages vii–viii to review the steps in the writing process.
- If you find yourself feeling nervous or unable to focus, close your eyes for a minute or two and take a few deep breaths. Then return to the test.

Pacing is important, so use these tips to manage your time:

- Difficult questions may precede easy ones. Because all of the questions have equal point value, make sure you have an opportunity to answer all of the easy questions. Don't spend a lot of time on a difficult question. If you find yourself spending a lot of time on a single item, stop working on that item. Write the question number on your scratch paper. Then mark the answer you think is correct, and go on to the next question. If you have time at the end of the test, return to the difficult questions and check your answers.
- Allow yourself 75 minutes to complete the 50 multiple-choice items and 45 minutes to answer the essay question. If you finish the essay before time is up, you may return to the multiple-choice questions.

About the GED Posttest

This GED Posttest is a review of the 50 skills presented in this book. It is parallel in form to the Pretest you took at the beginning of this book. The first 30 multiple-choice items address the four areas tested in Part I of the GED Language Arts, Writing Test:

- Mechanics
- Usage
- Sentence Structure
- Organization

The essay addresses the five areas assessed on Part II of the test, as identified on the GED Testing Service's Essay Scoring Guide:

- Response to the Prompt
- Organization
- Development and Details
- Conventions of Edited (Standard) American English
- Word Choice

The GED Posttest will demonstrate what you learned from the specific skills you practiced throughout this book, and it will help you identify what areas to review prior to taking the GED test.

Take this test just as you would the GED test. On the GED test, you will have 75 minutes to answer 50 multiple-choice questions and 45 minutes to write the essay. On this test, take 45 minutes to answer the 30 multiple-choice questions and 45 minutes to write the essay.

Answer every question on this GED Posttest. Follow the instructions for effective test-taking on the previous page.

When time is up, mark the items you did not finish. Then take extra time to answer those items, too. That will give you an idea of how much faster you need to work on the actual test. After you finish, turn to the Answer Key (pages 146–174) and the GED Essay Scoring Guide (pages x–xi) to check your answers. Then use the GED Posttest Evaluation Charts (pages 140–141) to figure out which skills to review in the instruction section of this book (pages 20–121). Use the additional essay topics on page 142 for additional practice writing essays.

GED Posttest

Part I

Directions: Choose the <u>one best answer</u> to each question.
<u>Questions 1 through 8</u> refer to the following letter.

Dear Springfield Resident,

A

(1) The Twenty-Fifth Annual Downtown Jazz and Blues Music Festival is scheduled to take place the Weekend of June 17 at Davis Park. (2) The festival will kick off on Friday night at 7:30 with a concert by the Dixieland Jazz Ensemble. (3) During the festival, over 80 different music groups representing many varieties of jazz and blues music will perform.

B

(4) Evening concerts on our main stage, the band shell in Davis Park, starting at 7:00 P.M. on Friday, Saturday, and Sunday nights. (5) Concerts there will last until 10:30. (6) To celebrate the festival's twenty-fifth anniversary a special fireworks show will close the last concert on Sunday night.

C

(7) The community stage, which is north of the band shell, will highlight amateur and up-and-coming performers from our local community. (8) The Acoustic Stage will feature performers who work without artificial amplification.

D

(9) Singers and performers of numerous varieties of music will perform— including jazz, blues, and bluegrass, as well as many other styles. (10) On Saturday night, festivalgoers can hear a special tribute to the late Latin jazz great, Tito Puente. (11) Sunday night features hip-hop/jazz fusion artist Tahiri.

E

(12) All of the concerts and events at the Downtown Jazz and Blues Music Festival is free, and no tickets are required. (13) Food, drinks, and other refreshments will be available from 20 of the cities' best restaurants. (14) You can sample ribs from Howie's Barbecue, roasted corn on the cob from Organic Marketplace, or homemade desserts from Cheesecake and More.

F

(15) You can walk or take public transportation to the festival, or one can drive and use the city parking garage beneath Davis Park or any of the private lots nearby.

1 Sentence 1: **The Twenty-Fifth Annual Downtown Jazz and Blues Music Festival is scheduled to take place the Weekend of June 17 at Davis Park.**

Which correction should be made to sentence 1?

(1) replace <u>Downtown</u> with <u>downtown</u>
(2) change <u>is</u> to <u>are</u>
(3) change <u>scheduled</u> to <u>schedule</u>
(4) replace <u>to</u> with <u>too</u>
(5) replace <u>Weekend</u> with <u>weekend</u>

2 Sentence 4: **Evening concerts on our main stage, the band shell in Davis Park, starting at 7:00 P.M. on Friday, Saturday, and Sunday nights.**

Which correction should be made to sentence 4?

(1) remove the commas after <u>stage</u> and <u>Park</u>
(2) replace <u>band shell</u> with <u>Band Shell</u>
(3) change <u>starting</u> to <u>will start</u>
(4) remove the commas after <u>Friday</u> and <u>Saturday</u>
(5) insert a comma after <u>and</u>

3 Sentence 6: **To celebrate the festival's twenty-fifth anniversary a special fireworks show will close the last concert on Sunday night.**

Which correction should be made to sentence 6?

(1) insert a comma after <u>celebrate</u>
(2) replace <u>festival's</u> with <u>festivals'</u>
(3) insert a comma after <u>anniversary</u>
(4) change <u>fireworks</u> to <u>firework's</u>
(5) no correction is necessary

4 Which sentence would be most effective if inserted at the beginning of paragraph C?

(1) Many great local performers are featured in this year's festival, too.
(2) Two special acts will perform during the day on Friday and Saturday.
(3) There will be food, performances, and events for children during the day.
(4) During the day, festival goers can enjoy a variety of acts at our two day stages.
(5) Everyone should plan to come to the festival early and stay late.

5 Sentences 10 and 11: **On Saturday night, festivalgoers can hear a special tribute to the late Latin jazz great, Tito Puente. Sunday night features hip-hop/jazz fusion artist Tahiri.**

The most effective combination of sentences 10 and 11 would include which group of words?

(1) Tito Puente Sunday
(2) Tito Puente, Sunday
(3) Tito Puente and Sunday
(4) Tito Puente, and Sunday
(5) Tito Puente, moreover, Sunday

The letter is repeated for your use in answering the remaining questions.

Dear Springfield Resident,

A

(1) The Twenty-Fifth Annual Downtown Jazz and Blues Music Festival is scheduled to take place the Weekend of June 17 at Davis Park. (2) The festival will kick off on Friday night at 7:30 with a concert by the Dixieland Jazz Ensemble. (3) During the festival, over 80 different music groups representing many varieties of jazz and blues music will perform.

B

(4) Evening concerts on our main stage, the band shell in Davis Park, starting at 7:00 P.M. on Friday, Saturday, and Sunday nights. (5) Concerts there will last until 10:30. (6) To celebrate the festival's twenty-fifth anniversary a special fireworks show will close the last concert on Sunday night.

C

(7) The community stage, which is north of the band shell, will highlight amateur and up-and-coming performers from our local community. (8) The Acoustic Stage will feature performers who work without artificial amplification.

D

(9) Singers and performers of numerous varieties of music will perform— including jazz, blues, and bluegrass, as well as many other styles. (10) On Saturday night, festivalgoers can hear a special tribute to the late Latin jazz great, Tito Puente. (11) Sunday night features hip-hop/jazz fusion artist Tahiri.

E

(12) All of the concerts and events at the Downtown Jazz and Blues Music Festival is free, and no tickets are required. (13) Food, drinks, and other refreshments will be available from 20 of the cities' best restaurants. (14) You can sample ribs from Howie's Barbecue, roasted corn on the cob from Organic Marketplace, or homemade desserts from Cheesecake and More.

F

(15) You can walk or take public transportation to the festival, or one can drive and use the city parking garage beneath Davis Park or any of the private lots nearby.

6 Sentence 12: **All of the concerts and events at the Downtown Jazz and Blues Music Festival is free, and no tickets are required.**

Which correction should be made to sentence 12?

① replace <u>concerts and events</u> with <u>Concerts and Events</u>
② change <u>is</u> to <u>are</u>
③ remove the comma after <u>free</u>
④ remove <u>and</u> after <u>free</u>
⑤ no correction is necessary

7 Sentence 13: **Food, drinks, and other refreshments will be available from 20 of the <u>cities'</u> best restaurants.**

Which is the best way to write the underlined portion of this sentence? If the original is the best way, choose option (1).

① cities'
② cities's
③ city's
④ citys'
⑤ cities

8 Sentence 15: **You can walk or take public transportation to the festival, or one can drive and use the city parking garage beneath Davis Park or any of the private lots nearby.**

Which correction should be made to sentence 15?

① insert a comma after <u>walk</u>
② replace <u>to</u> with <u>too</u>
③ replace <u>one</u> with <u>you</u>
④ insert a comma after <u>drive</u>
⑤ insert a comma after <u>Park</u>

A

(1) Picking a pair of athletic shoes used to be easy. (2) There were only a few brands and styles of shoes in those days, one just chose the pair that seemed the most comfortable and stylish. (3) But today, athletic shoes are a multi-billion dollar business that offers thousands of different styles and colors, and have special features that make picking a pair of athletic shoes difficult. (4) Nevertheless, there are ways to help you find your ideal shoes.

B

(5) First, you should wear different shoes for working out than for everyday use. (6) For everyday shoes, comfort and appearance are the most important criteria. (7) For exercising, finding the right shoe involves several factors. (8) First, consider the type of activities you will engage in. (9) If you mainly participate in a specific sport or activity, such as running, walking, or playing tennis, you will want to get shoes designed specifically for that activity. (10) Running shoes, for example, contain extra padding to make running easier on your feet. (11) Tennis shoes contain extra padding in the tow area to provide extra cushioning while serving. (12) Walking shoes are specially designed to help you walk quickly and effortlessly. (13) If you participates in many sports, a pair of cross-training shoes is a good idea. (14) These shoes have enough padding for runners, but they also meet the needs of other common sports and activities.

C

(15) After you had selected a kind of shoe, begin to look at individual pairs of shoes. (16) Try to find shoes that are lightweight and comfortable. (17) When you try on shoes, make sure you are wearing the same kind of socks you will be wearing when you work out. (18) It's important to put on clean, white cotton socks each time you exercise. (19) When you try on shoes, make sure you do more than just look at them in a mirror. (20) Take a short walk around the shoe department, and see how they feel. (21) Make sure they fit snugly but are not too tight. (22) Also make sure that there is extra room at the tip of the shoe. (23) If your feet are jammed too closely to the tip of the shoe, your feet will hurt and you run the risk of injuring yours.

D

(24) Finally, look for style and special features. (25) For example, if you run early in the morning or late at night, you should look for shoes with reflective material on them so that drivers can see you in the dark. (26) If you are interested in measuring the distance you run or walk, you could consider shoes with a built-in pedometer. (27) If you have trouble with your feet, look for special padding. (28) Some shoes are filled with air or gel that provide extra cushioning. (29) After you get your shoes, make sure you break them in before your first workout. (30) As you continue to wear them, watch for signs of wear and tear. (31) Worn out shoes can be just as harmful to your feet as improper footwear.

9 Sentence 2: **There were only a few brands and styles of shoes in those <u>days, one</u> just chose the pair that seemed the most comfortable and stylish.**

Which is the best way to write the underlined portion of this sentence? If the original is the best way, choose option (1).

(1) days, one
(2) days one
(3) days, since one
(4) days, so one
(5) days, or one

10 Sentence 3: **But today, athletic shoes are a multi-billion dollar business that offers thousands of different styles and colors, and have special features that make picking a pair of athletic shoes difficult.**

The most effective revision of sentence 3 would include which group of words?

(1) styles, colors, and have special features
(2) styles, have colors and special features
(3) styles, have colors, and have special features
(4) styles, colors, and special features
(5) styles, colors, special features

11 Sentence 6: **For everyday shoes, comfort and appearance are the most important criteria.**

Which correction should be made to sentence 6?

(1) remove the comma after <u>shoes</u>
(2) insert a comma after <u>comfort</u>
(3) insert a comma after <u>appearance</u>
(4) change <u>are</u> to <u>is</u>
(5) no correction is necessary

12 Sentence 11: **Tennis shoes contain extra padding in the tow area to provide extra cushioning while serving.**

Which correction should be made to sentence 11?

(1) replace <u>shoes</u> with <u>Shoes</u>
(2) replace <u>contain</u> with <u>contains</u>
(3) replace <u>tow</u> with <u>toe</u>
(4) replace <u>to</u> with <u>two</u>
(5) insert a comma after <u>cushioning</u>

13 Sentence 13: **If you participates in many sports, a pair of cross-training shoes is a good idea.**

Which correction should be made to sentence 13?

(1) replace <u>participates</u> with <u>participate</u>
(2) remove the comma after <u>sports</u>
(3) replace <u>pair</u> with <u>pear</u>
(4) change <u>is</u> to <u>are</u>
(5) no correction is necessary

The information is repeated for your use in answering the remaining questions.

A

(1) Picking a pair of athletic shoes used to be easy. (2) There were only a few brands and styles of shoes in those days, one just chose the pair that seemed the most comfortable and stylish. (3) But today, athletic shoes are a multi-billion dollar business that offers thousands of different styles and colors, and have special features that make picking a pair of athletic shoes difficult. (4) Nevertheless, there are ways to help you find your ideal shoes.

B

(5) First, you should wear different shoes for working out than for everyday use. (6) For everyday shoes, comfort and appearance are the most important criteria. (7) For exercising, finding the right shoe involves several factors. (8) First, consider the type of activities you will engage in. (9) If you mainly participate in a specific sport or activity, such as running, walking, or playing tennis, you will want to get shoes designed specifically for that activity. (10) Running shoes, for example, contain extra padding to make running easier on your feet. (11) Tennis shoes contain extra padding in the tow area to provide extra cushioning while serving. (12) Walking shoes are specially designed to help you walk quickly and effortlessly. (13) If you participates in many sports, a pair of cross-training shoes is a good idea. (14) These shoes have enough padding for runners, but they also meet the needs of other common sports and activities.

C

(15) After you had selected a kind of shoe, begin to look at individual pairs of shoes. (16) Try to find shoes that are lightweight and comfortable. (17) When you try on shoes, make sure you are wearing the same kind of socks you will be wearing when you work out. (18) It's important to put on clean, white cotton socks each time you exercise. (19) When you try on shoes, make sure you do more than just look at them in a mirror. (20) Take a short walk around the shoe department, and see how they feel. (21) Make sure they fit snugly but are not too tight. (22) Also make sure that there is extra room at the tip of the shoe. (23) If your feet are jammed too closely to the tip of the shoe, your feet will hurt and you run the risk of injuring yours.

D

(24) Finally, look for style and special features. (25) For example, if you run early in the morning or late at night, you should look for shoes with reflective material on them so that drivers can see you in the dark. (26) If you are interested in measuring the distance you run or walk, you could consider shoes with a built-in pedometer. (27) If you have trouble with your feet, look for special padding. (28) Some shoes are filled with air or gel that provide extra cushioning. (29) After you get your shoes, make sure you break them in before your first workout. (30) As you continue to wear them, watch for signs of wear and tear. (31) Worn-out shoes can be just as harmful to your feet as improper footwear.

14 Sentence 15: **After you <u>had selected</u> a kind of shoe, begin to look at individual pairs of shoes.**

Which is the best way to write the underlined portion of this sentence? If the original is the best way, choose option (1).

① had selected
② selected
③ selecting
④ selects
⑤ have selected

15 Sentence 18: **It's important to put on clean, white cotton socks each time you exercise.**

Which revision should be made to the placement of sentence 18?

① move sentence 18 to the beginning of paragraph A
② move sentence 18 to follow sentence 16
③ move sentence 18 to follow sentence 19
④ remove sentence 18
⑤ no revision is necessary

16 Sentence 23: **If your feet are jammed too closely to the tip of the shoe, your feet will hurt and you run the risk of injuring yours.**

Which correction should be made to sentence 23?

① change <u>jammed</u> to <u>jam</u>
② replace <u>too</u> with <u>to</u>
③ replace <u>shoe, your</u> with <u>shoe, you're</u>
④ change <u>run</u> to <u>ran</u>
⑤ change <u>yours</u> to <u>yourself</u>

17 Which revision would improve the effectiveness of the information?

① begin a new paragraph with sentence 26
② begin a new paragraph with sentence 27
③ begin a new paragraph with sentence 28
④ begin a new paragraph with sentence 29
⑤ begin a new paragraph with sentence 30

Questions 18 through 24 refer to the following information.

(1) Have you ever wondered how a mobile phone works? (2) The cell phone, a truly amazing example of technology, uses a highly complex system so that me and you can use our mobile phones to make calls from almost anywhere.

(3) A mobile phone is really a special kind of radio. (4) A regular radio only receives sound. (5) Other kinds of radios, such as a walkie-talkie, communicate with a single radio signal that can either send or receive a message at the same time. (6) That's why walkie-talkie users have to keep saying "over" each time they are finished speaking and are ready to listen. (7) A mobile phone uses two signals, one for speaking and one for listening. (8) Therefore, unlike a walkie-talkie, a mobile phone user does not have to keep saying "over."

(9) Mobile phone companies use a network of towers with radio transmitters, and receivers throughout the city. (10) In a typical mobile phone network, the land is divided into areas called "cells," each of which is about ten square miles large. (11) When a customer turns on his or her phone, it sends a signal to the tower in that cell. (12) Computers then check the phone's number. (13) If the phone belongs to a paying customer, then the phone is ready to make a call.

(14) A customer makes a call, and a message is sent to the tower. (15) The tower then sends the call to central computers where they're connected to the regular phone system. (16) From there, the call is routed to the number being called.

(17) Mobile phones also continue to work as callers move about. (18) That's because the tower keeps track of the strength of the signal from the phone. (19) At the same time, other towers keep track of the signal, too. (20) The first tower notices the signal getting weaker. (21) The second tower notices the signal getting stronger. (22) At some point, the first tower will tell the phone to switch towers and start communicating with the second tower. (23) If a call is long enough, it can switch towers several times.

(24) These facts about mobile phones explain why calls sometimes get lost. (25) The mobile phone is in a place where the signal isn't strong or is blocked by a building. (26) The result is the common question, "Can you hear me now?"

18 Sentence 2: **The cell phone, a truly amazing example of technology, uses a highly complex system so that <u>me and you</u> can use our mobile phones to make calls from almost anywhere.**

Which is the best way to write the underlined portion of this sentence? If the original is the best way, choose option (1).

① me and you
② myself and I
③ you and myself
④ you and I
⑤ myself and yourself

19 Sentence 7: **A mobile phone uses two signals, one for speaking and one for listening.**

The most effective revision of sentence 7 would begin with which group of words?

① In contrast,
② In addition,
③ In sum,
④ Second,
⑤ For example,

20 Sentence 8: **Therefore, unlike a walkie-talkie, a mobile phone user does not have to keep saying "over."**

Which correction should be made to sentence 8?

① remove the comma after <u>walkie-talkie</u>
② insert the word <u>user</u> after <u>walkie-talkie</u>
③ remove the word <u>user</u>
④ change <u>does</u> to <u>do</u>
⑤ change <u>have</u> to <u>has</u>

21 Sentence 9: **Mobile phone companies use a network of towers with radio transmitters, and receivers throughout the city.**

Which correction should be made to sentence 9?

① insert a comma after <u>companies</u>
② change <u>use</u> to <u>uses</u>
③ insert a comma after <u>towers</u>
④ remove the comma after <u>transmitters</u>
⑤ no correction is necessary

The information is repeated for your use in answering the remaining questions.

(1) Have you ever wondered how a mobile phone works? (2) The cell phone, a truly amazing example of technology, uses a highly complex system so that me and you can use our mobile phones to make calls from almost anywhere.

(3) A mobile phone is really a special kind of radio. (4) A regular radio only receives sound. (5) Other kinds of radios, such as a walkie-talkie, communicate with a single radio signal that can either send or receive a message at the same time. (6) That's why walkie-talkie users have to keep saying "over" each time they are finished speaking and are ready to listen. (7) A mobile phone uses two signals, one for speaking and one for listening. (8) Therefore, unlike a walkie-talkie, a mobile phone user does not have to keep saying "over."

(9) Mobile phone companies use a network of towers with radio transmitters, and receivers throughout the city. (10) In a typical mobile phone network, the land is divided into areas called "cells," each of which is about ten square miles large. (11) When a customer turns on his or her phone, it sends a signal to the tower in that cell. (12) Computers then check the phone's number. (13) If the phone belongs to a paying customer, then the phone is ready to make a call.

(14) A customer makes a call, and a message is sent to the tower. (15) The tower then sends the call to central computers where they're connected to the regular phone system. (16) From there, the call is routed to the number being called.

(17) Mobile phones also continue to work as callers move about. (18) That's because the tower keeps track of the strength of the signal from the phone. (19) At the same time, other towers keep track of the signal, too. (20) The first tower notices the signal getting weaker. (21) The second tower notices the signal getting stronger. (22) At some point, the first tower will tell the phone to switch towers and start communicating with the second tower. (23) If a call is long enough, it can switch towers several times.

(24) These facts about mobile phones explain why calls sometimes get lost. (25) The mobile phone is in a place where the signal isn't strong or is blocked by a building. (26) The result is the common question, "Can you hear me now?"

22 Sentence 11: **When a customer turns on <u>his or her</u> phone, it sends a signal to the tower in that cell.**

Which is the best way to write the underlined portion of this sentence? If the original is the best way, choose option (1).

(1) his or her
(2) his or hers
(3) him or her
(4) him or hers
(5) his or her's

23 Sentence 15: **The tower then sends the call to central computers where <u>they're</u> connected to the regular phone system.**

Which is the best way to write the underlined portion of this sentence? If the original is the best way, choose option (1).

(1) they're
(2) there
(3) its
(4) it's
(5) their

24 Sentences 20 and 21: **The first tower notices the signal getting weaker. The second tower notices the signal getting stronger.**

The most effective combination of sentences 20 and 21 would include which group of words?

(1) weaker, the
(2) weaker and the
(3) weaker while the
(4) weaker, however, the
(5) weaker the

Louise M. Holst, Mayor
City Hall
Allerton, TX 98923

Dear Mayor Holst:

(1) I am a lifelong resident of Allerton. (2) I am writing to you today to inform you of some problems we are experiencing in the West End neighborhood. (3) As you know, traffic in the West End had been increasing for the last few years. (4) In our neighborhood is several new stores and a new car wash. (5) We have also added over 100 homes, and many apartment buildings, and a small hotel.

(6) Now, during rush hour and on weekends, traffic on Enfield Road has increased dramatically at busy times, the line of cars in front of the new car wash is often two blocks long. (7) Sometimes the line even blocks the intersection of Enfield Road and Highway 66. (8) As a result, traffic on both Enfield and the highway backs up, and several accidents have occurred. (9) When traffic is heavy, ambulances and fire trucks have trouble getting through. (10) Just last week, a fire in an empty store burned out of control because fire trucks could not get there in time. (11) The increased traffic has caused other problems. (12) Parking is now almost impossible to find after 6:00 P.M., and noise and litter have gone up dramatically.

(13) I would like the city to take action. (14) The problem is getting worse and worse by the day. (15) I believe that the city should ban parking on Enfield Road during rush hour. (16) That would create an additional lane for traffic and for cars waiting to enter the car wash. (17) In addition, the city should make it illegal for the line of cars entering the car wash to extend for more than one block. (18) Furthermore, the city should make all businesses, hotels, and apartment buildings provide off-street parking for their customers. (19) That way, visitors will not be competing with residents for parking spaces. (20) Finally, street cleaning needs to take place more often. (21) That would reduce the amount of litter and trash in sidewalks and streets.

(22) I hope that the city will be able to take these steps which are needed to keep our neighborhood nice. (23) I look forward to hearing about the city's plans to address these issues.

Sincerely,

Ralph Williams

Ralph Williams

25 Sentence 3: **As you know, traffic in the West End** <u>had been increasing</u> **for the last few years.**

Which is the best way to write the underlined portion of this sentence? If the original is the best way, choose option (1).

① had been increasing
② has been increasing
③ is increasing
④ will be increasing
⑤ increases

26 Sentence 4: **In our neighborhood is several new stores and a new car wash.**

Which correction should be made to sentence 4?

① insert a comma after <u>our</u>
② change <u>is</u> to <u>are</u>
③ replace <u>new</u> with <u>knew</u>
④ insert a comma after <u>stores</u>
⑤ no correction is necessary

27 Sentence 5: **We have also added over 100 homes, and many apartment buildings, and a small hotel.**

Which correction should be made to sentence 5?

① remove <u>have</u>
② remove the comma after <u>homes</u>
③ remove <u>and</u> after <u>homes</u>
④ remove the comma after <u>buildings</u>
⑤ remove <u>and</u> after <u>buildings</u>

28 Sentence 6: **Now, during rush hour and on weekends, traffic on Enfield Road has increased** <u>dramatically at busy times,</u> **the line of cars in front of the new car wash is often two blocks long.**

Which is the best way to write the underlined portion of this sentence? If the original is the best way, choose option (1).

① dramatically at busy times,
② dramatically, at busy times,
③ dramatically. At busy times,
④ dramatically and at busy times,
⑤ dramatically, but at busy times,

29 Sentence 12: **Parking is now almost impossible to find after 6:00 P.M., and noise and litter have** <u>gone</u> **up dramatically.**

Which is the best way to write the underlined portion of this sentence? If the original is the best way, choose option (1).

① gone
② went
③ go
④ goes
⑤ going

30 Sentence 13 and 14: **I would like the city to take action. The problem is getting worse and worse by the day.**

The most effective combination of sentences 13 and 14 would include which group of words?

① action because
② action, because
③ action, or
④ action, while
⑤ action, since

Essay Directions and Topic

Part II

Look at the box on page 139. In the box is the assigned topic.

You must write on the assigned topic **ONLY.**

You will have 45 minutes to write on your assigned essay topic.

After you write your essay, you or your instructor will score your essay according to its overall effectiveness. Follow the evaluation instructions on page ix. The evaluation will be based on the following criteria:

- Well-focused main points
- Clear organization
- Specific development of your ideas
- Control of sentence structure, punctuation, grammar, word choice, and spelling

Be sure to do the following:

- Write legibly in ink so that readers will be able to read your writing.
- Write on the assigned topic.
- Write your essay on ordinary lined paper or the Essay Answer Sheet (page 143).

IMPORTANT:

On the GED, you may return to the multiple-choice section after you complete your essay if you have time remaining in the test period.

Essay Topic

Many people prefer to take public transportation. Others prefer to walk or drive.

What kind of transportation do you prefer? Why? In your essay, tell what kind of transportation you prefer. Give reasons to explain your answer. Use your personal observations, experience, and knowledge to support your essay.

Part II is a test to determine how well you can use written language to explain your ideas.

In preparing your essay, you should take the following steps:

- Read the **DIRECTIONS** and the **TOPIC** carefully.
- Plan your essay before you write. Use scratch paper to make any notes.
- Before you turn in your essay, re-read what you have written and make any changes that will improve your essay.

Your essay should be long enough to develop the topic adequately.

GED Posttest Evaluation Chart

After you complete the GED Posttest, use these charts to figure out which skills you need to review in the instruction section of this book.

To complete the charts, use results from the Answer Key pages, 146–174, and the GED Essay Scoring Guide, pages x–xi.

Part I

Circle the numbers of the questions you missed in column 1. The second and third columns tell you the name of the skill and its number in the instruction section of this book. Focus your review on those skills. The fourth column tells you the pages to review in the instruction section. The last column indicates the pages in Contemporary's *GED Language Arts, Writing* where the skill is taught in greater detail.

Question Number	Skill Name	Skill Number	Pages	*GED Language Arts, Writing*
1	Capitalization	18	54–55	177–178
2	Sentence Fragments	1	20–21	20, 23–24
3	Comma Details	23	64–65	183–184
4	Topic Sentences and Paragraphs	27	72–73	115
5	Commas Joining Independent Clauses	20	58–59	83, 89
6	Agreement with Interrupting Structures	8	34–35	68–69
7	Using Apostrophes	25	68–69	36–37, 43
8	Avoiding Pronoun Shift	17	52–53	159–160
9	Comma Splice	3	24–25	96
10	Parallel Structure	6	30–31	154–156
11	Commas After Introductory Prepositional Phrases	22	62–63	68–70
12	Homonyms	26	70–71	179–182
13	Subject-Verb Agreement	7	32–33	62–63
14	Sequence of Verb Tense	12	42–43	101–102
15	Unity and Coherence	28	74–75	248–249
16	Reflexive and Indefinite Pronouns	16	50–51	71–73
17	Joining and Dividing Paragraphs	29	76–77	120–126
18	Subject and Object Pronouns	13	44–45	39–40
19	Transitions Within Paragraphs	30	78–79	286–287
20	Misplaced and Dangling Modifiers	5	28–29	149–152
21	Avoiding Excess Commas	24	66–67	183–184
22	Possessive Pronouns	14	46–47	39–43
23	Pronoun Agreement	15	48–49	38–40
24	Subordination	4	26–27	89–92
25	Using Word Clues to Figure Out Verb Tense	11	40–41	51–53
26	Agreement with Inverted Structures	9	36–37	66–67
27	Commas in a Series	19	56–57	183
28	Run-On Sentences	2	22–23	86
29	Correct Verb Forms	10	38–39	54–56
30	Commas with Subordinate Clauses	21	60–61	83–85

Part II

After you evaluate your essay using the instructions on pages ix–xi, circle your score for each part of the GED Essay Scoring Guide in this chart. Then review the skills with a score of 2 or lower. The remaining columns tell you each skill's name, number, and page numbers to review. The last column lists the pages in Contemporary's *GED Language Arts, Writing* book for additional instruction. For extra practice writing essays, see More GED Essay Topics on page 142.

Criteria	My Score	Skill Name	Skill Number	Pages	GED Language Arts, Writing
Response to the Prompt	1 2 3 4	What Is an Essay?	31	80–81	208
		Understanding the Topic	32	82–83	220–222
Organization	1 2 3 4	Parts of the Paragraph	35	88–91	115–116
		Description	36	92–93	220–221
		Narration	39	98–99	220–221
		How-To	40	100–101	220–221
		Giving Reasons	41	102–103	233–234
		Checking the Organization	42	104–105	232
		The Three-Paragraph Essay	44	108–109	– – –
		The Introductory Paragraph and Thesis Statement	45	110–111	255–258
		Writing Body Paragraphs	46	112–113	259–263
		Writing Concluding Paragraphs	47	114–115	265–266
		Writing Longer Essays	48	116–117	214–216
Development and Details	1 2 3 4	Brainstorming	33	84–85	224–227
		Support and Relevance	38	96–97	248–249
		Raising Your Score: Content and Organization	49	118–119	250–251
Conventions of Edited American English	1 2 3 4	Complete Sentences	34	86–87	19–20
		Revising Mechanics	43	106–107	293–294
		Raising Your Score: Sentence Structure	50	120–121	83–85 89–92
Word Choice	1 2 3 4	Word Choice	37	94–95	283–285

More GED Essay Topics

Use these topics to gain additional experience writing essays. You or your instructor should use the GED Essay Scoring Rubric on page x to evaluate your work.

Topic 1

Each of our lives has exciting and memorable moments. What is the most exciting or memorable moment in your life?

In your essay, identify that time or moment. Why was it so exciting? Give reasons to explain your answer. Use your personal observations, experience, and knowledge to support your essay.

Topic 2

Each of us likes to do certain things on a day off. For you, what's a perfect day off?

In your essay, describe a perfect day off. Tell what you would do on your day off. Use your personal observations, experience, and knowledge to support your essay.

Topic 3

Cell phones are becoming more and more common. But many people feel that cell phone users are an annoyance in restaurants, buses, and other public places.

Do you think that people should be allowed to use cell phones in places such as restaurants, buses, and public places? Give reasons to explain your answer. Use your personal observations, experience, and knowledge to support your essay.

Topic 4

If you could live anywhere, where would you live?

In your essay, state where you would live. Give reasons to back up your choice. Use your personal observations, experience, and knowledge to support your essay.

Topic 5

Each of us has a job or occupation. But our present jobs might not be ideal for us. For you, what is your ideal job?

In your essay, identify your dream job. Why is it so special? Why is it the perfect job for you? Give reasons to explain your answer. Use your personal observations, experience, and knowledge to support your essay.

Essay Answer Sheet

Annotated Answer Key

Pretest

Part I (Pages 3–15)

1. ② reservation until
   When I finally reached the desk, the employee was unable to find my reservation until I spelled my name several times and gave her my reservation number. Option ② is correct because the subordinating conjunction <u>until</u> indicates the relationship of the clauses. The subordinating conjunctions in Options ① and ⑤ do not indicate the relationship of the clauses. Option ③ incorrectly uses the transition <u>however</u> to join the clauses. <u>However</u> does not indicate the relationship of the clauses and is not punctuated correctly: when using <u>however</u>, a semicolon is needed after <u>reservation</u> to join the two clauses. Joining the clauses with <u>but</u> results in a sentence that does not make sense (Option ④). Option ⑤ also has an unnecessary comma after <u>reservation</u>. A comma is not needed when a dependent clause follows an independent clause.

2. ① insert a comma after <u>lower floor</u>
   My reservation was also for a room on a lower floor, but she told me that only rooms on the twenty-second floor were available. Option ① is correct because a comma is needed to join two independent clauses with <u>but</u>. There is also no reason to insert a comma after <u>but</u> (Option ②). Option ③ is incorrect because the pronoun refers to a woman, so <u>she</u> is needed. There is no reason to change <u>were</u> to <u>was</u> (Option ④). <u>Were</u> agrees with the plural subject <u>rooms</u>.

3. ③ change <u>their</u> to <u>there</u>
   The clerk who checked me in wasn't there, and another clerk was on duty. Option ③ is correct because the adverb <u>there</u> is needed in this sentence to refer to a place, not the possessive word <u>their</u>. Option ① is incorrect because the preposition <u>in</u> is needed in this part of the sentence, not the noun <u>inn</u> ("hotel"). Option ② moves the apostrophe to an incorrect position. The apostrophe should be in the same place as the letter removed from the contraction, <u>o</u>. Option ④ removes a comma needed to join two independent clauses with the coordinating conjunction <u>and</u>.

4. ① insert a comma after <u>Angrily</u>
   Angrily, he told me to wait in line with the others, so I had to wait 15 more minutes to get a key to my room. Option ① is correct because a comma is needed after the introductory adverb <u>Angrily</u>. There is no reason to insert a comma after <u>line</u> (Option ②) or <u>minutes</u> (Option ④). Option ③ removes a comma needed to join two independent clauses with the coordinating conjunction <u>so</u>.

5. ④ Unfortunately, my problems did not end there.
   Option ④ is the best topic sentence for paragraph C. Paragraph C is about several more problems, and Option ④ provides a good, general introduction to the paragraph. Options ① and ③ are too specific. The Internet and the pool were not the only problems mentioned in the paragraph, and there is nothing in the paragraph to indicate that Internet access was the biggest problem. Option ② does not sum up the problems mentioned in the paragraph, which includes more than problems with the room. Option ⑤ does not sum up the main idea of the paragraph.

6. ⑤ replace <u>memorial day</u> with <u>Memorial Day</u>
   However, employees told me that the pool was not scheduled to open until the following weekend, which was Memorial Day. Option ⑤ is correct because holidays, such as Memorial Day, are proper nouns, so the first letter of each word should be capitalized. Option ① removes a comma required after the introductory transition <u>However</u>. The paragraph takes place in the past, so there is no reason to change <u>was</u> to the present tense (Options ② and ④). <u>Weekend</u> is not a proper noun in this sentence, so it does not need to be capitalized (Option ③).

7. ② a warm, airless, and uncomfortable room
   Since there were no other rooms available, I had to sleep in a warm, airless, and uncomfortable room. Option ② correctly uses parallel structure to join three adjectives (<u>warm</u>, <u>airless</u>, and <u>uncomfortable</u>) in a list using commas and <u>and</u>. Option ③ is incorrect because there is no reason to use <u>and</u> after each of the adjectives to join them in a list. Option ④ needs commas and <u>and</u> to join the three adjectives in a list. Option ⑤ is awkward and wordy.

8. ⑤ change <u>can</u> to <u>could</u>
   I complained to a desk clerk about all of these problems, but she said that there was nothing she could do to solve them. Option ⑤ is correct because the sentence is in the past, so the past form of <u>can</u> ("be able"), could, is needed. Therefore, Options ① and ③, which introduce more present tense verbs, are incorrect. Option ② is incorrect because the verb <u>was</u> agrees with its singular subject, <u>nothing</u>. There is no reason to remove <u>can</u> (Option ④).

9. **④** replace <u>they</u> with <u>you</u>
Each service has advantages and disadvantages, so it's important to choose wisely so that you and your family can see the programs you like. Option ④ is correct because the subject pronoun <u>you</u> is needed to refer to the people who like the TV programs, <u>you and your family</u>. <u>Has</u> agrees with its singular subject <u>service</u>, so there is no reason to change it (Option ①). <u>It's</u> is correctly used as a contraction for <u>it is</u> in this sentence, so Option ② is incorrect. There is no reason to change the possessive pronoun <u>your</u> to the contraction <u>you're</u> (Option ③).

10. **②** insert a comma after <u>locations</u>
In some locations, your choices may be limited to four or five channels. Option ② is correct because a comma is needed after the introductory prepositional phrase <u>In some locations</u>. There is no reason to insert a comma after <u>some</u> (Option ①). There is no reason to change the possessive pronoun <u>your</u> to the contraction <u>you're</u> (Option ③) or the emphatic possessive <u>yours</u> (Option ④).

11. **③** move sentence 10 to follow sentence 6
Option ③ is correct because sentence 10 names an advantage of broadcast TV, so the sentence should go with the other advantages. The transition <u>In addition</u> indicates that the sentence should go after another advantage, so the best place for this sentence is after sentence 6. For this reason, Options ② and ④ are incorrect. Option ① is incorrect because the sentence belongs in paragraph B, which is about broadcast TV. The sentence gives a relevant detail about the advantages of broadcast TV, so Option ⑤ is incorrect.

12. **②** improves
As technology improves, cable companies plan to increase the number of channels even more. Option ② is correct because the singular subject <u>technology</u> requires a singular verb, <u>improves</u>. There is no reason to change the verb to the simple past (Option ③) or the present perfect (Option ④). Option ⑤ creates a sentence fragment because <u>improving</u> is not a complete verb.

13. **②** insert a comma and <u>and</u> after <u>offerings</u>
Standard packages have more offerings, and other packages can include many more channels, including premium channels. Option ② is correct because sentence 18 is a run-on. Two independent clauses are run together without any punctuation or coordinating conjunctions. Option ② correctly inserts a comma

and the coordinating conjunction <u>and</u> to join the two clauses. Option ① is incorrect because <u>have</u> agrees with the plural subject <u>packages</u>. There is no reason to change the tense of <u>can include</u> (Option ③) or to remove the comma after <u>more channels</u> (Option ④).

14. **⑤** replace <u>them</u> with <u>it</u>
Parents can simply not order an objectionable channel, or they can use blocking technology to prevent their children from watching it. Option ⑤ is correct because the word the pronoun refers to is singular (<u>channel</u>), so the singular object pronoun <u>it</u> is needed. There is no reason to capitalize <u>objectionable channel</u> (Option ①) or to insert a comma after <u>technology</u> (Option ③). A comma is needed after <u>channel</u> to join two independent clauses with <u>or</u> (Option ②). There is no reason to change the possessive pronoun <u>their</u> to <u>there</u> (Option ④).

15. **①** When you use a satellite network,
When you use a satellite network, a special satellite dish is installed outside your home. Sentence 23 has a dangling modifier—the phrase <u>Using a satellite network</u> modifies the phrase <u>satellite dish</u>, and is the implied subject of the phrase, which does not make sense. Option ① corrects the problem by changing the phrase to a clause with a subject that makes sense, <u>you</u>. Option ② is also a dangling modifier. Options ③, ④, and ⑤ result in sentences that do not make sense.

16. **②** cost
Satellite networks, offering the largest selection of programming, often cost more than cable. Option ② is correct because the subject <u>networks</u> is plural, so the plural verb <u>cost</u> is needed. Option ③ is not a full verb, changing the sentence to a fragment. Options ④ and ⑤ result in sentences that do not make sense.

17. **③** join paragraphs C and D
Option ③ is correct because paragraphs C and D are on the same topic, cable television, so they should be joined together. Options ① and ② are incorrect because paragraphs A and B and B and C are on different topics so they should not be joined together. Paragraph D provides important information about the main idea of the passage, so Option ④ is incorrect. There is no reason to move sentence 16 (Option ⑤), which belongs before the discussion of the various kinds of cable packages.

18. ❷ puppy that

In addition, you want to pick a healthy puppy that will grow up to be a loyal pet for many years. Sentence 5 is a fragment. Option ② fixes it by joining it to sentence 4 as a dependent clause. Option ③ results in a sentence that does not make sense. Options ④ and ⑤ do not fix the sentence fragment. It is not possible to join a dependent clause to an independent clause with <u>and</u> (Option ⑤).

19. ❸ change <u>is</u> to <u>are</u>

Experts agree that there are several steps you should follow to ensure you choose the right pet. Option ③ is correct because the plural form of <u>be</u>, <u>are</u>, is needed to agree with the plural subject <u>steps</u>. There is no reason to change <u>agree</u> to <u>agrees</u>. (Option ①) or to change the adverb <u>there</u> to the possessive pronoun <u>their</u> (Option ②). There is no reason to change <u>choose</u> to <u>choosing</u> (Option ④). There is no reason to replace the adjective <u>right</u> ("correct") with the verb <u>write</u> ("record on paper") (Option ⑤).

20. ❶ On the other hand,

On the other hand, the dog you choose should not be a large or aggressive breed if your children are very small. Option ① is correct because it has the only transition that makes sense in this sentence. Sentence 12 contrasts with the previous sentences, and only <u>On the other hand</u> indicates contrast. For this reason, the remaining options are incorrect.

21. ❷ remove the comma after <u>breeder</u>

You might get advice from a dog breeder or veterinarian before making a choice. Option ② is correct because a comma is not needed to join two nouns (<u>breeder</u> and <u>veterinarian</u>) with <u>or</u>. Commas are only needed when three or more items are involved. Option ① is incorrect because there is no reason to replace <u>might</u> ("may perhaps") with <u>mite</u> ("a small insect"). There is no reason to insert a comma after <u>veterinarian</u> (Option ③). Option ④ results in a sentence that does not make sense.

22. ❷ insert a comma after <u>shelter</u>

When you get a dog from the animal shelter, you often only have to pay for the dog's license and required shots. Option ② is correct because a comma is needed to join a dependent clause to an independent clause when the dependent clause is first. There is no reason to insert a comma after <u>dog</u> (Option ①). Option ③ results in a pronoun shift: the pronouns in the sentence change from <u>you</u> to <u>one</u>. There is no reason to change the

singular possessive <u>dog's</u> to the plural possessive <u>dogs'</u> (Option ④) because the sentence is only talking about one dog. There is no reason to insert a comma after <u>license</u> (Option ⑤). A comma is not needed to join two nouns (<u>license</u> and <u>shots</u>) with <u>and</u>. Commas are only needed when three or more items are involved.

23. ❸ its

Look over the dog to make sure its skin and fur look healthy. Option ③ is correct because the pronoun replaces the singular noun <u>dog</u>, so the singular possessive pronoun <u>its</u> is needed. Option ② is incorrect because the possessive pronoun <u>its</u>, not the contraction <u>it's</u> ("it is") is needed. Option ④ is incorrect because there is no reason to insert the adverb <u>there</u> into this sentence. Option ⑤ is incorrect because a possessive pronoun, not an emphatic possessive, is needed before the nouns <u>skin</u> and <u>fur</u>.

24. ❶ puppy's

Check the puppy's gums. Option ① is correct because the singular possessive form of <u>puppy</u> is needed in this sentence. In the preceding sentences, <u>puppy</u> is singular, so it should be singular in this sentence. For this reason, the remaining options, which are all plural, are incorrect. Option ② is the plural possessive form. Option ③ is the plural form. Option ④ is the plural possessive form with an extra <u>s</u>. Option ⑤ is a misspelling of the plural form.

25. ❺ rock, dust, gases, and water

A comet is a frozen chunk of rock, dust, gases, and water that orbits around the sun. Option ⑤ is correct because it uses commas and <u>and</u> correctly to join the list of four items: <u>rock</u>, <u>dust</u>, <u>gases</u>, and <u>water</u>. Option ① is incorrect because it omits a comma after <u>dust</u>. Option ② is missing commas after all of the nouns in the list. Option ③ has an unneeded comma after <u>and</u>. Option ④ omits necessary commas after <u>rock</u> and <u>dust</u>.

26. ❷ are so large that they

Some comets' orbits are so large that they travel millions of miles beyond Pluto, the planet farthest from the sun. Option ② is correct because it successfully joins the sentences with the correct subject pronoun <u>they</u>. Option ① is incorrect because the subject pronoun <u>they</u>, not the object pronoun <u>them</u>, is needed in this sentence. Option ③ is incorrect because the pronoun refers to a plural noun, so a plural pronoun is needed. Options ④ and ⑤ result in sentences that do not make sense.

27. ② was

In fact, for many years people thought that the appearance of a comet in the sky meant that something terrible was going to happen. Option ② is correct because the sentence is in the past tense, so a past tense verb is needed. The other options result in sentences that do not make sense.

28. ③ insert <u>and</u> before <u>one</u>

He predicted that the comet would reappear in about 1758, and one year later the comet reappeared in March, 1759. Sentence 13 is a comma splice (two clauses joined together with only a comma). Option ③ fixes the problem by adding the coordinating conjunction <u>and</u>. Option ① is incorrect because there is no reason to change <u>reappear</u> to a past participle. Option ② changes the comma splice to a run-on sentence. Option ④ results in a sentence that does not make sense. Option ⑤ removes a necessary comma between the month and the year in a date.

29. ③ have cataloged

However, until now, they have cataloged only about 1,000 of them. Option ③ is correct because the present perfect tense, which consists of a form of the verb <u>have</u> and a past participle (<u>cataloged</u>), is needed here. Option ② results in an incomplete verb. There is no reason to use the past perfect tense in this sentence (Option ④). Option ⑤ does not make sense.

30. ④ themselves

Many of the discoverers, such as Hyakutake, choose to name their comets after themselves. Option ④ is correct because a reflexive pronoun is needed in this sentence, since the object pronoun and the subject of the sentence refer to the same person, in this case, the discoverers of the comets. <u>Themselves</u> agrees with the plural noun it replaces, <u>discoverers</u>. Options ②, ③, and ⑤ are incorrect because the pronoun refers to a plural subject, so a plural reflexive pronoun is necessary. In addition, Option ⑤ is incorrect because the pronoun replaces a person, so a pronoun that refers to a person is required. (<u>It</u> refers to animals and objects.)

Part II (Page 17)

Give your instructor your essay to evaluate. You will find his or her objective comments helpful in assessing your essay. If this is not possible, have another learner evaluate your paper. If you cannot find another learner to help you, review your paper yourself. If you do this, it's better to let your paper "sit" for a few days before you evaluate it. This way, you will experience your essay much the same way a first-time reader will experience it. Whoever reads your paper should use the GED Essay Scoring Guide on pages ix–xi to evaluate your essay and give it a score on each of the five criteria on the Scoring Guide using this scale:

1. Inadequate
2. Marginal
3. Adequate
4. Effective

Then write your score for each criteria on the Pretest Evaluation Chart on page 19. Use that chart to figure out which skills to study in the instruction section of this book.

Skill 1 (Page 21)

1. ③ change <u>discussing</u> to <u>will be discussing</u>

We will be discussing a number of important issues about the upcoming fall sales campaign. Option ③ is correct because it uses a complete verb to fix the sentence fragment. Option ① fixes the fragment but is incorrect because there is no reason to change the meaning of the sentence from future to past. Option ② is incorrect because <u>is</u> does not agree with the subject <u>we</u>. Option ④ is incorrect because <u>be discussing</u> is still an incomplete verb.

2. ⑤ no correction is necessary

Beginning next month, the campaign will run for six weeks. Option ⑤ is correct because the sentence is not a fragment. It has a complete subject (<u>campaign</u>) and verb (<u>will run</u>). Options ① and ③ create sentences that do not make sense. Option ② creates a sentence fragment and a comma splice. (For information on comma splices, see Skill 2). There is no reason to remove the introductory phrase <u>Beginning next month,</u> (Option ④).

3. **④** customers, which we
   The campaign is an important time for the company to get new customers, which we need to increase our income. Option ④ is correct because it correctly uses a comma to join sentence 5, which is a relative clause that cannot stand on its own, with the previous sentence. Options ②, ③, and ⑤ create sentences that do not make sense.

4. **⑤** from 2:00 to 4:00 although we
   The meeting is in Conference Room A from 2:00 to 4:00 although we might have to move to the Executive Conference Room because of another meeting scheduled for Conference Room A. Option ⑤ correctly joins the dependent clause in Sentence 7 to the independent clause in Sentence 6. Option ② is incorrect because it creates a run-on sentence. (For more information on run-on sentences, see Skill 2.) Option ③ creates a comma splice. (For more information on comma splices, see Skill 3.)
   Option ④ creates a comma splice and is missing a comma after *however*.

5. **❸** replace <u>Hoped</u> with <u>I hope</u>
   I hope you have a lot of good ideas to share. Option ③ is correct because it fixes the sentence fragment by giving the sentence a subject (<u>I</u>) and a verb that makes sense (<u>hope</u>). Option ① does not fix the sentence fragment. Option ② is incorrect because this sentence should be in the present tense. Option ④ creates a sentence that does not make sense.

Skill 2 (Page 23)

1. **❶** replace <u>down it</u> with <u>down. It</u>
   Nothing is more frustrating than having your car break down. It can ruin your entire day. Option ① fixes the run-on sentence by dividing it into two separate sentences. Option ② is incorrect because <u>brake</u> (meaning "slow a car by using the brakes") is not needed in this sentence. There is no reason to change <u>break</u> to the simple past (Option ③). This change does not fix the run-on sentence. Option ④ creates a comma splice. (For more information on comma splices, see Skill 3).

2. **❶** inscrt <u>will keep</u> after <u>steps</u>
   Several steps will keep your car in good operating condition and help you avoid trouble on the road. Sentence 2 is a fragment because it lacks a complete verb. Option ① supplies the missing verb. The other options do not correct the sentence fragment.

3. **❶** oil changed and your fluid levels, air filter, and battery checked
   First, you should have your oil changed and your fluid levels, air filter, and battery checked every three months or 3,000 miles. Option ① is correct because the sentence is correct as written. Option ② is not correct because it causes faulty parallel structure. (For more information on parallel structure, see Skill 6.) A comma is not needed after <u>changed</u> because <u>and</u> is not joining independent clauses and commas are needed after <u>fluid levels</u> and <u>air filter</u> (Option ③). Options ④ and ⑤ remove a needed comma for items in a series. (For more information on commas in a series, see Skill 19.)

4. **❷** insert a semicolon after <u>regularly</u>
   Second, check your tire pressure regularly; you should put air in your tires whenever the pressure looks low. Sentence 4 is a run-on. Option ② fixes the problem by joining the two independent clauses with a semicolon. Option ① creates a comma splice. (See Skill 3 for information on comma splices.) Option ④ removes the subject and part of the verb of the second clause. Option ③ is incorrect because an adverb is required to modify the verb <u>check</u>.

5. **❹** your tires, make sure
   When you check your tires, make sure you check the air pressure in your spare tire, too. Option ④ is correct because it correctly uses a comma after a dependent clause to join it to the following independent clause. Option ① omits essential information, <u>your tires</u>. Options ②, ③, and ⑤ create sentences that do not make sense.

Skill 3 (Page 25)

1. **❸** job whether we
   Good customer service is part of our job whether we work directly with customers or not. Option ③ is correct because it removes an unneeded comma. Option ② creates a run-on. (See Skill 2 for more information about run-ons.) Option ④ creates a sentence that does not make sense. Option ⑤ creates another error: a semicolon can join two independent clauses, not an independent clause and a dependent clause.

2. ⑤ customers, so we must

Our company exists because of our customers, so we must provide excellent customer service to keep their business. Option ⑤ fixes the comma splice by using the coordinating conjunction <u>so</u> to join the two independent clauses. Option ② is a run-on sentence. (For more information on run-on sentences, see Skill 2.) Option ③ omits the subject of the second clause. Option ④ creates a new comma splice.

3. ❶ insert <u>when</u> after <u>carefully</u>

Third, listen carefully when a customer has a complaint. Option ① is correct because it adds a subordinating conjunction, <u>when</u>, joining an independent clause to the dependent clause that follows. Option ② creates a comma splice. Options ③ and ④ create sentences that do not make sense.

4. ❷ customer; it's

Remember, it's easy to lose a customer; it's much harder to get a new one. Option ② is correct because it fixes the comma splice by joining the two independent clauses with a semicolon. Option ③ creates a run-on sentence. (For more information on run-on sentences, see Skill 2.) Option ④ creates a new comma splice. Option ⑤ tries to correct the comma splice by joining the independent clauses with a coordinating conjunction, but the conjunction does not make sense.

Skill 4 (Page 27)

1. ❸ the day of the show while on other shows

On some shows, contestants are selected from the audience the day of the show while on other shows, contestants are selected months in advance. Option ③ correctly joins the clauses with the subordinating conjunction <u>while</u>. The subordinating conjunctions in the other options do not make sense. Option ② also adds an unneeded comma after <u>show</u>.

2. ❹ You run to the front of the studio when your name is called.

Option ④ is correct because it uses the subordinating conjunction <u>when</u> to show the relationship between the two clauses. Option ① does not show the relationship between the two clauses. Option ② creates a run-on sentence. Option ③ creates a comma splice. Option ⑤ uses the correct subordinating conjunction, but adds an unneeded comma.

3. ⑤ no correction is necessary

Of course, before the show is taped, you will need to fill out forms in case you are selected and win a prize. Option ⑤ is correct because the subordinating conjunction <u>before</u> and a comma are used correctly to join the sentences. Options ① and ② are not correct because the subordinating conjunctions <u>until</u> and <u>while</u> do not make sense in this sentence. Option ③ removes a necessary comma. Option ④ creates a sentence that does not make sense.

4. ❷ replace <u>unless</u> with <u>until</u>

People have to take a written test and then wait until they are called for a screen test. Option ② is correct because the subordinating conjunction <u>until</u> indicates the correct relationship between the independent and subordinate clause. A comma is not needed when an independent clause comes before a subordinate clause (Option ①). The subordinating conjunctions <u>when</u> (Option ③), <u>after</u> (Option ④), and <u>although</u> (Option ⑤) do not make sense in this sentence.

Skill 5 (Page 29)

1. ❸ work, Marcus saw a dog run

Driving home from work, Marcus saw a dog run across the highway in front of his car. Sentence 2 has a dangling modifier, <u>Driving home from work</u>. As written, the sentence seems to say that the dog was driving home from work and ran across the road. Option ③ fixes the sentence by giving the modifier a logical word to describe, <u>Marcus</u>. Option ② doesn't correct the dangling modifiers and also omits a necessary comma. Option ④ creates a sentence that does not make sense. Marcus can't drive home and run across the highway. Option ⑤ creates a sentence fragment by deleting the subject of the sentence. (For more information on sentence fragments, see Skill 1.)

2. ❷ move <u>sharply</u> to follow <u>veered</u>

Marcus braked and veered sharply to the right to avoid the dog. Option ② corrects the misplaced modifier <u>sharply</u> by moving it next to the verb it modifies, <u>veered</u>. Option ① is not correct because <u>sharply</u> needs to be near the verb it modifies, <u>veered</u>. Option ③ is not correct because an adverb is needed to modify the verb <u>veered</u>, not an adjective. There is no reason to change <u>sharply</u> to <u>sharper</u>. (Option ④).

3. **⑤** no correction is necessary
Confused, the dog turned and ran back into the path of Marcus's car. Option ⑤ is correct because the sentence is correct as written. The modifier <u>Confused</u>, is correctly placed before the word it modifies, <u>dog</u>. Option ① removes a necessary comma. There is no reason to remove the word <u>Confused</u> (Option ②). Options ③ and ④ are incorrect because the dog is confused, not the path or the car.

4. **④** move <u>completely</u> to follow <u>highway</u>
Realizing that the dog was hurt, Marcus pulled off the highway completely and approached the dog. Option ④ is correct because the misplaced adverb <u>completely</u> is now near the phrase it modifies, <u>pulled off the highway</u>. Option ① does not correct the misplaced modifier. There is no reason to remove the comma after <u>hurt</u> (Option ②) or to insert a comma after <u>highway</u> (Option ③).

5. **③** When the owner picked up the dog at Marcus's house, the dog was glad to see him.
Sentence 9 contains a dangling modifier. According to the sentence, the dog was picking himself up at Marcus's house, which does not make sense. Option ③ corrects this error by providing a subject that makes sense for the phrase <u>picked up the dog</u>. The other options do not make sense because they fail to correct the dangling modifier.

Skill 6 (Page 31)

1. **③** replace <u>in an organized state</u> with <u>organized</u>
Keeping your closets clean and organized is not easy. In sentence 1, the two modifiers are not in parallel structure (<u>Clean</u> is an adjective and <u>in an organized state</u> is a prepositional phrase). Option ③ corrects the lack of parallelism by changing the prepositional phrase to an adjective, <u>organized</u>. There is no reason to change <u>Keeping</u> to <u>Keep</u> (Option ①). There is no reason to change <u>clean</u> to <u>cleaned</u> (Option ②). Option ④ introduces a new error in parallel structure (<u>Organization</u> is a noun, and <u>clean</u> is an adjective).

2. **③** change <u>organizing</u> to <u>organize</u>
In fact, there are now closet consultants, experts who will tell you how to clean and organize your closets. Option ③ corrects the faulty parallel structure in Sentence 2 by changing <u>organizing</u> to <u>organize</u> to match the form of the verb <u>clean</u>. The other options do not correct the faulty parallel structure.

3. **④** replace <u>very</u> with <u>too</u>
First, get rid of any clothes that are too small or too large. Option ④ corrects the faulty parallel structure in Sentence 4 by changing <u>very large</u> to <u>too large</u>, which matches the form of <u>too small</u>. The other options do not correct the faulty parallel structure.

4. **①** don't want or need
Donate everything you don't want or need to charity. Option ① is correct because the sentence is correct as written. The verbs <u>want</u> and <u>need</u> are already in parallel structure. Options ②, ③, and ④ introduce errors in parallel structure. Option ⑤ creates a sentence that does not make sense.

5. **④** remove <u>to spend</u>
Having an organized closet will help you find the right outfit for a night on the town or a day at the park. Option ④ corrects the error in parallel structure by removing the infinitive <u>to spend</u>, leaving the remaining phrases <u>a night on the town</u> and <u>a day in the park</u> in parallel structure. The other options do not correct the faulty parallel structure. In addition, Option ② introduces a new error in parallel structure (<u>for spending</u> and <u>to spend</u> are not parallel). Option ③ also needlessly repeats the phrase <u>the right outfit</u>.

Skill 7 (Page 33)

1. **③** change <u>have</u> to <u>has</u>
The Modern and Contemporary Art Museum has offered an inviting setting for the community to experience works of art for over 50 years. Option ③ is correct because the subject of the sentence, <u>Museum</u>, is singular so the verb needs to be in the singular form. Option ① changes the verb to the simple past, which does not make sense. Option ② creates an incorrect verb form. Option ④ is incorrect because there is no reason to change the verb to the past perfect tense.

2. **①** Suggested admission is $3.00 for seniors and children.
Option ① is correct because it combines the two sentences without creating any errors. Option ② is incorrect because the verb <u>are</u> does not agree with the singular subject <u>admission</u>. Option ③ is a run-on sentence. Option ④ is a comma splice. Option ⑤ is not the best choice because it is awkward.

3. ❸ change is to are
Visitors may pay more or less than the suggested donation, but all are required to pay something. Option ③ is correct because all refers to a plural noun, visitors. Therefore, the plural verb are is required. Option ① is incorrect because pays does not agree with the plural subject visitors. Option ② is not correct because the sentence is about what visitors pay every day for admission, not about what they have paid in the past. Option ④ results in a sentence that does not make sense.

4. ❷ helps
A trained guide always helps teachers plan their visits. Option ② is correct because the singular verb helps agrees with the singular subject guide. Option ① is not correct because the subject of the sentence is guide, which is singular, not guides, which is plural, so a singular verb form is required. Option ③ is not a complete verb, and creates a sentence fragment. Option ④ is not correct because it changes the meaning of the sentence. Option ⑤ results in a sentence that does not make sense.

Skill 8 (Page 35)

1. ❸ change are to is
Learning to use computers is easy in this one-day class at City Community College. Option ③ is correct because the subject of the sentence, learning, is singular, so it requires a singular verb, is. Option ① does not correct the lack of agreement between learning and are. Option ② creates a sentence fragment because be is not a complete verb. Option ④ changes the meaning of the sentence.

2. ❶ change learns to will learn
Students in this class will learn how to start a computer and use basic software. Option ① is correct because will learn agrees with the plural subject of this sentence, Students, and makes sense in this sentence. Option ② is incorrect because there is no reason to change the verb to the past tense. Options ③ and ④ are incorrect because the simple present tense is not used after to; to start and (to) use are infinitives, which have no added endings.

3. ❹ Using computers to send e-mails is
Using computers to send e-mails is also a topic. Option ④ is correct because the subject of the sentence is using, which is singular, and the singular verb is agrees with that subject. Option ② is incorrect because the subject of the sentence is

using, which is singular, not computers or e-mails, which are plural. Option ③ does not correct the agreement problem with using and are. Option ⑤ omits the verb completely, creating a sentence fragment.

4. ❷ change have to has
Our instructor, David Bell, a trainer for several area companies, has experience in helping beginners become successful computer users. Option ② is correct because the subject of the sentence, David Bell, is singular, and has agrees with this subject. Option ① is incorrect because the sentence already has a verb, but the verb does not agree with the subject. Option ③ creates a sentence that does not make sense. Option ④ does not correct the agreement error in the sentence, and creates another agreement error—the plural verb become agrees with the plural subject beginners.

5. ❺ no correction is necessary
Students wanting to learn keyboarding skills can take Keyboarding for Beginners, another six–week course. Option ⑤ is correct because the sentence contains no errors. All of the other options introduce errors into the sentence. Options ① and ② are incorrect because a verb is not needed before wanting, which is an adjective that describes learners. Option ③ is not correct because the plural verb can take agrees with the subject of the sentence, Students. Option ④ introduces another agreement error. The subject, Keyboarding for Beginners, is singular, but are is plural.

Skill 9 (Page 37)

1. ❺ no correction is needed
Do you and your family want to have a fun family vacation? Option ⑤ is correct because the sentence contains no errors. The other options introduce errors. Option ① creates an agreement error. Do agrees with the subject you and your family. There is no reason to change the verb Do to are (Option ②). Option ③ is incorrect because in questions such as this one, endings such as -s are not added to the main verb but to a verb like do. Option ④ is incorrect because the simple present tense is not used after to; to have is an infinitive, which has a verb with no added endings.

2. **②** change <u>is</u> to <u>are</u>

There are many reasons to vacation in a state or national park. Option ② is correct because the plural verb <u>are</u> agrees with the plural subject <u>reasons</u>. Option ① removes the sentence's verb, creating a sentence fragment. There is no reason to add a verb before <u>national park</u> (Options ③ and ④).

3. **⑤** no correction is necessary

Yellowstone National Park, for example, has geysers, such as the famous Old Faithful, that frequently spew water into the air. Option ⑤ is correct because the sentence contains no errors. Option ① is not correct because the singular verb <u>has</u> already agrees with its subject, <u>Yellowstone National Park</u>. There is no reason to change <u>has</u> to <u>is</u> or <u>are</u> (Options ② and ③). There is no reason to change <u>spew</u> to <u>spews</u> (Option ④) because the plural verb <u>spew</u> agrees with the plural subject <u>geysers</u>.

4. **①** change <u>are</u> to <u>is</u>

At Grand Canyon National Park is one of the most amazing sights in the world, the Grand Canyon. Option ① is correct because in this sentence with inverted order, <u>is</u> agrees with the singular subject <u>one</u>. There is no reason to change <u>are</u> to <u>has</u> or <u>have</u> (Options ② and ③) or to add verbs after <u>sights</u> (Options ④ and ⑤).

5. **③** change <u>offer</u> to <u>offers</u>

Third, the park system, which includes hundreds of parks in all 50 states and Puerto Rico, offers plenty of activities. Option ③ is correct. <u>Offer</u> should agree with the singular subject, <u>park system</u>, not with the plural interrupting phrase. Option ① is incorrect because this verb agrees with the singular noun it refers to, <u>park system</u>. Option ② is not correct because a full verb, not a participle, is needed here. Option ④ is not correct because there is no reason to change <u>offer</u> to the past tense.

Skill 10 (Page 39)

1. **④** are having

We are having several problems with data loss on the company's personal computers. Option ④ is correct because the present progressive tense is formed with <u>is</u> or <u>are</u> and a verb that ends in –ing. Options ①, ②, ③, and ⑤ are not correct because <u>have having</u>, <u>had having</u>, <u>has having</u>, and <u>are had</u> are not possible verb forms.

2. **③** change <u>losing</u> to <u>are losing</u>

In some cases, workers are losing a day or more of work because their computer's hard drive crashed. Option ③ is correct because this option fixes the sentence fragment by providing a complete verb that is formed correctly. Option ① is incorrect because the verb <u>has lost</u> does not agree with the subject, <u>workers</u>. Option ② is incorrect because <u>had losing</u> is not a possible verb form. Option ④ does not introduce a new error, but does not correct the sentence fragment. Option ⑤ removes the complete verb from the dependent clause.

3. **①** lost

One department lost a database of 10,000 customer names, addresses, and phone numbers. Option ① is correct because the sentence is correct as written. Option ② is not correct because the plural verb <u>have lost</u> does not agree with the singular subject <u>department</u>. Option ③ is not correct because there is no reason to use the past perfect tense in this sentence. Option ④ is not correct because there is no reason to use the present progressive tense in this sentence. Option ⑤ creates a sentence fragment because <u>losing</u> is not a complete verb.

4. **②** change <u>requesting</u> to <u>requests</u>

To stop these losses, the company requests that employees back up important files on a separate floppy disk. The participle <u>requesting</u> is not a complete verb. Option ② corrects the problem by inserting the complete verb <u>requests</u>. Option ① is not correct because there is no reason to change <u>stop</u> to <u>have stopped</u>. There is also no reason to change the tense of <u>back up</u> to the past perfect or present progressive tenses (Options ③ and ④).

5. **②** are working

If you are working on a file over a period of several days, back up the file regularly. Option ② is correct because <u>working</u> is not a complete verb. <u>Are working</u> is a complete verb that makes sense in the sentence and agrees with the subject, <u>you</u>. Options ③, ④, and ⑤ are not correct because the meaning of this sentence clearly calls for the present tense. There is no reason to use the simple past, past perfect, or past progressive tenses in this sentence.

Skill 11 (Page 41)

1. **④** is
   Collecting baseball cards is one of the most popular hobbies today. Option ④ is correct because the word <u>today</u> indicates that a present tense is required. <u>Is</u> is in the present tense and agrees with the subject of the sentence, <u>Collecting</u>. Options ①, ②, and ⑤ are in tenses that do not make sense in this sentence: simple past, present perfect, and future. Though in the present tense, Option ③ does not agree with the subject of the sentence, <u>Collecting</u>.

2. **③** were
   These original cards were not sold with gum or any other product. Option ③ is correct because clues in the sentence and preceding sentence indicate that this sentence is about how original baseball cards were sold when first issued. Therefore, the past tense is required. Option ② is in the past tense, but does not agree with the plural subject <u>cards</u>. There is no reason to use the present perfect or future tenses in this sentence (Options ④ and ⑤).

3. **①** had
   The front of each card had a picture of a baseball player, and the back had an advertisement. Option ① is correct because the sentence is correct as written. The sentence is clearly about the past, and both verbs should be in the past tense. There is no reason to use the present and future tense verbs in the remaining options.

4. **③** change <u>found</u> to <u>find</u>
   The companies produced over 2,000 kinds of cards, and occasionally collectors still find new cards from that time today. Option ③ is correct because the word <u>today</u> indicates that the second clause of this sentence is about the present, so the present tense is required. Therefore, Option ④, which uses the past perfect tense, is incorrect. Options ① and ② are incorrect because the first clause is about the companies' original production of the cards in the past, so the past tense is used correctly.

5. **③** change <u>start</u> to <u>started</u>
   Today, many adults have collections of baseball cards that they started when they were children, and many more continue to collect them. Option ③ is correct because the clause <u>that they started when they were children</u> clearly refers to the past, so a past tense verb is required. Option ① is incorrect because this

clause, introduced with the adverb <u>today</u>, correctly uses the present tense. Option ② creates a sentence fragment, since <u>having</u> is not a complete verb. Option ④ is incorrect because the present tense is required in this sentence, since it talks about what people collect now.

Skill 12 (Page 43)

1. **②** showed that it is
   At last Saturday's concert, the Parkville Chorus showed that it is one of the best musical groups in our city. Option ② is correct because the fact that the chorus is one of the best musical groups in the city is something that is true today, so the present tense makes sense for this verb. Option ④ correctly uses the present tense <u>is</u>, but incorrectly uses the present progressive tense, <u>is showing</u>, for an action that took place in the past. Options ① and ⑤, which use the past perfect and future tenses, do not make sense in this sentence. Option ③ replaces the verb with an incomplete verb form, <u>be</u>.

2. **⑤** no correction is necessary
   The Parkville Chorus sang 20 popular songs, and a smaller group, The Clip Notes, entertained with barbershop quartet favorites. Option ⑤ is correct because the sentence contains no errors. The sentence is about the past, and the verbs are in the simple past tense. Option ① is incorrect because inserting <u>sung</u>, a past participle, creates a sentence fragment. Options ②, ③, and ④ are incorrect because there is no reason to change the verbs to the past progressive tense (Options ② and ③) or the future tense (Option ④).

3. **③** change <u>was lasting</u> to <u>lasted</u>
   The concert started at 7:30 on the main stage of the Pickwick Theater, and it lasted until about 10:00 at night. Option ③ is correct because there is no reason to use the past progressive tense in this sentence, which refers to a finished action, not to an action that was in progress. Option ③ correctly replaces the past progressive with the simple past tense. Option ① does not correct the error with the verb <u>was lasting</u>, and introduces another, similar error with the verb <u>started</u>. There is no reason to use the future tense (Options ② and ④) in this sentence, which is about actions that took place in the past.

4. ① change <u>were</u> to <u>was</u>
The performance was so energetic that while the chorus was singing, most of the audience was tapping their feet along with the music. Option ① is correct because <u>were</u> does not agree with its subject, <u>audience</u>, a singular noun. <u>Was</u> agrees with this subject. There is no reason to change the verb to the past perfect tense (Option ②). Option ③ and ⑤ remove part of the verbs, leaving sentence fragments. Option ④ is a possible change to the sentence, but this option fails to correct the agreement error in the sentence.

5. ⑤ change <u>had been</u> to <u>will be</u>
At the end of the concert, the chorus announced that their next performance will be at 7:30 on Saturday, April 30. Option ⑤ is correct because the word <u>next</u> indicates that the future tense is called for in this context. Options ① and ② fail to correct this error and introduce additional errors. Option ① is incorrect because the simple past tense is used correctly to refer to a single, completed action. Option ② is incorrect because there is no reason to use the future tense in this part of the sentence. Option ③ creates an incomplete verb in a place where a complete verb is needed. Option ④ uses the past tense instead of the future tense, which is needed in this part of the sentence to state the chorus's future plans.

Skill 13 (Page 45)

1. ⑤ no correction is necessary
Thieves accessed her checking and savings accounts and emptied them. Option ⑤ is correct because the sentence contains no errors. The plural pronoun <u>them</u> correctly agrees with the plural noun <u>accounts</u>. Option ① is incorrect because there is no reason to insert the object pronoun <u>them</u> as subject of the verb <u>emptied</u>. Option ② is incorrect because the thieves emptied the woman's accounts, not the woman. Option ③ is incorrect because an object pronoun is required after the preposition <u>of</u>, not the singular pronoun <u>they</u>. Option ④ is not correct because a plural pronoun is required to replace the plural noun <u>accounts</u>.

2. ④ She and her husband
She and her husband spent six months and over $500 of their own money to get everything back. Option ④ is correct because both <u>She</u> and <u>husband</u> are the subjects of the sentence. Therefore, the pronoun <u>her</u> must be changed to a subject pronoun, <u>she</u>. Option ②, which reverses the order of the pronouns, is

incorrect because it doesn't correct the pronoun error. Option ③ replaces the phrase with another object pronoun, instead of a subject pronoun. Option ⑤ is not correct because the phrase <u>her husband</u> refers to a man, so the pronoun <u>it</u> should not be used.

3. ③ you or me
Identity theft can happen to you or me. Option ③ is correct because the pronoun <u>I</u> follows a preposition, so should be changed to the object pronoun <u>me</u>. There is no reason to change to pronouns that refer to completely different people (Options ②, ④, and ⑤), and Options ② and ⑤ also use the subject pronouns <u>they</u> and <u>we</u> instead of object pronouns.

4. ⑤ no correction is necessary
What can we do to stop it from happening to us? Option ⑤ is correct because the sentence is correct as written. Option ① is incorrect because there is no reason to change <u>we</u>, which is the subject of the sentence, to <u>us</u>, which is an object pronoun. Option ② is incorrect because there is no reason to change <u>we</u> to a pronoun that refers to completely different people. In addition, <u>them</u> is an object pronoun, and a subject pronoun is required in this part of the sentence. Option ③ is incorrect because <u>it</u>, a singular pronoun, agrees with the singular noun it replaces, <u>identity theft</u>. Option ④ is incorrect because <u>us</u> is object of the preposition <u>to</u>; therefore, there is no reason to change it to the subject pronoun <u>we</u>.

5. ② insert <u>you</u> before <u>should</u>
Finally, if you use the Internet for banking, you should keep your passwords secret and change them frequently. Option ② is correct because the sentence lacks a subject and is, therefore, a fragment. Option ② provides the necessary subject. There is no reason to replace <u>you</u> with <u>they</u> (Option ①). Option ③ creates a pronoun shift. Option ④ is incorrect because <u>them</u> is object of the verb <u>change</u> and, therefore, should not be changed to the subject pronoun <u>they</u>.

Skill 14 (Page 47)

1. **③** replace <u>his</u> with <u>their</u>
   All employees need to have their company ID cards with them at all times while at work. Option ③ is correct because the pronoun refers to a plural noun, the owners of the ID cards. The plural pronoun <u>their</u> agrees with this noun. Options ① and ② are incorrect because there is no reason to change the subject <u>All employees</u> to the possessive pronoun <u>your</u> or the emphatic possessive <u>yours</u>. Option ④ is incorrect because <u>them</u> is an object pronoun because it follows the preposition <u>with</u>. Therefore, there is no reason to change <u>them</u> to the possessive pronoun <u>their</u>. There is also no reason to insert the pronoun <u>their</u> after <u>while</u> (Option ⑤).

2. **⑤** no correction is necessary
   Employees in the warehouse should keep them in their pockets. Option ⑤ is correct because the sentence contains no errors. There is no reason to use the possessive pronoun <u>their</u>, since <u>them</u> is the object of the verb (Option ①). There is no reason to use the object pronoun <u>them</u> because a possessive pronoun is needed to show whose pockets the sentence is talking about (Option ②). Option ③ is incorrect because <u>his</u> does not agree with the noun it replaces, <u>Employees</u>. Option ④ is incorrect because the possessive pronoun <u>their</u>, not the emphatic possessive <u>theirs</u>, is used before a noun.

3. **①** your card
   If you leave the building without your card, the security guard must call your manager before you can reenter the building. Option ① is correct because the sentence contains no errors. The possessive pronoun <u>your</u> is correct because it occurs before the noun <u>card</u> and agrees with the noun it refers to, <u>you</u>. Option ② uses a subject pronoun incorrectly. Option ③ uses an emphatic possessive incorrectly. The pronouns <u>their</u> (Option ④) and <u>his or her</u> (Option ⑤) do not agree with the noun they replace, <u>you</u>, so they are incorrect.

4. **③** yours
   Do not try to enter the building using a company ID that is not yours. Option ③ is correct because an emphatic possessive is needed because it appears alone. Therefore, <u>you</u> (Option ①), which is a subject pronoun, is incorrect. The possessive pronoun <u>your</u> (Option ②) is incorrect because a possessive pronoun must occur before another noun. <u>His or hers</u> (Option ④)

and <u>theirs</u> (Option ⑤) are emphatic possessives but are incorrect because they do not agree with the possessor the pronoun refers to, <u>you</u>.

5. **⑤** his or hers
   An employee can be dismissed for using an ID that is not his or hers. Option ⑤ is correct because emphatic possessives are needed here because they appear alone. The pronouns in the phrase <u>his or hers</u> agree with the noun they replace, <u>employee</u>. Therefore, Option ①, which uses the object pronoun <u>him</u>, is incorrect. Option ② is incorrect because <u>her</u> is a possessive pronoun, not an emphatic possessive. Option ③ is incorrect because <u>him</u> and <u>her</u> are object pronouns, not emphatic possessives. Option ④ is incorrect because <u>he</u> is a subject pronoun and <u>her</u> is a possessive pronoun.

Skill 15 (Page 49)

1. **④** them
   You want to give the bride and groom a gift, but you don't know what to get them. Option ④ is correct because an object pronoun is needed since the pronoun is the object of the verb <u>get</u>. <u>Them</u> agrees with the phrase it refers to, <u>bride and groom</u>. Option ① is wordy and repetitive. Option ②, <u>it</u>, a singular object pronoun, and Option ⑤, <u>us</u>, a plural object pronoun, do not agree with the phrase they replace, <u>bride and groom</u>. Option ③ is incorrect because <u>she</u> is a subject pronoun.

2. **②** replace <u>them</u> with <u>it</u>
   You just choose it from a list of items that the couple selected. Option ② is correct because the singular object pronoun <u>it</u> agrees with the noun it replaces, <u>gift</u>. <u>We</u> (Option ①) is incorrect because there is no reason to change the subject of the sentence from <u>You</u>; the entire passage is directed to the reader using <u>You</u>. Option ③ is incorrect because <u>him</u> does not agree with the noun it replaces, <u>gift</u>. Options ④ and ⑤ do not correct the faulty agreement of <u>them</u>. In addition, replacing <u>items</u> and <u>the couple</u> with pronouns does not make sense because it is not clear what nouns the pronouns refer to in the passage.

3. **③** them
   If the couple is not registered, then ask someone close to them for advice. Option ③ is correct because <u>them</u> is an object pronoun and it replaces a noun that is the object of a preposition. <u>Them</u> agrees with the noun it replaces, <u>couple</u>. <u>Couple</u> is an unusual noun because it takes a singular verb (<u>is</u>) but is replaced by plural

157

pronouns. <u>Her</u> (Option ①) is an object pronoun but does not agree with <u>couple</u>. <u>Hers</u> (Option ②) is an emphatic possessive, not an object pronoun, and does not agree with <u>couple</u>. Option ④ agrees with <u>couple</u> but is a subject pronoun, not an object pronoun. Option ⑤ agrees with <u>couple</u> but is a possessive pronoun, not an object pronoun.

4. ❸ replace <u>they</u> with <u>she</u>
Usually, the maid of honor is a good friend of the bride and groom, so she may have some ideas for you. Option ③ is correct because the pronoun <u>she</u> agrees with the noun it replaces, <u>maid of honor</u>. Option ① and ② are incorrect because <u>he</u> and <u>it</u> do not agree with the noun they replace, <u>maid of honor</u>. Options ④ and ⑤ are incorrect because the passage is directed to the reader (using the pronoun <u>you</u>), not <u>her</u> or <u>them</u>.

5. ❹ replace <u>from them</u> with <u>yours</u>
That way, the couple will know it is yours and will be able to thank you. Option ④ is correct because this emphatic possessive occurs alone and agrees with the person it refers to, in this case the reader of the advice, <u>you</u>. Option ① is incorrect because <u>they</u> does not agree with the noun it replaces, <u>gift</u>. Option ② is incorrect because a possessive word is needed to show who the gift is from. Option ③ does not make sense because the couple does not need a card to tell them that the gift is for them. They need it to know who sent the gift. Option ⑤ is incorrect because the object pronoun <u>you</u> is needed, since the pronoun is the object of the verb <u>thank</u>.

Skill 16 (Page 51)

1. ❺ no correction is necessary
I Love Lucy **is one of the biggest success stories of television.** Option ⑤ is correct because the sentence contains no errors. Option ① is incorrect because the subject of the sentence, *I Love Lucy,* is singular. For this reason, <u>some</u> (Option ②), which refers to *I Love Lucy,* is incorrect. Options ③ and ④ result in sentences that do not make sense.

2. ❸ everyone
Almost everyone has heard of the loveable redhead Lucy and her Cuban bandleader husband, Ricky. Option ③ is correct because the paragraph is about how the popularity of the TV show has resulted in most people knowing about the TV character Lucy. Options ①, ② and ⑤ result in sentences that do not make sense. Option ④ is incorrect because <u>everything</u> cannot be used to refer to people.

3. ❶ replace <u>themselves</u> with <u>herself</u>
In one famous episode, Lucy stuffed herself with chocolate in order to avoid losing her job at a candy factory. Option ① is correct because <u>herself</u> agrees with the noun it replaces, <u>Lucy</u>, and is a reflexive pronoun because it refers to the same person as the subject of the sentence. <u>Itself</u> (Option ②) does not agree with the noun it replaces, <u>Lucy</u>. There is no reason to insert <u>herself</u> after <u>losing</u> (Option ③). Option ④ is incorrect because the possessive pronoun <u>her</u>, not a reflexive pronoun <u>herself</u>, is needed before <u>job</u> to show whose job it was.

4. ❸ replace <u>us</u> with <u>ourselves</u>
But, more importantly, experts say that we can see ourselves in the program. Option ③ is correct because a reflexive pronoun is needed here because the noun it replaces is the same as the subject of the clause, <u>we</u>. There is no reason to change the subject of the clause (Option ①). Options ② and ④ do not agree with the noun the pronoun refers to, <u>us</u>.

5. ❹ change <u>face</u> to <u>faces</u>
Each episode focused on real problems that everyone faces. Option ④ is correct because <u>faces</u> agrees with its singular subject, <u>everyone</u>. There is no reason to remove <u>Each</u> (Option ①). Options ② and ③ result in sentences that do not make sense. Option ⑤ replaces the verb <u>face</u> with a present participle, <u>facing</u>, which is not a complete verb, resulting in a sentence fragment.

Skill 17 (Page 53)

1. ❹ replace <u>their</u> with <u>our</u>
We are proud to announce that after 49 years in downtown Parkville, Ryan-Park Home Theater is moving from our original location to our new, larger location in Parkville Mall. Option ④ is correct because <u>their</u> is a pronoun shift. The sentence first refers to <u>We</u> and <u>our original location</u> and then shifts to <u>their new location</u>. The remaining options are not correct because the subject of the sentence is <u>We</u>, so the pronouns that refer to the subject of the sentence should agree with this subject.

2. ❸ replace <u>one orders</u> with <u>you order</u>
During this time, you can get 20 percent off all purchases of in-stock merchandise if you order by May 20. Option ③ is correct because the sentence first addresses the reader as <u>you</u> and then shifts to <u>one</u>. The passage is written to address the readers directly, using <u>you</u>, so the pronoun <u>you</u> is

correct in this sentence. For this reason, Options ①, ②, and ④, which use different pronouns, are incorrect.

3. **⑤** replace they with he or she
   If a name is called but that person is not present, he or she cannot win. Option ⑤ is correct because person is singular, so pronouns that refer to this noun must be singular. Option ① and ③ do not correct the pronoun shift with they, and introduce additional pronoun shifts, since your and you do not agree with that person or they. Option ② does not add an additional error to the sentence but does not correct the error with they. Option ④ is incorrect because they does not agree with the noun it replaces, that person.

4. **②** replace theirs with yours
   Our store has been serving Parkville families like yours for almost 50 years, and we hope to continue to do so from our new location for 50 more years. Option ② corrects the pronoun shift in this sentence. The passage directly addresses the reader using yours, so you should be used, not theirs. The other options do not correct this error and introduce additional pronoun shifts. The writer of the letter uses pronouns such as we and us to refer to the store, so the pronouns we and our should not change to my, one, its or their.

Skill 18 (Page 55)

1. **②** change Office Assistant to office assistant
   I am writing to you to apply for the position of office assistant at Heartland Printing Company. Option ② is correct because there is no reason to capitalize office assistant. Option ① is incorrect because there is no reason to capitalize the object pronoun you. Options ③ and ④ are incorrect because Printing Company is part of a proper noun so should remain capitalized.

2. **⑤** no correction is necessary
   I read about this opening in the Sunday, May 8, edition of the Daily News. Option ⑤ is correct because the sentence contains no errors. Options ① and ② are incorrect because days of the week and months of the year are proper nouns, so they should be capitalized. Option ③ is incorrect because there is no reason to capitalize edition. Option ④ is incorrect because the name of the newspaper is a proper noun and should be capitalized.

3. **②** change Doctor to doctor
   I am looking for a new job because the doctor is retiring at the end of this month. Option ② is correct because people's titles are capitalized only before their names. There is no reason to capitalize new job (Option ①) or end (Option ③). Option ④ is incorrect because there is no reason to capitalize the word month. Names of the months, such as July, are proper nouns and, therefore, capitalized, but the word month is a common noun and is not capitalized.

4. **④** change springfield to Springfield
   Prior to this position, I was a clerk in the purchasing office of Capitol Electric in Springfield. Option ④ is correct because Springfield, the name of a city, is a proper noun so it should be capitalized. Options ① and ② are incorrect because there is no reason to capitalize clerk or purchasing office. Option ③ is incorrect because Capitol Electric, the name of a specific company, is a proper noun, so it should remain capitalized.

5. **②** change High School to high school
   My education and training include graduation from high school, where I studied office occupations and keyboarding and took Accounting 1. Option ② is correct, since it is not necessary to capitalize high school in this sentence because it's not a proper noun. Only the name of a specific high school (such as Maine South High School) is a proper noun. Accounting is part of the name of a specific course, so it is a proper noun that should be capitalized. There is no reason to capitalize the words in the remaining options.

Skill 19 (Page 57)

1. **③** granola, corn flakes, raisin bran, or oatmeal
   Do you crave granola, corn flakes, raisin bran, or oatmeal at different times of the day? Option ③ is correct because it correctly uses commas to separate the items in the list. Option ② is incorrect because a comma is not needed after or. Option ④ has extra commas after corn and raisin. Option ⑤ has extra commas after raisin and oatmeal.

2. **①** of hundreds of hot and cold cereals
   The Cereal Bowl has a selection of hundreds of hot and cold cereals. Option ① is correct because the sentence contains no errors. The remaining options are incorrect because commas are not needed to separate a list of two items joined by and.

3. ④ insert or after bananas

You can also add raisins, nuts, strawberries, bananas, or blueberries to your cereal. Option ④ is correct because a conjunction such as and or or is needed. Option ① is incorrect because there is no reason to remove a needed comma and replace it with and. There is no reason to insert a comma after add (Option ②) or blueberries (Option ⑤). Option ③ results in a sentence that does not make sense.

4. ② insert buy before a cup

You can also get a bag of granola, order a breakfast tortilla, buy a cup of yogurt, or grab a donut to go. Option ② is correct because the items in a list joined by and or or need to be in the same grammatical form: all nouns, all verbs, etc. Option ② makes the items in the list parallel by adding a needed verb. Option ① removes another necessary verb. Option ③ removes a needed comma. There is no reason to add a comma after donut (Option ④).

Skill 20 (Page 59)

1 ⑤ no correction is necessary

You may have a lot of old clothes that your children outgrew, or maybe you have household items and collectables that you no longer need. Option ⑤ is correct because the sentence contains no errors. Option ① is incorrect because a comma is needed after outgrew to join the two independent clauses into a single sentence. There is no reason to add the commas in Options ②, ③, or ④.

2. ② them, but you

You want to sell them, but you don't want to have a garage sale. Option ② is correct because a comma is needed to join the two independent clauses into a single sentence. Option ③ creates a run-on sentence, and Option ④ creates a comma splice. Option ⑤ is incorrect because there is no reason to insert a comma after but.

3. ② insert a comma after bids

At the end of the auction, you simply examine the bids, and the customer with the highest bid gets the item. Option ② is correct because a comma is needed to join the two independent clauses into a single sentence. Option ① is incorrect because a comma is needed after the introductory prepositional phrase. Option ③ creates a run-on sentence. Option ④ results in a sentence that does not make sense.

4. ③ online payment system, and you ship

The customer sends you a payment using a credit card or an online payment system, and you ship the customer his or her purchase. Option ③ is correct because a comma is needed to join the two independent clauses into a single sentence with the coordinating conjunction and. Option ① is a comma splice. Option ② is a run-on sentence. Option ④ results in a sentence that does not make sense. Option ⑤ is incorrect because the seller, not the customer, ships the item.

5. ⑤ no correction is necessary

You will soon find out that buying and selling things on the Internet is easy and fun. Option ⑤ is correct because the sentence contains no errors. Commas are not needed after buying (Option ①) or easy (Option ④) because these lists only contain two items. There is no reason in add commas after things (Option ②) or Internet (Option ③).

Skill 21 (Page 61)

1. ⑤ no correction is necessary

Although all adult citizens can vote, voter turnout has been low in recent elections. Option ⑤ is correct because the sentence contains no errors. There is no reason to insert a comma after Although (Option ①). Option ② removes a comma needed after the dependent clause to join it to the following independent clause. Option ③ results in a sentence that does not make sense. There is no reason to add a comma before turnout (Option ④).

2. ② remove the comma after decrease

Voter participation will continue to decrease unless we take action and reverse this trend. Option ② is correct because a comma is not needed after decrease. In this sentence, the independent clause is first, so no comma is needed to join it to the following dependent clause. Option ① is incorrect because a comma is not needed after participation. Option ③ results in a sentence that does not make sense. Option ④ is incorrect because a comma is not needed after action.

3. ② to vote, they often do not
Even though people are registered to vote, they often do not exercise this vital right. Option ② is correct because it completes the dependent clause and uses a comma to join it to the following independent clause. Option ① results in a sentence that does not make sense. Option ③ omits the comma necessary after the initial dependent clause to join it to the following independent clause. Option ④ is incorrect because it omits the subject of the independent clause, <u>they</u>, making the clause into a fragment. There is no reason to use the coordinating conjunction <u>but</u> to join a dependent clause to the following independent clause (Option ⑤).

4. ③ Many citizens fail to vote because they think that voting is time-consuming.
Option ③ is correct because it joins the two sentences with a subordinating conjunction that indicates the relationship between the two clauses. Option ① is a run-on. Option ② is a comma splice. Option ④ uses an unnecessary comma after <u>vote</u>. (A comma is not needed to join an initial independent clause to a dependent clause.) Option ⑤ is not correct because the subordinating conjunction <u>although</u> does not make sense in this sentence.

5. ④ insert <u>so that</u> after <u>work</u>
In addition, people should get time off from work so that they can vote. Option ④ is correct because it adds a subordinating conjunction that correctly expresses the relationship between the independent and dependent clauses. Option ① is incorrect because there is no reason to remove the comma after the introductory prepositional phrase <u>In addition</u>. Option ② creates a comma splice. A comma is not needed before <u>so that</u> because the dependent clause introduced by <u>so that</u> follows the initial independent clause (Option ③).

Skill 22 (Page 63)

1. ① insert a comma after <u>auditoriums</u>
With two auditoriums, the complex has seats for 1,800 people in its main auditorium. Option ① is correct because the introductory prepositional phrase <u>With two auditoriums</u> needs to be followed by a comma. There is no reason to capitalize <u>complex</u> (Option ②) or follow it with a comma. (Option ③). There is also no reason to insert a comma after <u>people</u> (Option ④).

2. ① insert a comma after <u>Grandville</u>
In downtown Grandville, the beautiful white stone building with large windows looks out onto the large plaza on Main Street. Option ① is correct because <u>In downtown Grandville</u> is an introductory prepositional phrase, so it should be followed by a comma. Options ② and ③ are incorrect because the complete introductory phrase is <u>In downtown Grandville.</u> There is no reason to insert commas in the remaining options.

3. ③ insert a comma after <u>play</u>
Before or after a concert or play, enjoy a meal, a snack, or a delicious dessert. Option ③ is correct because the introductory prepositional phrase <u>Before or after a concert or play</u> should be followed by a comma. There is no reason to insert a comma after <u>Before</u> (Option ①). <u>Concert</u> is not the last word in the introductory prepositional phrase, so Option ② is incorrect. There is no reason to remove the comma after <u>meal</u> (Option ④). It is possible to remove the comma after <u>snack</u> (because a comma before <u>or</u> is optional), but the error with the missing comma after <u>play</u> is still uncorrected (Option ⑤).

4. ② insert a comma after <u>14</u>
On Saturday, May 14, residents can take a tour of the complex. Option ② is correct because a comma is needed after the introductory prepositional phrase <u>On Saturday, May 14</u>. Option ① removes a comma needed to write the date correctly. There is no reason to insert commas after <u>residents</u> (Option ③) or <u>tour</u> (Option ④).

Skill 23 (Page 65)

1. ① insert a comma after <u>However</u>
However, finding a credit card that offers a good deal is also important. Option ① is correct because a comma is needed after an introductory adverb such as <u>However</u>. There is no reason to add commas after <u>card</u> and/or <u>deal</u> (Options ② and ③) or after <u>is</u> and <u>also</u> (Option ④).

2. ⑤ no correction is necessary
The annual percentage rate, or APR, is the interest rate you pay each month. Option ⑤ is correct because the sentence contains no errors. There is no reason to insert commas after <u>percentage</u> and/or <u>annual</u> (Options ① and ②). There is also no reason to remove the commas after <u>percentage rate</u> or <u>APR</u> (Options ③ and ④) because they are needed to set off the appositive <u>or APR</u>.

3. ⑤ insert a comma after cards

Typically, annual fees range from $29 to $50, but some premium plastic, such as gold credit cards, may cost more. Option ⑤ is correct because commas are needed before and after the appositive such as gold credit cards. A comma is needed after the introductory adverb Typically (Option ①). A comma is also needed after $50 (Option ②) because two independent clauses are joined by but. A comma after plastic (Option ③) is needed to set off the appositive that follows, such as a gold card. There is no reason to add a comma after gold (Option ④).

4. ⑤ no correction is necessary

The grace period, usually 30 days, is the time you have to pay the charges before interest starts. Option ⑤ is correct because the sentence contains no errors. Commas are needed after period and days (Options ① and ②) to set off the appositive usually 30 days. There is no reason to insert commas after have or charges (Options ③ and ④).

Skill 24 (Page 67)

1. ④ remove the comma after TV

Today, many parents worry that their children spend too much time watching TV and playing video games. Option ④ is correct because a comma is not needed in a list of only two items joined by and. Option ① is incorrect because a comma is needed after the introductory word Today. Option ② is incorrect because a comma is not needed in a list of two items joined by and. Option ③ is incorrect because there is no reason to add a comma after children. Option ⑤ is incorrect because a comma is not needed after and when it is used to join items in a list.

2. ① remove the comma after daughter

Your son or daughter might like to participate in an organized sport, such as an after-school soccer. Option ① is correct because a comma is not needed between the subject (Your son or daughter) and the verb (might like). A comma is needed after sport (Option ③) to set off the following appositive. There is no reason to insert a comma after participate or school (Options ② and ④).

3. ② remove the comma after dancing

Your child might be interested in dancing or collecting coins and stamps. Option ② is correct because a comma is not needed to join two items (dancing and collecting) joined by and. There is no need to insert a comma after in (Option ①), or collecting (Option ③). And joins two items, coins and stamps, so a comma is not needed after coins (Option ④).

4. ① insert a comma after places

In many places, community centers offer classes for kids on interesting subjects, such as acting and magic. Option ① is correct because a comma is needed after the introductory prepositional phrase In many places. There is no reason to insert a comma after centers (Option ②). A comma is not needed between the subject and the verb. The comma after subjects (Option ③) is needed to set off the following appositive. Option ④ adds an unnecessary comma to a list of two items joined by and. There is no reason to insert a comma after and. (Option ⑤).

5. ① add a comma after interested

If your child is interested, he or she might want to learn to play a musical instrument. Option ① is correct because a comma is needed to join an initial dependent clause to the following independent clause. Option ② is incorrect because a comma is not needed in lists of two items joined with or. Option ③ is not correct because a comma is not needed between the subject and the verb of a sentence. There is no reason to insert a comma after musical (Option ④).

Skill 25 (Page 69)

1. ③ replace it's with its

The Friends of Lakeview will have its next regular meeting on Monday, May 23, at 7:30 P.M. Option ③ is correct because in this sentence, its is a possessive pronoun, not a contraction, so an apostrophe is not needed. For this reason, Option ④, which uses an apostrophe in an incorrect place, is also incorrect. Options ① and ② are incorrect because Friends is plural, not possessive, in this sentence, so an apostrophe is not needed.

2. **④** replace <u>Schools</u> with <u>School's</u>
The meeting will take place in Wallace O. Williams High School's community room. Option ④ is correct because <u>School</u> is possessive in this sentence, so it needs an apostrophe and an <u>-s</u>. Options ① and ② are incorrect because <u>Williams</u> is not possessive in this sentence. The school is named after Williams; it doesn't belong to him. Option ③ is incorrect because this word is singular and possessive, not plural and possessive.

3. **②** replace <u>cities</u> with <u>city's</u>
Also on the agenda is a discussion of the city's plan for its annual back-to-school parade. Option ② is correct because a singular possessive is needed in this sentence. Only one city sponsors the parade. Therefore, Option ①, which is a plural possessive, is incorrect. Option ③ misspells the plural possessive form of <u>city</u>, which is <u>cities'</u>. Option ④ is incorrect because in this sentence, <u>its</u> is a possessive pronoun, not a contraction, so an apostrophe is not needed.

4. **②** replace <u>well'</u> with <u>we'll</u>
Finally, we'll be joined by Bernie Hansen, a representative from the local branch of Commerce Bank, who will update us on the construction of the bank's new branch. Option ② is correct because the apostrophe should be inserted to take the place of the letters deleted from the contraction, in this case, <u>wi</u>. Option ① is incorrect because <u>we will</u>, or the contraction <u>we'll</u>, are needed here, not the noun <u>well</u>. Options ③ and ④ are incorrect because the sentence is about a single bank, so the singular possessive <u>bank's</u> is correct here.

5. **①** replace <u>Were</u> with <u>We're</u>
We're going to postpone the tour of the new school auditorium until June's meeting. Option ① is correct because an apostrophe is needed in the contraction <u>We're</u>, <u>we are</u>. Option ② is incorrect because the apostrophe is misplaced. The apostrophe should replace the letter deleted from the contraction, <u>a</u>. Options ③ and ④ are incorrect because there is no reason to use plural or plural possessive forms of <u>June</u> in this sentence.

Skill 26 (Page 71)

1. **②** replace <u>knew</u> with <u>new</u>
You want a great new personal music player. Option ② is correct because the adjective <u>new</u> is required to modify the noun phrase <u>personal music player</u>. Option ① is incorrect because the word <u>grate</u> ("metal grill" or "make into fine pieces") does not make sense in this sentence. Option ③ is incorrect because there is no reason to replace <u>personal</u> ("belonging to one person") with <u>personnel</u> ("human resources"). There is no reason to capitalize <u>player</u> (Option ④).

2. **④** replace <u>won</u> with <u>one</u>
How can you buy the right one? Option ④ is correct because the noun <u>one</u> is needed in this place, not the past tense form of the verb <u>win</u>, <u>won</u>. Option ① is incorrect because there is no reason to capitalize <u>you</u>. Option ② is incorrect because there is no reason to replace the verb <u>buy</u> with the preposition <u>by</u>. Option ③ is incorrect because the adjective <u>right</u> ("correct") is needed in this place in the sentence, not the verb <u>write</u>.

3. **①** replace <u>Sum</u> with <u>Some</u>
Some people have put their whole music libraries on their players. Option ① is correct because the adjective <u>Some</u> ("a few"), not the noun <u>sum</u> ("the result of addition") is needed in this sentence. There is no reason to replace the possessive pronoun <u>their</u> with the adverb <u>there</u> (Option ②) or the contraction <u>they're</u> (Option ③). Option ④ is incorrect because the adjective <u>whole</u> ("complete") is needed in this sentence rather than the noun <u>hole</u> ("opening in the ground").

4. **⑤** replace <u>week</u> with <u>weak</u>
You wouldn't want the music to sound weak when you play it back. Option ⑤ is correct because the adjective <u>weak</u> ("not strong") is required here, not the noun <u>week</u> ("period of seven days"). Option ① incorrectly forms the contraction <u>wouldn't</u> with the noun <u>wood</u> instead of the auxiliary verb <u>would</u>. Option ② is not correct because the apostrophe is misplaced. The apostrophe should replace the letter removed from the word <u>not</u>, <u>o</u> to form a contraction. There is no reason to replace <u>to</u>, (which is needed to form an infinitive with the following verb, <u>sound</u>) with the adverb <u>too</u> ("in addition") or the number <u>two</u> (Options ③ and ④).

5. ⑤ no correction is necessary

There is no telling when you will want to share your music with a friend. Option ⑤ is correct because the sentence contains no errors. There is no reason to replace the adverb <u>There</u> with the contraction <u>They're</u> (Option ①) or the possessive pronoun <u>Their</u> (Option ②). There is no reason to replace <u>to</u> (which is needed to form an infinitive with the following verb, <u>share</u>) with the number <u>two</u> (Option ③) or the adverb <u>too</u> ("in addition") (Option ④).

Skill 27 (Page 73)

1. ④ The merry-go-round has a long, surprising history. Option ④ is the best topic sentence for the paragraph. It sums up the main idea of the paragraph: that merry-go-rounds were developed many years ago. Option ① is too specific. The paragraph covers more than the initial invention of the merry-go-round. Option ② is too broad and may not be true. The paragraph covers only the initial history of the merry-go-round, not just the time of its invention, and says nothing about the importance of its invention. Option ③ is too broad and not related to the main idea of the passage, the invention of the merry-go-round. Option ⑤ is not related to the main idea of the paragraph, the history of the invention of merry-go-rounds.

2. ⑤ no correction is necessary

In fact, the period from about 1860 to 1930 was called the "Golden Age" of the merry-go-round because of the many beautiful rides created during this time. Option ⑤ is correct because the sentence is placed correctly. It gives an additional detail related to the sentence that comes before it, sentence 6. Therefore, Options ③ and ④ are incorrect. Option ① is incorrect because sentence 7 belongs in paragraph B with information about modern merry-go-rounds. Option ② is incorrect because sentence 7 is too detailed to be the topic sentence.

3. ② move sentence 8 to the beginning of paragraph B
Option ② is correct because paragraph B needs a topic sentence, and sentence 8 is an effective topic sentence for the paragraph. Option ① is incorrect because sentence 8 belongs in paragraph B, which is about merry-go-rounds in the United States. Options ③ and ④ are incorrect because sentence 8 is most effective as introduction to paragraph B.

4. ④ These beloved machines are now less and less common.
Option ④ is the best topic sentence for paragraph C because it provides the best statement of the main idea of the paragraph: that now there are fewer merry-go-rounds now than in the past. For this reason, Options ② and ⑤ are incorrect. Options ① and ③ are too specific, and Option ① is contradicted by the last sentence of paragraph C.

Skill 28 (Page 75)

1. ⑤ no correction is necessary

The track between Green Street and Flynn Street will be repaired. Option ⑤ is correct because sentence 3 is placed correctly in the paragraph. Repairing the track is one of the improvements that is causing the station to close temporarily. Option ① is incorrect because sentence 1, the topic sentence, is most effective first in the paragraph. Sentence 3 contains a detail that logically comes after sentence 1. Sentence 3 does not belong in paragraph B (Option ②), because that paragraph is about alternate travel arrangements while the station is closed. Sentence 3 does not belong after sentence 10 (Option ③), because that sentence is about new bus lines, not track repair. Option ④ removes a key detail from the passage: a main cause for the station to close is the track maintenance.

2. ⑤ remove sentence 6
Option ⑤ is correct because the sentence is not relevant to the main idea of the announcement: the repairs being made to the station. For this reason, the remaining options are incorrect.

3. ⑤ remove sentence 8
Sentence 8, which is about people who do not use the transit system, is not relevant to the main idea of paragraph B, or any of the other paragraphs, so should be removed. For this reason, the remaining options are incorrect.

4. ① move sentence 12 to follow sentence 5
Option ① is correct because paragraph A is about improvements to the station, and the sentence lists one of the improvements, a new exit with access to the new Skyline Tower Mall. Sentence 12 also begins with the word <u>Finally</u>, which means it should be toward the end of the paragraph. For this reason, Option ② is incorrect. Sentence 12 does not belong in paragraph B (Option ③) because that paragraph is about alternate transportation for subway riders. Option ④ removes a relevant idea from the selection.

Skill 29 (Page 77)

1. ⑤ remove sentence 3

   Option ⑤ is correct because sentence 3 is about insurance benefits, and not the topic of the memo, direct deposit. Option ① removes the introductory paragraph from the memo. There is no reason to combine the introduction to the memo and the first body paragraph (Option ②). Options ③ and ④ remove necessary sentences from paragraph A.

2. ❸ join paragraphs B and C

   Option ③ is correct because paragraphs B and C are both about the same main idea, the advantages of direct deposit, so they should be joined together. Options ① and ② remove needed information from the memo. There is no reason to join paragraphs C and D (Option ④) because these paragraphs are on different main ideas: advantages of direct deposit and instructions for signing up.

3. ❷ sentence 13

   Option ② is correct because starting with sentence 13, the paragraph shifts focus from how to sign up to how to make changes to direct deposit. Sentence 12 (Option ①), contains an idea related to signing up for direct deposit, so a new paragraph should not begin with that sentence. The remaining options result in dividing up information on changing or stopping direct deposit, which belong in a single paragraph.

4. ❹ remove sentence 20

   Option ④ is correct because sentence 20 introduces a new topic not related to direct deposit, so should be removed from the memo. Options ①, ②, and ③ remove necessary information from the memo.

Skill 30 (Page 79)

1. ❶ location, make all of the necessary arrangements, and plan fun activities for everyone.
   To have a successful reunion, select a date and location, make all of the necessary arrangements, and plan fun activities for everyone. Option ① is correct because it is the most effective combination of the clauses into a single sentence. The clauses are in parallel structure, use a transition that makes sense, and are correctly joined by commas and <u>and</u>. The remaining options use incorrect transitions.

2. ❺ If, for example,
   If, for example, a relative who lives in Canada will be visiting at a certain time, that might be a good time to have the reunion. Option ⑤ is correct because a transition indicating an example is needed in this sentence. Options ①, ②, ③ and ④ use incorrect transitions.

3. ❸ insert <u>also</u> after <u>You</u>
   You also might hire a babysitter. Option ③ is correct because the word <u>also</u> indicates that sentence 10 is an additional suggestion about how to deal with children at the reunion. Options ①, ②, and ⑤ use transitions that do not make sense. There is no reason to change <u>might</u> (auxiliary verb) to <u>mite</u> ("a small insect") (Option ④).

4. ❹ As a result, people
   As a result, people at the reunion will get a better understanding of the family and its history. Option ④ is correct because the transition <u>As a result</u> indicates the correct relationship between sentence 12 and the information that came before: studying family history will result in a better understanding of the family. Option ① is incorrect because a transition is needed to indicate the relationship between sentences 11 and 12. Options ②, ③, and ⑤ use transitions that do not make sense.

Skill 31 (Page 81)

Check Your Knowledge

1. no
2. yes
3. no
4. yes
5. yes
6. no
7. no
8. yes

Practice

1. Checked: none

2. Checked: It's on a specific subject; The ideas are organized; It has a beginning, a middle, and an end; It's written in complete sentences and in one paragraph; It has good spelling, grammar, and punctuation.

3. Checked: It's on a specific subject; The ideas are organized; It has a beginning, a middle, and an end; It's written in complete sentences and in one paragraph; It has good spelling, grammar, and punctuation.

Write

Many answers are possible. Share your list of topics with your instructor or another learner.

Skill 32 (Page 83)
Check Your Knowledge

1. false
2. true
3. false
4. true
5. false
6. true
7. true
8. true

Practice

Many answers are possible. Compare your answers with these possible answers:

1. Topic: whether it's important to vote
   How you will answer: give reasons

2. Topic: my favorite food
   How you will answer: give a description

3. Topic: a really good day
   How you will answer: tell what happened

Write

Many answers are possible. Share your answers with your instructor or another learner.

Skill 33 (Page 85)
Check Your Knowledge

1. no
2. yes
3. no
4. no
5. no
6. yes

Practice

1. Many answers are possible. Compare your answers with these possible answers.

   loving
   sets limits
   encouraging
   meets regularly with teachers
   helps with homework
   disciplines when necessary
   makes sure children have nutritious meals
   makes sure children have plenty of good clothes

2. Many answers are possible. Use your answers to improve your brainstorming in the future.

Write

Many answers are possible. Share your answers with your instructor or another learner.

Skill 34 (Page 87)
Check Your Knowledge

1. I have a great neighbor, Carmen Mendoza.

2. Carmen is very friendly.

3. Sometimes we spend hours talking.

4. Her home is always beautiful.

5. She has beautiful flowers in her garden.

6. She's very helpful.

7. Carmen always checks on our oldest neighbor, Ms. Espinoza.

8. Carmen babysits for me when I have to work late.

Practice

1. Many answers are possible. Share your answers with your instructor or another learner.

2. Use your answers to improve your writing in the future.

Write

Many answers are possible. Share your answers with your instructor or another learner.

Skill 35 (Pages 90–91)
Check Your Knowledge

1. a healthful meal is low in fat and has fresh ingredients

2. Underlined: A healthful meal should be low in fat and contain plenty of fresh, natural ingredients.

3. 5

4. The tacos were filled with spicy chicken and plenty of lettuce, tomatoes, and chopped onions. For dessert, we had fresh grapes.

5. Underlined: My husband and kids loved everything, and I was happy because everything was good for them.

Practice

B3: Still others enjoy treating themselves to a favorite food such as a pizza or a burger and fries.

TS: If we watch our diets, we don't have to eat sensible foods all the time—sometimes we can splurge on a favorite food.

B1: Some people really enjoy chocolate as a splurge.

CS: So even if you are watching your diet, leave some room for an occasional treat.

B2: Other people enjoy salty snacks, such as potato chips or tortilla chips.

Write

Many answers are possible. Share your answers with your instructor or another learner.

Skill 36 (Page 93)
Check Your Knowledge

1. no

2. yes

3. no

4. yes

5. no

6. yes

7. yes

8. no

Practice

Many answers are possible. Compare your answers with these possible answers.

1 Favorite food is salad

5 Ripe red tomatoes

6 Chopped onions

8 Top it off with blue cheese dressing

2 Like to eat salad for lunch or dinner

3 Sometimes eat it for lunch and dinner

7 Always add special ingredients—nuts, cheese, fresh vegetables

4 Fresh lettuce

Write

1. Many answers are possible. Share your answers with your instructor or another learner.

2. Many answers are possible. Follow the instructions on pages ix–xi to evaluate your essay.

Skill 37 (Page 95)
Check Your Knowledge

Many answers are possible. Compare your answers with these possible answers.

1. Mr. Chun made a delicious and healthful tuna salad sandwich for lunch.

2. The fresh air smells as good as an ocean breeze.

3. She drove to the new supermarket at 70 miles per hour.

4. He read a fascinating novel about the Civil War.

5. I need a red plaid work shirt for the freezing cold winter weather.

6. It's pouring rain right now.

7. Going to the movies is great entertainment for the whole family.

8. His kitchen has dirty dishes piled everywhere.

Practice

Many answers are possible. Share your answers with your instructor or another learner.

Write

Many answers are possible. Follow the instructions on pages ix–xi to evaluate your essay.

Skill 38 (Page 97)

Check Your Knowledge

Many answers are possible. Compare your answers with these possible answers.

1. Crossed off: can get sick and die easily; Added: Nice for people who live in apartments

2. Crossed off: some dogs are very lazy; Added: keep their owners safe

3. Crossed off: dogs are very friendly; Added: skunks can bite or scratch

4. Crossed off: cats like to catch birds; Added: she always says "hello" to guests

Practice

Many answers are possible. Share your answers with your instructor or another learner.

Write

Many answers are possible. Follow the instructions on pages ix–xi to evaluate your essay. Use your answers to ③ to improve your writing in the future.

Skill 39 (Page 99)

Check Your Knowledge

6 I had to work through lunch.

4 Then the bus was late.

2 First, when I got up, I stepped on my glasses and broke them.

8 I had to pay my landlord $25 to come over and let me in my apartment.

3 After that, I had to repair them with tape.

1 I had a terrible day yesterday.

5 When I got to work, my boss yelled at me for being late.

7 When I got home after work, I found out I'd lost my keys.

Practice

Many answers are possible. Share your answers with your instructor or another learner.

Write

Many answers are possible. Follow the instructions on pages ix–xi to evaluate your essay. Use your answers to ② to improve your writing in the future.

Skill 40 (Page 101)

Check Your Knowledge

4 After the word "Ready" appears, dial the number you want to call.

7 When you are finished using the phone, hold down the red on-off button until you hear another musical chime.

2 When the phone turns on, you will hear a short musical chime.

1 Turn on the phone by holding down the red on-off button.

3 Watch the display panel for the word "Ready" to appear.

6 When you are finished talking, press the red on-off button again.

5 Press the Talk button after you dial.

Practice

Many answers are possible. Share your answers with your instructor or another learner.

Write

Many answers are possible. Follow the instructions on pages ix–xi to evaluate your essay. Use your answers to ② to improve your writing in the future.

Skill 41 (Page 103)

Check Your Knowledge

1. Circled: give reasons, explain

2. Circled: specific reasons and examples

3. Circled: specific reasons and examples

Practice

Many answers are possible. Share your answers with your instructor or another learner.

Write

Many answers are possible. Follow the instructions on pages ix–xi to evaluate your essay. Use your answers to ② to improve your writing in the future.

Skill 42 (Page 105)

Check Your Knowledge

1. how-to; Move *Always wash cooking pots last,* to after the sentence, *Then rinse the silverware.*

2. narration; Move *I signed a lease right after I looked at the apartment the first time,* to after the sentence, *It was small but nice, and the price was right.*

3. description; Move *I keep all of my materials for the GED on my desk,* to after the sentence, *My desk is in the hall.*

Practice

Many answers are possible. Share your answers with your instructor or another learner.

Write

Many answers are possible. Follow the instructions on pages ix–xi to evaluate your essay. Use your answers to ② to improve your writing in the future.

Skill 43 (Page 107)

Check Your Knowledge

1. **All young people** should do a year or more of public service.

2. For example, joining the **Peace** Corps is a great way to serve the country.

3. **Other young people** might want to join the military.

4. Joining the army or the navy **are** great ways to serve the country and see the world.

5. **Young people** should get **benefits** for serving the country.

6. One **benefit** could be a year of free college education for each year of service.

7. The biggest benefit **is** that young people will develop a sense of **r**esponsibility.

8. Doing a year of public service **benefits** the whole **c**ountry and all of its citizens.

Practice

Many answers are possible. Share your answers with your instructor or another learner. Use your answers to improve your mechanics in the future.

Write

Many answers are possible. Follow the instructions on pages ix–xi to evaluate your essay. Use your answers to ③ to improve your writing in the future.

Skill 44 (Page 109)

Check Your Knowledge

1. body

2. conclusion

3. introduction

Practice

1. conclusion

2. body

3. introduction

Write

Many answers are possible. Share your answers with your instructor or another learner. Use your answers to ② to improve your writing in the future.

Skill 45 (Page 111)

Check Your Knowledge

Checked: build interest in the essay, have a thesis statement; be organized from general to specific

Practice

❶ Many answers are possible. Compare your answers with these possible answers.

1. Collecting stamps is an enjoyable hobby for several reasons.

2. People keep pets for companionship and fun.

3. My favorite pastimes are reading and swimming.

4. My least favorite task is vacuuming.

5. I would like my next car to be a sleek sports car.

❷ Many answers are possible. Share your answers with your instructor or another learner. Use your answers to improve your writing in the future.

Write

Many answers are possible. Share your answers with your instructor or another learner. Use your answers to ② to improve your writing in the future.

Skill 46 (Page 113)

Check Your Knowledge

❶ Many answers are possible. Compare your answers with these possible answers.

1. the first paragraph of an essay; provides an overview of the topic and states the main idea, builds interest, and has a thesis statement.

2. provides detail and examples to back up the main idea

3. usually the last sentence of the introduction; states the main idea of the essay

4. usually the first sentence of a body paragraph; states the main idea of the paragraph

❷

1. introduction

2. introduction

3. body

4. body

Practice

Many answers are possible. Compare your answers with these possible answers.

1. Pancakes are easy to make.

2. Camping is a great way to spend a family vacation.

Write

Many answers are possible. Share your answers with your instructor or another learner. Use your answers to ② to improve your writing in the future.

Skill 47 (Page 115)

Check Your Knowledge

1. conclusion

2. body

3. introduction

4. body

5. introduction

6. conclusion

7. introduction

8. conclusion

9. conclusion

Practice

Many answers are possible. Follow the instructions on pages ix–xi to evaluate your essay. Use your answers to ② to improve your writing in the future.

Write

Many answers are possible. Follow the instructions on pages ix–xi to evaluate your essay. Use your answers to ③ to improve your writing in the future.

Skill 48 (Page 117)

Check Your Knowledge

E Introductory paragraph

B Thesis statement

I Topic sentence 1

G Body paragraph 1

F Topic sentence 2

A Body paragraph 2

D Topic sentence 3

H Body paragraph 3

C Concluding paragraph

Practice

Group 1: learned to drive; needed to learn because I moved to Los Angeles; in Los Angeles many people have cars; I needed to drive to work

Group 2: now can drive to work; can drive kids to school, too; can drive to the beach on weekends

Group 3: had to learn other new skills; pumping gas; changing a flat

Write

Many answers are possible. Follow the instructions on pages ix–xi to evaluate your essay.

Skill 49 (Page 119)

Check Your Knowledge

Many answers are possible. Share your answers with your instructor or another learner.

Practice

Many answers are possible. Share your answers with your instructor or another learner.

Write

Many answers are possible. Follow the instructions on pages ix–xi to evaluate your essay. Use your answers to ② to improve your writing in the future.

Skill 50 (Page 121)

Check Your Knowledge

1. I had a lot of fun last weekend, and I got a lot of work done, too.

2. On Saturday morning, I cleaned the kitchen and bathroom, but I didn't vacuum.

3. I was washing the dishes when the phone rang.

4. My brother was calling because he wanted to go to the mall with me.

5. He wanted me to go to the mall with him since he needed to buy a new suit.

6. I didn't have any plans for the afternoon, so I went with him to the mall.

7. He didn't want to buy a suit unless it was on sale.

8. After we bought him a nice suit on sale, we went to a restaurant for dinner.

9. On Sunday, I studied for the GED, and I got ready for work on Monday.

10. On Sunday night, I read a magazine while my children were doing their homework.

Practice

Many answers are possible. Share your answers with your instructor or another learner. Use your answers to ② to improve your writing in the future.

Write

Many answers are possible. Follow the instructions on pages ix–xi to evaluate your essay. Use your answers to ④ to improve your writing in the future.

Posttest

Part I (Pages 125–137)

1. ⑤ replace Weekend with weekend
   The Twenty-Fifth Annual Downtown Jazz and Blues Music Festival is scheduled to take place on the weekend of June 17 at Davis Park.
   Option ⑤ is correct because weekend is not a proper noun, so there is no reason to capitalize it. Option ① is incorrect because downtown is a proper noun in this passage, part of the name of the event, so there is no reason to change it to lower case. Option ② is incorrect because the subject of the sentence, Festival, is singular, so it needs the singular form of be (is). Option ③ results in a sentence that does not make sense. Option ④ is incorrect because the word to is used to form an infinitive, not too ("also").

2. ③ change starting to will start
   Evening concerts on our main stage, the band shell in Davis Park, will start at 7:00 P.M. on Friday, Saturday, and Sunday nights. Sentence 4 is a sentence fragment because starting is not a complete verb. Option ③ corrects this problem by providing a complete verb, will start. Option ① incorrectly removes the commas that set off the appositive the band shell in Davis Park. Band shell is a common noun, so there is no reason to capitalize it (Option ②). Option ④ removes commas that are needed for three or more items in a series. Option ⑤ adds an unnecessary comma.

3. ③ insert a comma after anniversary
   To celebrate the festival's twenty-fifth anniversary, a special fireworks show will close the last concert on Sunday night.
   Option ③ is correct because a comma is required after an introductory prepositional phrase. There is no reason to insert a comma after celebrate (Option ①). Festival is a singular noun, so the possessive is formed correctly (Option ②). Fireworks is a plural noun and not a possessive, so Option ④ is incorrect.

4. ④ During the day, festivalgoers can enjoy a variety of acts at our two day stages.
   Option ④ is the best topic sentence for paragraph C, which focuses on the activities at the two day stages. The remaining options do not state this main idea.

5. **④** Tito Puente, and Sunday

On Saturday night, festivalgoers can hear a special tribute to the late Latin jazz great, Tito Puente, and Sunday night features hip-hop/jazz fusion artist Tahiri. Option ④ is correct because it joins the two independent clauses with the coordinating conjunction <u>and</u> and a comma. Option ① is a run-on sentence. Options ② and ⑤ are comma splices. Option ③ omits a comma required after <u>Puente</u> to join two independent clauses with the coordinating conjunction <u>and</u>.

6. **②** change <u>is</u> to <u>are</u>

All of the concerts and events at the Downtown Jazz and Blues Music Festival are free, and no tickets are required. Option ② is correct because the subject of this sentence, <u>concerts and events</u>, is plural, so the plural form of <u>be</u> (<u>are</u>) is needed. Option ① is incorrect because there is no reason to capitalize <u>concerts and events</u>. Option ③ removes a comma required after <u>free</u> to join two independent clauses with the coordinating conjunction <u>and</u>. Option ④ results in a comma splice.

7. **③** city's

Food, drinks, and other refreshments will be available from 20 of our city's best restaurants. Option ③ is correct because the information is about a festival in a particular city, and the singular possessive form of <u>city</u> is <u>city's</u>. <u>Cities'</u> (Option ①) is the plural possessive form of <u>city</u>. Option ② is the plural possessive form of <u>city</u> with an extra -<u>s</u> after the apostrophe. Option ④ is a misspelling of the plural possessive form of <u>city</u>. Option ⑤ is the plural form of <u>city</u>.

8. **③** replace <u>one</u> with <u>you</u>

You can walk or take public transportation to the festival, or you can drive and use the city parking garage beneath Davis Park or any of the private lots nearby. Option ③ is correct because sentence 15 contains a pronoun shift, changing from <u>you</u> to <u>one</u>. A comma is not needed after <u>walk</u> (Option ①), <u>drive</u> (Option ④), or <u>Park</u> (Option ⑤) because a comma is needed only when joining three or more items with <u>and</u> or <u>or</u>. Option ② is incorrect because the preposition <u>to</u> is required here, not <u>too</u> ("also").

9. **④** days, so one

There were only a few brands and styles of shoes in those days, so one just chose the pair that seemed the most comfortable and stylish. Sentence 2 is a comma splice, and Option ④ fixes the problem by adding a comma and the

appropriate coordinating conjunction, <u>so</u>. Option ② is a run-on. Option ③ joins the clauses with the subordinating conjunction <u>since</u>, which does not make sense. Option ⑤ joins the clauses with the coordinating conjunction <u>or</u>, which does not make sense.

10. **④** styles, colors, and special features

But today, athletic shoes are a multi-billion dollar business that offers thousands of different styles, colors, and special features that make picking a pair of athletic shoes difficult. Sentence 3 has faulty parallelism. The three phrases joined by <u>and</u> (<u>styles</u>, <u>colors</u>, and <u>special features</u>) should all be in the same grammatical form, as in Option ④. Options ①, ②, and ③ all have faulty parallelism. Option ⑤ omits <u>and</u> before <u>special features</u>, which is needed when joining three items in a list.

11. **⑤** no correction is necessary

For everyday shoes, comfort and appearance are the most important criteria. Option ⑤ is correct because the sentence contains no errors. Option ① is incorrect because a comma is needed after the introductory prepositional phrase, <u>For everyday shoes</u>. Option ② is incorrect because a comma is not needed in a list of two items joined by <u>and</u>. There is no reason to insert a comma between subject and verb (Option ③). The subject of this sentence, <u>comfort and appearance</u>, is plural, so the plural verb <u>are</u> is needed, not <u>is</u> (Option ④).

12. **③** replace <u>tow</u> with <u>toe</u>

Tennis shoes contain extra padding in the toe area to provide extra cushioning while serving. Option ③ is correct because the noun <u>toe</u>, a part of the foot, not the verb <u>tow</u> ("move a vehicle by pulling it") is needed in this sentence. There is no reason to capitalize <u>shoes</u>, which is a common noun (Option ①). Option ② is incorrect because the plural verb <u>contain</u> is needed to agree with the plural subject <u>Tennis shoes</u>. Option ④ is incorrect because <u>to</u>, not the number <u>two</u>, is needed to form the infinitive <u>to provide</u>. There is no reason to add a comma after <u>cushioning</u>.

13. **①** replace <u>participates</u> with <u>participate</u>

If you participate in many sports, a pair of cross-training shoes is a good idea. Option ① is correct because a singular verb is needed to agree with the singular subject <u>you</u>. Option ② is incorrect because a comma is needed to join a dependent clause to a subsequent independent clause. Option ③ is incorrect because <u>pear</u>, a kind of fruit, does not make sense in this sentence. <u>Pair</u> ("a set of two") is the correct word. Option ④ is incorrect because the subject of the clause, pair, is singular, so the singular form of the verb, is, is needed in this sentence.

14. ⑤ have selected
After you have selected a kind of shoe, begin to look at individual pairs of shoes. Option ⑤ is correct because a present tense verb is required in this sentence, and have selected is the only complete present tense verb among the options that agrees with the subject you. Therefore, Options ① and ②, which are past tenses, are incorrect. Option ③, which is a present participle and not a complete verb, is also incorrect. Option ④, selects, is incorrect because it does not agree with the subject of the clause, you.

15. ④ remove sentence 18
Option ④ is correct because this sentence is on a topic unrelated to the main idea of the information, choosing athletic shoes wisely, so it should be removed. For this reason, the remaining options are all incorrect.

16. ⑤ replace yours with yourself
If your feet are jammed too closely to the tip of the shoe, your feet will hurt and you run the risk of injuring yourself. Option ⑤ is correct because the subject of the clause and the direct object of the verb refer to the same person, you, so the reflexive pronoun yourself is needed. There is no reason to change jammed to jam (Option ①). Option ② is incorrect because too ("very"), not the preposition to, makes sense in this sentence. There is no reason to change the possessive pronoun your to the contraction of you are, (you're) (Option ③). There is no reason to change run to the past tense (Option ④).

17. ④ begin a new paragraph with sentence 29
Option ④ is correct because paragraph D is on two topics: style and special features, and using your new shoes. Sentence 29 is where the new topic begins, so it's a logical place for a new paragraph to begin. For this reason, the remaining options are incorrect.

18. ④ you and I
The cell phone, a truly amazing example of technology, uses a highly complex system so that you and I can use our mobile phones to make calls from almost anywhere. Option ④ is correct because the pronouns are the subject of the clause, so the subject pronouns you and I are needed. Therefore, Option ①, which has the object

pronoun me, and Options ②, ③, and ⑤, which have the reflexive pronouns myself and/or yourself, are incorrect.

19. ① In contrast,
In contrast, a mobile phone uses two signals, one for speaking and one for listening. Option ① is correct because the information in sentence 7 contrasts with the information in the previous sentence, and Option ① is the only transition word that signals this meaning. Therefore, the remaining options are incorrect.

20. ② insert the word user after walkie-talkie
Therefore, unlike a walkie-talkie user, a mobile phone user does not have to keep saying "over." Sentence 8 has a dangling modifier: the phrase unlike a walkie-talkie implies that the mobile phone user is unlike a walkie-talkie, which is not the meaning of the sentence. Option ② is correct because inserting user shows that walkie-talkie users are being compared to mobile phone users, which makes sense. Option ① removes a comma required after the introductory prepositional phrase unlike a walkie-talkie. Option ③ does not make sense because a mobile phone cannot talk. Option ④ is incorrect because the verb does already agrees with its singular subject user. There is no reason to change have to has (Option ⑤).

21. ④ remove the comma after transmitters
Mobile phone companies use a network of towers with radio transmitters and receivers throughout the city. Option ④ is correct because a comma is not needed in a list of two items joined by and. Option ① is incorrect because a comma is not needed between a subject and a verb. Option ② is incorrect because the plural verb use agrees with its plural subject companies. There is no reason to insert a comma after towers (Option ③).

22. ① his or her
When a customer turns on his or her phone, it sends a signal to the tower in that cell. Option ① is correct in this sentence because two possessive pronouns are required in this sentence. Option ② is incorrect because there is no reason to use the emphatic possessives hers. Option ③ is incorrect because there is no reason to use the object pronoun him. Option ④ is incorrect because there is no reason to use the object pronoun him or the emphatic possessives hers. Option ⑤ misspells the emphatic pronoun hers.

23. ④ it's

The tower then sends the call to central computers where it's connected to the regular phone system. Option ④ is correct because the singular pronoun <u>it</u> is needed to agree with the noun it replaces, <u>signal</u>, and the verb <u>is</u> (<u>it's</u>) agrees with this subject. There is no reason to replace the pronoun with the adverb <u>there</u> (Option ②), the possessive pronoun <u>its</u> (Option ③), or the plural possessive <u>their</u> (Option ⑤).

24. ③ weaker while the

The first tower notices the signal getting weaker while the second tower notices the signal getting stronger. Option ③ correctly joins the two clauses with the subordinating conjunction <u>while</u>, which makes sense in this context, since the two actions are happening at the same time. Option ① creates a comma splice. Option ② is missing a comma after <u>weaker</u>, which is required when joining independent clauses with a coordinating conjunction such as <u>and</u>. Option ④ creates a comma splice. Option ⑤ creates a run-on sentence.

25. ② has been increasing

As you know, traffic in the West End has been increasing for the last few years. Option ② is correct because the present perfect tense is required when talking about an action that began in the past and has continued into the present. For this reason, the remaining options are incorrect.

26. ② change <u>is</u> to <u>are</u>

In our neighborhood are several new stores and a new car wash. Sentence 4 has inverted structure, and the plural subject of this sentence is <u>several new stores and new car wash</u>, and <u>are</u> agrees with this plural subject (Option ②). A comma after <u>our</u> results in a sentence that does not make sense (Option ①). There is no reason to change <u>new</u> ("not old") to <u>knew</u> (the past tense of <u>know</u>) (Option ③). A comma is not needed after <u>stores</u> because only two items are joined with <u>and</u> (Option ④).

27. ③ remove <u>and</u> after <u>homes</u>

We have also added over 100 homes, many apartment buildings, and a small hotel. Option ③ is correct because <u>and</u> is used only once (before the last item) when joining three or more items in a list. Option ① is a possible change to the sentence, but it does not correct the error with <u>and</u>. Option ② removes a comma required when joining three or more items with <u>and</u>. Option ④ is a possible change to the sentence, but does not correct the error with <u>and</u>. There is no reason to remove <u>and</u> after <u>buildings</u> (Option ⑤).

28. ③ dramatically. At busy times,

Now, during rush hour and on weekends, traffic on Enfield Road has increased dramatically. At busy times, the line of cars in front of the new carwash is often two blocks long. Option ③ is correct because sentence 6 is a run-on. Option ③ corrects the run-on by dividing it into two sentences. Option ② creates a comma splice. Option ④ is missing the comma required after <u>dramatically</u> when joining two independent clauses with <u>and</u>. Joining the two clauses with <u>but</u> (Option ⑤) does not make sense.

29. ① gone

Parking is now almost impossible to find after 6:00 P.M., and noise and litter have gone up dramatically. Option ① is correct because the past participle of <u>go</u> (<u>gone</u>) is required to form the present perfect tense. For this reason, the remaining options are incorrect.

30. ① action because

I would like the city to take action because the problems are getting worse and worse by the day. Option ① joins the sentences correctly by using the subordinating conjunction <u>because</u>, which makes sense in this sentence. Option ② also uses the subordinating conjunction <u>because</u>, but adds a comma, which is not needed to join an independent clause to a following dependent clause. Option ③ joins the sentences with the coordinating conjunction <u>or</u>, which does not make sense. The subordinating conjunction <u>while</u> (Option ④) does not make sense in this sentence. Option ⑤ uses the subordinating conjunction <u>since</u>, which makes sense, but adds an extra comma, which is not needed to join an independent clause to a following dependent clause.

Part II (Page 139)

Give your instructor your essay to evaluate. You will find his or her objective comments helpful in assessing your essay. If this is not possible, have another learner evaluate your paper. If you cannot find another learner to help you, review your paper yourself. If you do this, it's better to let your paper "sit" for a few days before you evaluate it. This way, you will experience your essay much the same way a first-time reader will experience it. Whoever reads your paper should use the GED Essay Scoring Guide on pages ix–xi to evaluate your essay and give it a score on each of the five criteria on the rubric using this scale:

1. Inadequate   3. Adequate
2. Marginal   4. Effective

Then write your score for each criteria on the Posttest Evaluation Chart on page 141. Use that chart to figure out which skills to study in the instruction section of this book.

Glossary

appositive An appositive is a phrase that re–names a noun using different words.

body paragraph The body paragraph is the second paragraph of a three-paragraph essay. A good body paragraph gives plenty of examples and details to support the main idea of the essay.

body sentence The sentences after the topic sentence called body sentences. Good body sentences are specific, are in a logical order, and support the main idea of the paragraph.

brainstorming Brainstorming is a way to gather ideas for an essay. When you brainstorm, write many ideas as quickly as possible.

chronological order In a narration essay, the events are usually arranged in order of time, or chronological order.

clause A clause is a group of words with a complete subject and verb.

coherence A paragraph has coherence when all of the body sentences are in logical order.

comma splice A comma splice occurs when two independent clauses are joined with a comma.

complete sentence A complete sentence has a subject and a verb, is a complete thought, and can stand alone. A complete sentence begins with a capital letter and ends with a period.

complex sentence A complex sentence consists of an independent clause and a dependent clause joined with a word such as *if, because, when, while,* or *unless.*

compound predicate A compound predicate is two predicates joined by a word such as *and* or *or.*

compound sentence A compound sentence consists of two independent clauses joined with a comma and a word such as *and, but, or,* or *so.*

concluding paragraph A concluding paragraph restates the main idea, summarizes the information in the body, and provides a final thought to the reader.

concluding sentence A concluding sentence sums up the information in the body of the paragraph.

contraction Contractions are words that are shortened by combining two words and leaving out letters. To write a contraction, put the apostrophe in the place where letters were omitted.

dangling modifier A dangling modifier occurs when a sentence lacks an appropriate word for the modifier to describe.

dependent clause A dependent clause cannot stand alone as a sentence. It is introduced by a word such as *after, although, because, before, if, since, unless, until, when,* or *where.* (see also: subordinate clause)

descriptive essay A descriptive essay is used to describe a person, place, thing, or feeling.

direct address A direct address is a word or phrase in a sentence that directly address someone.

Edited American English Edited American English uses complete sentences, and correct spelling, puncuation, and grammer.

emphatic possessive pronoun An emphatic possessive pronoun shows possession but stands alone, usually at the end of a sentence.

essay An essay is a written composition on a specific subject. The ideas in an essay are organized and have a beginning, middle, and end.

fragment A fragment is an incomplete sentence.

GED Essay Scoring Guide The GED Essay Scoring Guide is used by raters to evaluate GED essays. A score of 2 is a minimum passing grade on this part of the GED test.

give reasons When you give reasons in an essay, you explain the thinking behind an opinion, belief, or action.

homonym Homonyms are two or more words with the same (or similar) pronunciation but different spellings and meanings.

how-to essay A how-to essay explains the steps in a process.

idea map An idea map is a way to gather and organize your ideas.

indefinite pronoun An indefinite pronoun is a pronoun that refers to an unknown or unspecified noun. An indefinite pronoun can be singular or plural.

independent clause An independent clause has a complete subject and verb, is a complete thought, and can stand alone as a sentence.

introductory paragraph The introductory paragraph of an essay tells the reader what the essay will be about, builds interest, and prepares the reader for the information to come in the body paragraph.

inverted structure A sentence has inverted structure if the verb comes before the subject.

mechanics Mechanics includes spelling, punctuation, and grammar.

misplaced modifier A misplaced modifier is a modifier that is not placed near the word it modifies, causing confusion for readers.

multi-paragraph essay A multi-paragraph essay has more than one paragraph. An effective GED essay is usually four or five paragraphs long.

narration A narration essay tells what happened in the past. When you narrate, use chronological order—order your ideas by time.

object pronoun An object pronoun is a pronoun that takes the place of a noun that is the object of a verb or a preposition.

organization Organization is the order in which you present ideas. In an effective GED essay, the ideas are in an order that makes sense.

paragraph A paragraph is a group of sentences on a specific topic. It has a beginning, middle, and end, and the first line is indented.

parallel structure A sentence has parallel structure when the items joined by a conjunction are in the same grammatical form.

possessive noun Possessive nouns show who owns or possesses something.

possessive pronoun Possessive pronouns show who a noun belongs to. Possessive pronouns come before nouns.

prepositional phrase A prepositional phrase consists of a preposition and its object (the noun or pronoun that follows the preposition). Common prepositions include *on, at, for, in, with, without, before, after, to, during,* and *by*.

pronoun Pronouns must agree with the nouns they replace.

pronoun shift A pronoun shift occurs when the number or person of pronouns is changed when referring to the same person or thing.

proper adjective A proper adjective is an adjective derived from a proper noun. The important words in a proper adjective must be capitalized.

proper noun A proper noun is the name of a specific person, place, group, or thing. The important words in a proper noun must be capitalized.

reflexive pronoun A reflexive pronoun is a pronoun that refers to the same noun that is the subject of the sentence.

relative clause A relative clause does not express a complete thought and cannot stand alone. It is introduced by a relative pronoun such as *who, whom, which, that, whoever,* or *whatever.*

relevant An idea that tells about the main subject of your essay. In a good GED essay, all of the ideas should be relevant.

run-on sentence A run-on sentence is two or more independent clauses joined together without connecting words or punctuation.

sentence fragment A sentence fragment lacks a complete subject or verb, does not express a complete thought, and cannot stand alone.

sequence of tense Sequence of tense is when different tenses are used to show that the actions happened at different times.

subject pronoun A subject pronoun is a pronoun that takes the place of a noun that is the subject of a sentence.

subordinate clause A subordinate clause cannot stand alone as a sentence. It is introduced by a word such as *after, although, because, before, if, since, unless, until, when* or *where.* (see also: dependent clause)

subordinating conjunction A subordinating conjunction introduces a subordinate clause.

tense The tense of a verb can show the time of the action: past, present, or future.

thesis statement The thesis statement is the last sentence of the introductory paragraph. This sentence states the main idea of the essay and indicates the kind of information that will come later in the body paragraphs.

topic sentence The topic sentence is general and states the main idea of the paragraph.

transition Use transitions to show the relationship among the ideas in a paragraph. Transitions can be used to add an idea, show contrast among ideas, introduce an example, or introduce a result.

unity A paragraph has unity when all of the body sentences support the main idea.

writing prompt The writing prompt states the topic your essay should address. An effective GED essay should "present a clearly focused main idea that addresses the prompt."

Index